Early Praise for Karen Ge's
The Three-Year MathCounts Marathon

"You have done an incredible job in creating a resource others will find valuable, and, more importantly, be inspired by."

Albert Ni
MathCounts
2002 National Champion

"It's wonderful to see students sharing their paths to success so that others may follow! In *The Three-Year MathCounts Marathon*, Karen Ge shares her experience through carefully chosen problems, each of which offers more than stacks of routine exercises."

Richard Rusczyk
Founder and CEO
Art of Problem Solving

"This delightful problem book by Karen Ge is a must read for high flying middle schoolers. Anyone who wants to be a top flight mathematical problem solver can learn from her fine choices of problems and her conversational style of writing. The selection of topics is right on target and the consistent use of symbols makes the reading easy."

Harold Reiter
Professor of Mathematics
University of North Carolina at Charlotte

ALSO BY KAREN GE

*Dissecting the New CogAT: Full Length Test Prep with a
Perfect Scorer — CogAT 7 Traps and Pitfalls and How to Avoid Them*

THE THREE-YEAR
MATHCOUNTS®
MARATHON

THE THREE-YEAR
MATHCOUNTS®
MARATHON

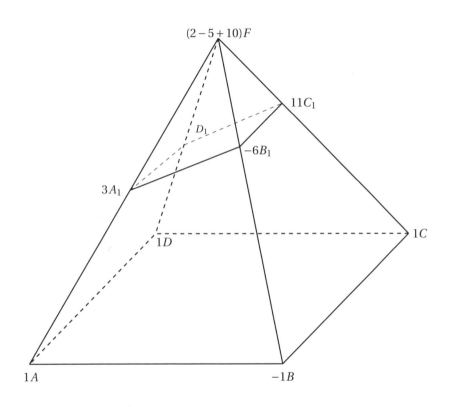

KAREN GE

FOREWORD BY ALBERT NI

 Aquahouse Publishing

Copyright ©2016 Aquahouse Publishing

Mathematics Subject Classification (2010): 00A07, 97U40

ISBN 978-0-9855068-9-6

All Rights Reserved

Printed in the United States of America. No part of this book may be translated or reproduced in any form without written permission from Aquahouse Publishing, P. O. Box 3320, Lisle, IL 60532, USA

MATHCOUNTS® and Mathlete® are registered trademarks of the MATHCOUNTS Foundation, which was not involved in the production of, and does not endorse, this work.

This book is printed on acid-free paper.

*To Mrs. Croco and Mr. Titus,
my MathCounts coaches*

Foreword

Math is funny. In spite of being firmly grounded in logic and rigor, the Queen of Sciences invokes a lot of emotions. For some, math is a sworn enemy — a source of fear, frustration, and contempt. For others, it's an enigmatic acquaintance — often around, occasionally helpful, but never fully understood. And then there are those for whom math is a trusted and beloved friend — eternally reliable, universally accessible, and impossibly consistent (literally impossible, it turns out, but that's a story for another book).

Mathematicians are funny too. You'd think if any group of people would have rigorous reasoning for their common interest, it would be them. Instead, "Why such a passion for math?" might be the only question mathematicians *don't* try to break down into a logical explanation. We just love it. Call it an axiom, if you will.

Growing up, I fancied myself a mathematician, and math was indeed a trusted and beloved friend. I loved math for all the "logical" reasons. I enjoyed the satisfaction of rigor, the insight into objective truth, and certainly the thrill of solution.

But where my appreciation has grown the most over time is of the people. Today, when I imagine someone who loves math, what comes to mind is not logic or rigor, words that could just as easily describe a robot. Instead, it's passion and altruism. Few fields consist of people so eager to share what they love, just so others can experience their joy. It's our unified cry to the world, "Math is so cool! I'd love to share it with you so you can enjoy it more too!"

That's why it was such an honor when Karen asked me to write the foreword for this book. People like her, and efforts like creating this book, define what I love about math more than any brilliant theorem, clever proof, or contest trophy.

This is more than a set of problems and solutions. It's the collection of an artist, painstakingly curated into a gallery celebrating the joy of math. Is that not the most heartfelt of gifts? I hope you enjoy it as much as I do.

Albert Ni
San Francisco, California

Preface

Introduction

Making it to national MathCounts is the goal of many middle school mathletes, and it was mine. Unfortunately, a healthy dose of reality almost shattered my lofty dream; I failed miserably in my first state MathCounts competition. The dozens and dozens of names ahead of my own forced me to understand that it would be an uphill battle if I ever wanted to earn a place on the 4-person state team. Upon examining the problems I had missed, I also realized my math knowledge was neither broad nor deep. Further aggravating the situation was my tendency to make thoughtless mistakes. I would forget the π when the problem asked for the area of a circle, give a four-digit integer answer when asked for a probability, etc.

To cut back on careless mistakes, I worked through every MathCounts problem that I could find, be it from a school handbook, a real competition, or an AoPS Mini. That made roughly 15,000 problems. I did them all, and not just once or twice. To broaden and deepen my mathematical knowledge, I learned all I could about algebra, geometry, number theory, and combinatorics, getting insight from my coaches, summer camps, and the internet. This book is the product of that learning process.

You might wonder why one would need a book for MathCounts practice. After all, isn't a 15,000-problem database enough? The uncomfortable truth is that it is not. Let's face it: real MathCounts competition problems are consistently getting harder each year. *Langley's Adventitious Angles*, for example, was once considered one of the hardest elementary math problems. But it is now conveniently included in a recent MathCounts national team round. Working through past competition and handbook problems can get you only so far; much more is required if you want to compete in earnest. For some mathletes, it is impossible to even earn a spot on their school team without advanced math knowledge, because their team selection tests are much harder than the actual MathCounts competitions.

This book contains more than 400 carefully selected problems ranging from MathCounts to IMO, each with a detailed solution. It is intended for advanced MathCounts mathletes, coaches, and parents. For MathCounts beginners, I highly recommend Jason Batterson's *Competition Math for Middle School*, published by Art of Problem Solving. Please note that although I included many problems from high school math competitions, the purpose of this book is not to prepare you for those contests. Rather, these problems are chosen to hone your MathCounts problem solving skills because today's high school math problems will appear in tomorrow's MathCounts competitions. Be prepared!

Definitions and notation

We use $\mathbb{N}$ to denote all nonnegative integers, $\mathbb{Z}$ to denote integers, $\mathbb{Z}^+$ to denote all positive integers, $\mathbb{Q}$ to denote rational numbers, $\mathbb{R}$ to denote all real numbers, and $\mathbb{C}$ to denote all complex numbers. Given a finite set S, we use $|S|$ to denote the number of elements in S. Given sets A and B, we use $A \cup B$ and $A \cap B$ to denote the union and intersection of A and B, respectively. Given integers d and n, $d|n$ means d divides n evenly. For any real number x, we use $\lfloor x \rfloor$ to denote the largest integer less than or equal to x, and call it the *floor* of x. We use $\lceil x \rceil$ to denote the smallest integer greater than or equal to x, and call it the *ceiling* of x.

Points with integer coordinates are called *lattice points*. A triangle is *scalene* if its three sides all have different lengths. A *cevian* is a line segment from a vertex of a triangle to the opposite side. Two or more lines are said to be *concurrent* if they intersect in a single point. Two or more points are said to be *collinear* if they lie on a single line. Given $\triangle ABC$, we use a, b, and c to denote the lengths of sides BC, CA, and AB, respectively. Given an n-sided polygon $A_1 A_2 ... A_n$, we use $[A_1 A_2 ... A_n]$ to denote its area.

Sources of problems used in this book

Most problems in this book come directly or are adapted from the following sources. However, sometimes the questions are formatted differently. For example, an AIME problem in this book does not necessarily have an integer answer in the range from 000 to 999. Figures are not necessarily drawn to scale. Occasionally the source is not acknowledged when I am not exactly sure where the problem came from. I sincerely apologize for any omission in mentioning a source.

AHSME
AIME
AMC 10
AMC 12
ARML
Art of Problem Solving
AwesomeMath
Berkeley Math Circle
CGMO

Chicago ARML
CMO
Colorado Math Circle
EGMO
German Problems
GMAT
HMMT
IMO
JBMO
Kennedy Junior High School MathCounts Team Selection Test (KMCTST)
Los Angles Math Circle
Mandelbrot
MathCounts
MAΘ
MathPath
Mathworks Math Contest
MOP
Moscow Mathematical Festival
MPfG
NIMO
Online Math Circle
PMWC
PUMaC
Purple Comet
Putnam
San Jose Math Circle
USAMO
USAMTS
WOOT

Engel, Arthur. *Problem-Solving Strategies*. New York: Springer, 1998. Print.
Fomin, Dmitri, et al. *Mathematical Circles: Russian Experience*. Rhode Island: American Mathematical Society, 1996. Print.
Prasolov, Viktor. *Problems in Plane and Solid Geometry v.1 Plane Geometry*. Trans. Dimitry Leites. 2001. PDF file.
Stankova, Zvezdelina and Tom Rike. *A Decade of the Berkeley Math Circle: The American Experience*. Rhode Island: American Mathematical Society, 2008. Print.
Yashchenko, Ivan. *Invitation to a Mathematical Festival*. Trans. Anna Fedorova. Rhode Island: American Mathematical Society, 2013. Print.
Zeitz, Paul. *The Art and Craft of Problem Solving*. 2nd. Ed. New Jersey: John Wiley and Sons, Inc., 2007. Print.

Acknowledgments

This book is dedicated to Mrs. Croco, my 6th and 7th grade MathCounts coach, and to Mr. Titus, my 8th grade coach at Kennedy Junior High School. Ever since

Mrs. Croco founded the KJHS MathCounts club in 1996, she worked tirelessly and sent many Kennedy students to the MathCounts National Competition. After her retirement in 2014, our new coach Mr. Titus has continued to uphold Mrs. Croco's high standards. Thank you, Mrs. Croco and Mr. Titus! Without your encouragement and challenges, I would never have made it to the national level. I would also like to thank my fellow mathletes from KJHS. During my three-year journey, I became a better problem solver because of our spirited competitions. I thank Sarah Youngquist for providing thousands of past MathCounts problems to help me practice, Kathryn Combs for proofreading the entire manuscript, and the MathCounts Foundation for granting me permission to use MathCounts problems and logos. Finally, my deepest gratitude goes to my parents for their steadfast love and support.

This book was prepared using LaTeX. The layout is an adaptation of the Springer Verlag's `svmono` document class.

Karen Ge
Lisle, Illinois

Contents

Foreword xi

Preface xiii

1 **Mathematical Principles** 1
   1.1 The Induction Principle 1
   1.2 The Pigeonhole Principle 2
   1.3 The Invariance Principle 3
   1.4 The Extremal Principle 4
   Problems for Chapter 1 5

2 **Functions and Representations** 7
   2.1 Functions 7
   2.2 Simon's Favorite Factoring Trick 8
   2.3 Egyptian Fractions 9
   2.4 Pascal's Triangle and Binomial Theorem 10
   Problems for Chapter 2 12

3 **Word Problems** 15
   3.1 Ratio and Percentage Problems 15
   3.2 Distance, Rate, and Time Problems 16
   3.3 Logic Problems 17
   3.4 Miscellaneous Problems 17
   Problems for Chapter 3 19

4 **Polynomials** 23
   4.1 Remainder and Factor Theorems 23
   4.2 Roots of a Polynomial 24
   4.3 Vieta's Formulas 26
   4.4 Newton's Sums 27
   Problems for Chapter 4 29

5 Sequences and Series 31
- 5.1 Arithmetic and Geometric Sequences 31
- 5.2 Telescoping Sums 33
- 5.3 Recurrence Relations 34
- 5.4 Characteristic Equations 34
- Problems for Chapter 5 37

6 Functional Equations 39
- 6.1 Evaluating Functional Equations 39
- 6.2 Properties of Functions and Polynomial Equations 41
- 6.3 Solving Single Variable Functional Equations 42
- 6.4 Solving Multi-Variable Functional Equations 43
- Problems for Chapter 6 45

7 Triangles and Polygons 47
- 7.1 MathCounts Trigonometry 47
- 7.2 Area Formulas and Theorems 49
- 7.3 Other Useful Theorems 51
- 7.4 The Triangle Inequality 53
- Problems for Chapter 7 54

8 Circles 59
- 8.1 Areas in a Circle 59
- 8.2 Cyclic quadrilaterals 62
- 8.3 Power of a Point 63
- 8.4 Ptolemy's Theorem 64
- Problems for Chapter 8 66

9 Three-Dimensional Geometry 71
- 9.1 Three Views of a 3D Object 71
- 9.2 Folding and Cutting 73
- 9.3 Angles and Distances 74
- 9.4 Higher Dimensions 77
- Problems for Chapter 9 78

10 Angle Chasing 83
- 10.1 Angles in a Polygon 83
- 10.2 Angles in a Circle 85
- 10.3 Trigonometric Form of Ceva's Theorem 86
- 10.4 Langley's Adventitious Angles 88
- Problems for Chapter 10 89

11 Mass Points 93
- 11.1 Mass Points and Cevians 94
- 11.2 Mass Points and Transversals 95
- 11.3 Multiple Mass Points Systems 96
- 11.4 Mass Points in Space 98

Problems for Chapter 11 100

12 Number Sense 105
12.1 Prime Factorization 105
12.2 Number Bases 107
12.3 Chicken McNugget Theorem 108
12.4 Euler's Theorem 109
Problems for Chapter 12 111

13 Modular Arithmetic 113
13.1 Chinese Remainder Theorem 113
13.2 Solving Linear Diophantine Equations 115
13.3 Solving Diophantine Equations Using Inequalities 116
13.4 The Floor Function 118
Problems for Chapter 13 119

14 Counting 121
14.1 Stars and Bars 121
14.2 Principle of Inclusion-Exclusion 123
14.3 Counting Using Recurrence Relations 125
14.4 Counting Geometric Objects 126
Problems for Chapter 14 129

15 Probability and Statistics 131
15.1 Conditional Probability 131
15.2 Geometric Probability 133
15.3 Mean, Median, Mode, and Range 134
15.4 Expected Value 134
Problems for Chapter 15 136

Answers 139
Answers for Chapter 1 139
Answers for Chapter 2 140
Answers for Chapter 3 140
Answers for Chapter 4 141
Answers for Chapter 5 141
Answers for Chapter 6 142
Answers for Chapter 7 142
Answers for Chapter 8 143
Answers for Chapter 9 143
Answers for Chapter 10 144
Answers for Chapter 11 144
Answers for Chapter 12 145
Answers for Chapter 13 145
Answers for Chapter 14 146
Answers for Chapter 15 146

Solutions 147
    Solutions for Chapter 1 147
    Solutions for Chapter 2 151
    Solutions for Chapter 3 157
    Solutions for Chapter 4 164
    Solutions for Chapter 5 169
    Solutions for Chapter 6 175
    Solutions for Chapter 7 180
    Solutions for Chapter 8 189
    Solutions for Chapter 9 197
    Solutions for Chapter 10 205
    Solutions for Chapter 11 212
    Solutions for Chapter 12 222
    Solutions for Chapter 13 227
    Solutions for Chapter 14 232
    Solutions for Chapter 15 237

Index 247

About the Author 251

Chapter 1
Mathematical Principles

Solving mathematical problems requires not only a pencil and paper, but also mental tools. These tools are not hard-to-remember facts, formulas, and tricks. Rather, they are so omnipresent that we tend to be oblivious to them. Because they are so fundamental, we refer to them as principles. The principles presented in this book are the induction principle, the pigeonhole principle, the invariance principle, and the extremal principle. As mathletes, we need to train ourselves to always ask if we can apply these principles to solve the problem at hand. It takes a lot of practice to master mathematical principles. In this chapter and every other chapter of this book, skimming through the examples of the chapter is far from enough. You need to work through each and every problem of the chapter by yourself to firmly master the concepts.

1.1 The Induction Principle

When dealing with sequences or patterns, we often need to use the induction principle. Proof by (simple) induction is a two step process. Step 1, also called the *base case*, we prove that the given statement is true for the first natural number. Step 2, the *inductive step*, we prove that if the statement is true for one natural number, then it is also true for the next natural number. Combining these two steps, we conclude that the given statement is true for all the natural numbers. Sometimes simple induction is not enough and we need strong induction where in step 2 we prove that if the statement is true for the first $k-1$ natural numbers, then it is also true for the kth number. Our first example uses strong induction.

Example 1.1. In the sequence 2001, 2002, 2003, ..., each term after the third is found by subtracting the previous term from the sum of the two terms that precede that term. For example, the fourth term is $2001 + 2002 - 2003 = 2000$. What is the 2004th term in this sequence? (AMC 12)

Answer: 0

Solution: To simplify calculations, we can get rid of the 2000 from each term and rewrite the sequence as $a_1 = 1$, $a_2 = 2$, $a_3 = 3$, $a_4 = a_1 + a_2 - a_3$, ..., $a_{n+3} = a_n + a_{n+1} - a_{n+2}$, ... After getting a_{2004}, we add 2000 back to get the 2004th term of the original sequence. Let's calculate the first a few terms of the new sequence: $a_1 = 1$, $a_2 = 2$, $a_3 = 3$, $a_4 = 0$, $a_5 = 5$, $a_6 = -2$, $a_7 = 7$, $a_8 = -4$, ... We guess that

$$a_{2n-1} = 2n - 1, \quad \text{and} \quad a_{2n} = 4 - 2n. \qquad (*)$$

Now we use the induction principle to prove that this is indeed the case. Step 1, we see that $(*)$ is true for $n = 1$. Step 2, assuming that for $n = 1, 2, ..., k$, we have

$$a_{2n-1} = 2n - 1, \quad \text{and} \quad a_{2n} = 4 - 2n.$$

Then

$$a_{2k+1} = a_{2k-2} + a_{2k-1} - a_{2k} = 4 - (2k-2) + 2k - 1 - (4 - 2k) = 2k + 1,$$
$$a_{2k+2} = a_{2k-1} + a_{2k} - a_{2k+1} = 2k - 1 + 4 - 2k - (2k+1) = 4 - (2k+2).$$

That is, $(*)$ is also true when $n = k + 1$. Thus, it is true for all natural numbers n. In particular, $a_{2004} = 4 - 2004$. Therefore, the 2004th term of the original sequence is $4 - 2004 + 2000 = \boxed{0}$.

1.2 The Pigeonhole Principle

Theorem 1.1. (Pigeonhole Principle) *If $n + 1$ or more pigeons are distributed among n pigeonholes, then at least one pigeonhole contains two or more pigeons.*

Although the pigeonhole principle seems obvious, its application is usually not trivial because we have to figure out what the "pigeons" are and what the "pigeonholes" are. Let's look at a WOOT problem.

Example 1.2. Fifteen chairs are evenly placed around a circular table on which are name cards for fifteen guests, also evenly spaced. The guests fail to notice these cards until after they have sat down, and it turns out that no one is sitting in front of his own card. Is it possible for the table to be rotated so that at least two of the guests are simultaneously sitting in front of their own cards?

Answer: It is possible.

Solution: Let's define the card-distance of each guest as follows: if a guest sits in front of his own card, then his card-distance is zero; for any guest, if there is a positive integer n, $1 \le n \le 14$, such that we need to rotate the table $\frac{n}{15}$ revolution counter-clockwise so that the guest can sit in front of his own card, then his card-distance is n. Since no one sits in front of his own card, each guest has a card-distance in the range from 1 to 14, inclusive. Since we have 15 guests (pigeons) and 14 possible card-distances (pigeonholes), at least two guests have the same card-distance. Let's call this common distance d. Now we rotate the table $\frac{d}{15}$ revolution counter-clockwise and these two guests will be simultaneously sitting in front of their own cards. Therefore, it is possible .

1.3 The Invariance Principle

In problems that involve transformations (not necessarily geometric ones), sometimes a certain quantity does not change. Such a quantity, called an *invariant*, is usually the key to solving this type of problem. When a transformation does not have any invariants, sometimes we can find a quantity that changes only in one direction, either always increasing, or always decreasing. Such a quantity is called a *monovariant*. Monovariants are also very helpful when we need to find out what is attainable after all the transformations.

One important example of invariance is parity. If a quantity is always even or always odd during transformations, then its final parity is the same as its initial parity after going through all the transformations.

Example 1.3. A grasshopper jumps along a line. His first jump takes him 1 cm, his second 2 cm, and so on. Each jump can take him to the right or to the left. Is it possible that after 2010 jumps the grasshopper returns to the point at which he started? (Russia)

Answer: It is impossible.

Solution: We see that the grasshopper jumps an even number of centimeters during his even steps and an odd number of centimeters during his odd steps. Among the 2010 jumps, there are 1005 odd steps and 1005 even steps. Adding together all the lengths he jumped, we get an odd number of centimeters. But returning to the starting point requires an even number, so it is impossible for the grasshopper to return to his starting point after 2010 jumps.

Example 1.4. A box has 300 matches. Two players take turns removing no more than half the matches in the box. The player who can't move loses. Who can guarantee a win?

Answer: Player 1

Solution: Let's start with only one match. In that case, the first player cannot remove anything and so loses. When there are two matches, the first player can remove one and let the second player be the loser. But when there are three matches, the first player can only remove one and the second player becomes the winner. We see that the losing number is always of the form $2^{n+1} - 1$. It is an invariant. For if there are $2^{n+1} - 1$ matches, then no matter how many matches, say x, where $1 \leq x \leq 2^n - 1$, the first player removes, the second player can always remove $2^n - x$ matches and leave $2^n - 1$ matches to the first player, forcing Player 1 to lose eventually. On the other hand, if the number of matches is of the form $2^n + a$, where $0 \leq a < 2^n - 1$, then the first player can always remove $a + 1$ matches, leaving $2^n - 1$ matches to the second player, forcing the second player to lose eventually. Since 300 is not of the form $2^{n+1} - 1$, the winner is $\boxed{\text{Player 1}}$.

1.4 The Extremal Principle

In problem solving, sometimes it is useful to focus on extreme objects, such as the largest or the smallest element. This technique is called the extremal principle and it can be quite useful. We know that any nonempty finite set of real numbers has a minimal element. This is also true for any nonempty set of natural numbers.

Theorem 1.2. (Well-ordering Principle) *Every nonempty subset of the natural numbers has a least element.*

Example 1.5. On a large, flat field, 15 people are positioned so that for each person the distances to all the other people are different. Each person holds a water gun and at a given signal fires and hits the person who is closest. Is it possible that everyone gets wet? (CMO)

Answer: It is impossible.

Solution: We first get rid of the pairs of people who fire at each other. Since we start with 15 people, some people must remain. If only one person remains, then we are done because this person would be dry. Otherwise, we pick one person from these remaining people, say A, whose distance to his closest neighbor B is maximal. We claim that A stays dry. Suppose this were not the case, then there would be a person C who fired at A. C is not B because we have excluded those who fire at each other. This means A is C's closest neighbor. But the distance between A and C is larger than the distance between A and B because B is A's closest neighbor and the distances from A to all the others are different. Thus, C's distance to his closest neighbor A is larger than A's distance to his closest neighbor B, contradicting to our choice of A. Therefore, A stays dry. So, it is $\boxed{\text{impossible}}$ that everyone gets wet.

Problems for Chapter 1

Problem 1.1. A basket of fruit is arranged out of apples, bananas, and oranges. What is the smallest number of fruit that should be put in the basket to guarantee that there are either at least 8 apples or at least 6 bananas or at least 9 oranges?

Problem 1.2. Six distinct positive integers are randomly chosen between 1 and 2006, inclusive. What is the probability that some pair of these integers has a difference that is a multiple of 5? (AMC 10)

Problem 1.3. Is it true that in any group of 8 people, there are two people in the group who have the same number of friends among the people in the group?

Problem 1.4. There are 100 soldiers in a detachment, and every evening three of them are on duty. Can it happen that after a certain period of time each soldier has shared duty with every other soldier exactly once? (Russia)

Problem 1.5. The sum of the ages of the 33 students in a class is 430 years. Are there 20 students in the class such that the sum of their ages is greater than 260?

Problem 1.6. Pete bought a notebook containing 96 pages, and numbered them from 1 through 192. Victor tore out 25 pages of Pete's notebook, and added the 50 numbers he found on the pages. Could Victor get 1990 as the sum? (Russia)

Problem 1.7. In the Parliament of Sikinia, each member has at most three enemies. Is it possible that the house be separated into two houses, so that each member has at most one enemy in his or her own house? (Engel)

Problem 1.8. There are 51 senators in a senate. The senate needs to be divided into n committees such that each senator is on exactly one committee. Each senator hates exactly three other senators. (If A hates B, then B does not necessarily hate A.) Find the smallest n such that it is always possible to arrange the committees so that no senator hates another senator on his or her committee. (MOP)

Problem 1.9. Of 101 coins, 50 are counterfeit, and differ from the genuine coins in weight by 1 gram. Dmitri has a balance scale which shows the difference in weights between the objects placed in each pan. He chooses one coin, and wants to find out in one weighing whether it is counterfeit or not. Can he do this? (Russia)

Problem 1.10. There are three piles of stones. The first has 19, the second has 8, and the third has 9 stones. You are allowed to choose two piles and transfer one stone from each of these two piles to the third pile. After several of these operations, is it possible that each of the three piles has 12 stones?

Problem 1.11. Is it true that every polyhedron has at least two faces with the same number of edges? (Engel)

Problem 1.12. There are 13 green, 15 blue, and 17 red chameleons on Camelot Island. Whenever two chameleons of different colors meet, they both swap to the third color. Is it possible for all chameleons to become one color? (Russia)

Problem 1.13. There is a positive integer in each square of a rectangular table. In each move, you may double each number in a row or subtract 1 from each number of a column. Can you reach a table of zeros with these moves? (Engel)

Problem 1.14. Initially, 9 of the 100 squares in a 10 × 10 grid are infected. During each unit time interval, each square which has 2 or more infected neighbors (a neighbor being a square which shares an edge) also become infected. Is it possible that all 100 squares will eventually become infected?

Problem 1.15. In a certain two-person game, each player, in turn, removes 1, 2, 3, 4, or 5 toothpicks from a common pile, until the pile is exhausted. The player who takes the last toothpick loses. If the starting pile contains 300 toothpicks, how many toothpicks must the first player take on the first turn to guarantee a win with perfect subsequent play? (KMCTST)

Problem 1.16. In a ping pong tournament with no ties allowed, each player plays with everyone else exactly once. Is there some unfortunate player such that every other player either beat him or beat someone who beat him? (Engel)

Problem 1.17. Starting with the set $\{3, 4, 12\}$, you are allowed to replace any two numbers a and b with the new pair $0.6a - 0.8b$ and $0.8a + 0.6b$. Can you transform the set into $\{4, 6, 12\}$? (Engel)

Problem 1.18. A chess player prepares for a tournament by playing some practice games over a period of eight weeks. She plays at least one game per day, but no more than 11 games per week. Is it true that there is a period of consecutive days during which she plays exactly 23 games? (Zeitz)

Problem 1.19. There are n identical cars on a circular track. Together they have just enough gas for one car to complete a lap. Is there a car that can complete a lap by collecting gas from the other cars on its way around? (Engel)

Problem 1.20. A king decides to give 100 of his prisoners a test. If they pass, they can go free. Otherwise, the king will execute all of them. The test goes as follows: the prisoners stand in a line, all facing forward. The king puts either a black or a white hat on each prisoner. The prisoners can only see the colors of the hats in front of them. Then, in any order they want, each one guesses the color of the hat on his head. Other than that, the prisoners can not speak. To pass, no more than one of them may guess incorrectly. If they can make their strategy beforehand, can they be assured that they will survive?

Chapter 2

Functions and Representations

In their book, *Calculus of a Single Variable*, Thomas Dick and Charles Patton state that "One of the most important concepts in all of mathematics is that of function." We will give an introduction of functions here. Later, in Chapter 13, we will revisit some special functions, such as the floor and ceiling functions.

2.1 Functions

A *function f* is a relation that associates members of an input set A to members of an output set B. Every member $a \in A$ is uniquely associated with a member $f(a) \in B$. The *range* of a function is the set of all possible output values. The *domain* is the set of all possible input values that can generate a valid output. In other words, the domain of a function is the set of all input values that make the function mathematically defined. Let's look at a MathCounts problem.

Example 2.1. What is the sum of all real values of x that are solutions to the equation
$$\left(\frac{2}{3}x^2 - x - \frac{2}{3}\right)^{(x^2-9x+20)} = 1?$$

Answer: $\dfrac{23}{2}$

Solution: For any nonzero real number a, $a^0 = 1$. So let us solve the equation $x^2 - 9x + 20 = 0$ first.

$$x^2 - 9x + 20 = 0, \quad (x-4)(x-5) = 0, \quad x = 4 \text{ or } x = 5.$$

Since neither $x = 4$ nor $x = 5$ is a solution to $\frac{2}{3}x^2 - x - \frac{2}{3} = 0$, both of them are solutions to our equation.

Since $1^a = 1$ for all real numbers a, our equation has a solution if $\frac{2}{3}x^2 - x - \frac{2}{3} = 1$.

$$\frac{2}{3}x^2 - x - \frac{2}{3} = 1, \qquad 2x^2 - 3x - 5 = 0, \qquad x = \frac{5}{2} \text{ or } x = -1.$$

Both are solutions to our equation.

Since for any integer n, $(-1)^{2n} = 1$, our equation has a solution if $\frac{2}{3}x^2 - x - \frac{2}{3} = -1$ and $x^2 - 9x + 20$ is an even integer.

$$\frac{2}{3}x^2 - x - \frac{2}{3} = -1, \qquad 2x^2 - 3x + 1 = 0, \qquad x = \frac{1}{2} \text{ or } x = 1.$$

When $x = \frac{1}{2}$, $x^2 - 9x + 20$ is not an integer. When $x = 1$, $x^2 - 9x + 20$ is an even integer. So $x = 1$ is a solution to our equation.

Therefore, the sum of all real solutions is $4 + 5 + \frac{5}{2} + (-1) + 1 = \boxed{\frac{23}{2}}$.

2.2 Simon's Favorite Factoring Trick

We complete the square when we need to solve a quadratic equation. Similarly, we *complete the rectangle* when we need to make an expression factorable. For example, to make an expression such as $xy + ax + by$ factorable, we add a term ab and now $xy + ax + by + ab = (x+b)(y+a)$. The general strategy of adding a constant or variable to an expression to make it factorable is called *Simon's Favorite Factoring Trick*. Let's look at an example from the Princeton University Mathematics Competition.

Example 2.2. Professor Conway collects a total of 58 midterms from the two sections of his introductory linear algebra course. He notices that the number of midterms from the smaller section is equal to the product of the digits of the number of midterms from his larger section. Assuming that everyone handed in a midterm, how many students are there in the smaller section?

Answer: 21 students

Solution: Since there are 58 students in total, the number of students in the larger section is a two-digit positive integer that is greater than or equal to 30. Let x be its tens digit and y its units digit. We have $xy + 10x + y = 58$. Therefore,

$$xy + 10x + y + 10 = 68, \qquad (x+1)(y+10) = 68.$$

Since $x \geq 3$, the only integer solution to $(x+1)(y+10) = 68$ is $x+1 = 4$ and $y+10 = 17$. So there are $xy = 3 \cdot 7 = \boxed{21 \text{ students}}$ in the smaller section.

In addition to Simon's Favorite Factoring Trick, we also need to know basic factorization formulas, including:

$$x^n - y^n = (x-y)(x^{n-1} + x^{n-2}y + \cdots + xy^{n-2} + y^{n-1}),$$
$$x^n + y^n = (x+y)(x^{n-1} - x^{n-2}y + \cdots - xy^{n-2} + y^{n-1}), \quad \text{if } n \text{ is odd},$$
$$x^3 + y^3 + z^3 - 3xyz = (x+y+z)(x^2 + y^2 + z^2 - xy - xz - yz),$$
$$a^4 + 4b^4 = (a^2 + 2b^2 + 2ab)(a^2 + 2b^2 - 2ab).$$

2.3 Egyptian Fractions

The ancient Egyptians did not use numerators and denominators to represent fractions. Instead, a positive proper fraction was represented as the sum of unit fractions in ancient Egypt. A *unit fraction* is a fraction where the numerator is 1 and the denominator is a natural number greater than 1.

Given relatively prime positive integers a and b with $b > a$, let $b = q \cdot a + r$, where q is the quotient and r is the remainder when b is divided by a. Then

$$\frac{a}{b} = \frac{1}{q+1} + \frac{a-r}{b(q+1)}. \qquad (*)$$

We repeat the process if needed and see that every positive proper fraction can be written as a finite sum of distinct unit fractions. The representation of a fraction as the sum of distinct unit fractions is called an *Egyptian representation*, or an *Egyptian fraction*.

We see from $(*)$ that for any positive integer $n > 1$, $\frac{1}{n}$ can be written as the sum of two unit fractions

$$\frac{1}{n} = \frac{1}{n+1} + \frac{1}{n(n+1)}.$$

Let's look at a MathCounts problem.

Example 2.3. Find the sum of all possible x values such that $\frac{1}{x} + \frac{1}{y} = \frac{1}{7}$, where x and y are positive integers.

Answer: 78

Solution: Multiplying both sides by $7xy$, we get $xy = 7x + 7y$, $xy - 7x - 7y + 49 = 49$. So $(x-7)(y-7) = 49$. Note that $x - 7 < 0$ and $y - 7 < 0$ does not give us any solutions. Thus there are only three possible cases:

$$\text{Case 1}: x - 7 = 1, \text{ and } y - 7 = 49.$$

This case gives us $x = 8$ and $y = 56$.

$$\text{Case 2}: x - 7 = 7, \text{ and } y - 7 = 7.$$

This case gives us $x = 14$ and $y = 14$.

$$\text{Case 3}: x - 7 = 49, \text{ and } y - 7 = 1.$$

This case gives us $x = 56$ and $y = 8$.

Therefore, the sum of all possible x values is $8 + 14 + 56 = \boxed{78}$.

2.4 Pascal's Triangle and Binomial Theorem

$$\begin{array}{c}
1 \\
1 \quad 1 \\
1 \quad 2 \quad 1 \\
1 \quad 3 \quad 3 \quad 1 \\
1 \quad 4 \quad 6 \quad 4 \quad 1 \\
1 \quad 5 \quad 10 \quad 10 \quad 5 \quad 1 \\
1 \quad 6 \quad 15 \quad 20 \quad 15 \quad 6 \quad 1 \\
1 \quad 7 \quad 21 \quad 35 \quad 35 \quad 21 \quad 7 \quad 1 \\
1 \quad 8 \quad 28 \quad 56 \quad 70 \quad 56 \quad 28 \quad 8 \quad 1
\end{array}$$

Pascal's triangle is a very important number pattern. Beginning with a 1 at the top (the 0th row), each number in the following rows of Pascal's triangle is the sum of two numbers: the number above and to the left and the number above and to the right. If the number above and to the left (right) is not present, we treat it as zero. There are $n + 1$ entries in the nth row of Pascal's triangle. They are:

$$\binom{n}{0}, \binom{n}{1}, \binom{n}{2}, \ldots, \binom{n}{n-1}, \binom{n}{n},$$

where

$$\binom{n}{k} = \frac{n!}{k!(n-k)!}$$

is called *n choose k*. These $n+1$ numbers sum to 2^n. As we will see in Theorem 2.1, these $n + 1$ numbers are the coefficients of the binomial expansion of $(a + b)^n$. Note that the third diagonal of Pascal's triangle is a list of triangular numbers: 1, 3, 6, 10, 15, 21, ... A triangular number is a number that can be represented by a triangular array of dots. Now let's look at an AIME problem.

2.4 Pascal's Triangle and Binomial Theorem

Example 2.4. In which row of Pascal's triangle do three consecutive entries occur that are in the ratio 3 : 4 : 5?

Answer: 62

Solution: Suppose these entries are in the nth row and there is an r with $1 \le r < n$ such that
$$\binom{n}{r-1} : \binom{n}{r} : \binom{n}{r+1} = 3 : 4 : 5.$$
Then there is a constant k such that
$$n! = 3k \cdot (r-1)!(n-r+1)! = 4k \cdot r!(n-r)! = 5k \cdot (r+1)!(n-r-1)!$$
Therefore,
$$3(n-r+1) = 4r,$$
$$5(r+1) = 4(n-r).$$
Solving the system, we get $r = 27$ and $n = \boxed{62}$.

The Binomial Theorem gives a way of expanding a binomial expression that has been raised to the nth power. Pascal's triangle plays a major role here.

Theorem 2.1. (Binomial Theorem)
$$(a+b)^n = \binom{n}{0}a^n + \binom{n}{1}a^{n-1}b + \binom{n}{2}a^{n-2}b^2 + \cdots + \binom{n}{n-1}ab^{n-1} + \binom{n}{n}b^n.$$

After $(a+b)^n$ is expanded, its coefficients, called *binomial coefficients*, are the entries of the nth row of Pascal's triangle. Let's look at another AIME problem.

Example 2.5. Find the smallest positive integer n for which the expansion of $(xy - 3x + 7y - 21)^n$, after like terms have been collected, has at least 1996 terms.

Answer: 44

Solution: By Simon's Favorite Factoring Trick,
$$xy - 3x + 7y - 21 = (x+7)(y-3),$$
$$(xy - 3x + 7y - 21)^n = (x+7)^n (y-3)^n.$$

The binomial expansions of $(x+7)^n$ and $(y-3)^n$ each has $n+1$ terms. The expansion of $(x+7)^n(y-3)^n$ has $(n+1)^2$ terms because the product of any term from $(x+7)^n$ and any term from $(y-3)^n$ produces a unique term in the final expansion. Since the smallest perfect square after 1996 is $2025 = 45^2$, $n = 45 - 1 = \boxed{44}$.

Problems for Chapter 2

Problem 2.1. If for three distinct positive numbers x, y, and z,
$$\frac{y}{x-z} = \frac{x+y}{z} = \frac{x}{y},$$
then find the numerical value of $\frac{x}{y}$. (AHSME)

Problem 2.2. Positive integers x and y satisfy $x < y$ and $\frac{1}{x} + \frac{1}{y} = \frac{5}{12}$. What is the sum of all possible x values?

Problem 2.3. Find all positive integral pairs (x, y) that satisfy the equation
$$xy + x - 2y = 9.$$

Problem 2.4. Find the sum of the roots of the equation
$$x^{2001} + \left(\frac{1}{2} - x\right)^{2001} = 0,$$
given that there are no multiple roots. (AIME)

Problem 2.5. If $f\left(\frac{2x-3}{x-2}\right) = 5x - 2$, compute $f^{-1}(27)$. (ARML)

Problem 2.6. Suppose
$$a + b + c = \frac{1}{a} + \frac{1}{b} + \frac{1}{c} = 5, \quad \text{and} \quad abc = 1.$$
Compute $a^3 + b^3 + c^3$. (ARML)

Problem 2.7. Let f be a function such that for $x \in \{-1, 0, 1\}$,
$$f(x^2) = 2(f(x))^2 - 1.$$
Compute all possible values of $f(-1)$. (ARML)

Problem 2.8. Let $a = 3^{\frac{1}{223}} + 1$ and for all $n \geq 3$ let
$$f(n) = \binom{n}{0}a^{n-1} - \binom{n}{1}a^{n-2} + \binom{n}{2}a^{n-3} - \cdots + (-1)^{n-1}\binom{n}{n-1}a^0.$$
Find $f(2007) + f(2008)$. (Purple Comet)

Problems for Chapter 2

Problem 2.9. (MathCounts) $\lfloor x \rfloor$ is the largest integer less than or equal to x. Find the sum of the three smallest positive solutions to

$$x - \lfloor x \rfloor = \frac{1}{\lfloor x \rfloor}.$$

Problem 2.10. If the tens digit of $(4A1)^{1A4}$ is 2, compute all possible values for the digit A. Here, $4A1$ and $1A4$ represent 3-digit numbers. (ARML)

Problem 2.11. The arithmetic mean of two distinct positive integers x and y is a two-digit integer. The geometric mean of x and y is obtained by reversing the digits of the arithmetic mean. What is $|x - y|$? (AMC 12)

Problem 2.12. Expanding $(1+0.2)^{1000}$ by the Binomial Theorem we get

$$\binom{1000}{0}(0.2)^0 + \binom{1000}{1}(0.2)^1 + \cdots + \binom{1000}{1000}(0.2)^{1000} = A_0 + A_1 + \cdots + A_{1000},$$

where

$$A_k = \binom{1000}{k}(0.2)^k$$

for $k = 0, 1, \ldots, 1000$. For which k is A_k the largest? (AIME)

Problem 2.13. For any a and b, we will define a "move that adds (a,b)" as a move from any point (c,d) to the point $(c+a, d+b)$. A particle moves according to the following rules. If a move added (p,q) to get to the current position, the next move will add either $(p-1, q)$ or $(p, q-1)$ to move to the next position. Neither p nor q can ever be negative. Particle A starts at $(0,0)$ and moves to $(3,4)$. Particle A will continue to move according to the preceding rules. When the particle can no longer move according to the preceding rules, it is located at point (r,r). What is the value of r? (MathCounts)

Problem 2.14. (MathCounts) What is the sum of all real numbers x such that

$$(x^2 - 5x + 5)^{(x^2 - 7x + 12)} = 1?$$

Problem 2.15. Kevin and Devin each makes one hat per day for charity, but they started on different days. Today, Kevin made his 520th hat, and Devin made his 50th. A celebration is planned for the next date that Kevin's hat count is evenly divisible by Devin's hat count. In how many days from today will they celebrate? (MathCounts)

Problem 2.16. When $(x + 2y - z)^8$ is expanded, and the like terms are combined, what is the coefficient of the term $x^3 y^2 z^3$? (MathCounts)

Problem 2.17. Ryan's letter weighs $\frac{9}{10}$ oz. Stamps weigh $\frac{1}{30}$ oz each. The cost of mailing the first ounce, or fraction thereof, costs 37 cents, and each additional ounce, or fraction thereof, costs 23 cents. If Ryan only has 1 cent stamps, how many stamps should he use? Remember that he is paying for the weight of the stamps, too. Assume there are no physical constraints regarding the number of stamps or the size of the envelope. (MathCounts)

Problem 2.18. (AIME) Compute

$$\frac{(10^4+324)(22^4+324)\cdots(58^4+324)}{(4^4+324)(16^4+324)\cdots(52^4+324)}.$$

Problem 2.19. The polynomial $1-x+x^2-x^3+\cdots+x^{16}-x^{17}$ may be written in the form

$$a_0+a_1y+a_2y^2+a_3y^3+\cdots+a_{16}y^{16}+a_{17}y^{17},$$

where $y=x+1$ and the a_i's are constants. Find the value of a_2. (AIME)

Problem 2.20. If f is a function such that

$$f(x)+\frac{1}{x}\cdot f\left(-\frac{1}{x}\right)=3,$$

what is the value of $f(2)$? (MathCounts)

Problem 2.21. If

$$f(x)=\begin{cases}-x, & \text{if } x<0\\-x^2, & \text{if } x\geq 0\end{cases}$$

and $f(f(f(x)))=4$, what is the value of x? (MathCounts)

Problem 2.22. What is the minimum value of

$$8x^3+36x+\frac{54}{x}+\frac{27}{x^3}$$

for positive real numbers x? (MathCounts)

Problem 2.23. How many of the first 1000 positive integers can be expressed in the form

$$\lfloor 2x\rfloor+\lfloor 4x\rfloor+\lfloor 6x\rfloor+\lfloor 8x\rfloor,$$

where x is a real number? (AIME)

Chapter 3
Word Problems

Word problems are some of the hardest MathCounts problems. Part of the challenge is translating the problem from plain English into mathematical equations. To solve word problems, we must read the problem carefully and write down what is given, what is unknown, and how the two are related. Typically, a word problem is written like a story and contains more information than is needed to solve it. Organizing information into a chart or a table can help us clear our minds so that we are not distracted by unnecessary information. After getting the answer, it is important to plug it back into the original problem to check if it makes sense and answers the question being asked.

3.1 Ratio and Percentage Problems

Sometimes, solving a problem directly will give us messy calculations. To avoid this pitfall, we can change our point of view and consider the problem from a different angle. Let's look at a problem from the Moscow Mathematical Festival.

Example 3.1. Gulliver came to the island country of Lilliput with 7,000,000 dollars. He spent all his money on bottles of milk at 7 dollars per bottle; at the time, an empty bottle cost 1 dollar. When he drank all the milk he returned the empty bottles and immediately used all the money he got back to buy more milk. While doing this, he noticed that both the price of milk and the price of an empty bottle doubled. Then he drank all the milk again, returned the bottles and used all the money again to buy more milk and so on. Every time he went back to the shop for more milk both the price of milk and the price of an empty bottle doubled. How many bottles of milk did Gulliver drink?

Answer: 1,166,666 bottles

Solution: Instead of calculating the amount of milk in terms of dollars, we can calculate it in terms of empty bottles because the ratio between the price of an empty bottle and that of the milk inside a bottle is always fixed. At the beginning, Gulliver's money is worth 7,000,000 empty bottles. With 7 empty bottles, we can buy one bottle of milk, leaving us with one empty bottle after Gulliver drank the milk. So, the price of 6 empty bottles is equal to that of the milk inside a bottle. Therefore 7,000,000 empty bottles can buy $\frac{7000000}{6} \approx 1,166,666$ bottles of milk with a leftover of 4 empty bottles. Since Gulliver cannot use the 4 empty bottles to buy any more milk, he drank $\boxed{1,166,666 \text{ bottles}}$ of milk.

3.2 Distance, Rate, and Time Problems

For as long as there have been human societies, there have been concerns about distance, rate, and time. A North American folktale goes like this:

> A traveler came upon an old farmer hoeing in his field beside the road. The wanderer hailed the countryman, who looked up from his work. "How long will it take me to get to the next town?" asked the stranger. "I can't rightly say," was the farmer's curt reply. Insulted, the traveler strode off. "About an hour," shouted the farmer after him. "Why didn't you say so when I first asked?" "Because I didn't know how fast you were walking."

Example 3.2. A certain car drives 40 miles per gallon of gas at a rate of 60 mph. It drives 35 miles per gallon of gas at a rate of 75 mph. So, traveling at the higher speed saves time, but uses more gas. Gas costs $3.50 per gallon. What is the cost for each hour of time saved when traveling at the higher speed? (MathCounts)

Answer: $3.75

Solution: Let's first find x, the number of hours such that the distance of driving at 75 mph for x hours is the same as the distance of driving at 60 mph for $x+1$ hours. Driving this distance at a rate of 75 mph could save one hour.

$$75x = 60(x+1), \qquad x = 4 \text{ hours.}$$

Next, let's organize the given information into a table:

speed	miles per gallon	gallons per hour	total time	total gas
60 mph	40 mi/g	$\frac{60}{40}$ g/h	5 hours	$5 \cdot \frac{60}{40}$ gallons
75 mph	35 mi/g	$\frac{75}{35}$ g/h	4 hours	$4 \cdot \frac{75}{35}$ gallons

Therefore, the expense for each hour of time saved is $3.50 \cdot (4 \cdot \frac{75}{35} - 5 \cdot \frac{60}{40}) = \boxed{\$3.75}$.

3.3 Logic Problems

Proof by contradiction is the most common method used to solve logic puzzles. We rule out a scenario by showing that if it were true, then we would have a contradiction. Let's look at an example.

Example 3.3. Before a soccer game between North and South, there were five predictions:
a) There won't be a draw.
b) North will score against South.
c) North will win.
d) North won't lose.
e) Three goals will be made in total.
After the match, it turned out that exactly three of these predictions were true. How many goals did South make in the game? (Moscow)

Answer: 2 goals

Solution: First let's see if North won. If this were the case, then predictions a), b), c), and d) were all correct, contradicting the fact that only three predictions were correct. So North did not win. Next let's see if it was a tie. If this were the case, then predictions a), c), and e) would not be true and so at most two predictions might be true. Again, this is a contradiction. Therefore, South won. Since predictions c) and d) cannot be true, predictions a), b), and e) must be true. So, North made one goal and South made $\boxed{2 \text{ goals}}$.

3.4 Miscellaneous Problems

Generally speaking, there are no fixed methods to solve word problems. So the best thing we can do is practice, practice, and practice. That said, sometimes working backwards is a better method than a direct approach, as we will see in the following MathCounts problem.

Example 3.4. Auggie spent all of his money in 5 stores. In each store, he spent $1 more than one-half of what he had when he went in. How many dollars did Auggie have when he entered the first store?

Answer: $62

Solution: Suppose Auggie had d_i dollars when he entered store i, where $1 \leq i \leq 5$. Let's work backwards. At the last store, Auggie used all his money. So
$$1 + \tfrac{1}{2}d_5 = d_5, \qquad d_5 = 2.$$

Next, we have

$$d_4 - \left(1 + \frac{1}{2}d_4\right) = 2, \quad d_4 = 6. \quad d_3 - \left(1 + \frac{1}{2}d_3\right) = 6, \quad d_3 = 14.$$

$$d_2 - \left(1 + \frac{1}{2}d_2\right) = 14, \quad d_2 = 30. \quad d_1 - \left(1 + \frac{1}{2}d_1\right) = 30, \quad d_1 = \boxed{\$62}.$$

Our next example comes from a KJHS MathCounts Team Selection Test.

Example 3.5. Alice, Betty, and Carol took the same series of exams. For each exam there was one score of x, one score of y, and one score of z, where x, y, and z are distinct positive integers. The total of the scores obtained by each of the girls was: Alice 20, Betty 10, and Carol 9. If Betty placed first in the algebra exam, who placed second in the geometry exam?

Answer: Carol

Solution: Without loss of generality, let's assume that $x > y > z$. Suppose the series had n exams in total, then

$$n(x + y + z) = 20 + 10 + 9 = 39.$$

So n is a factor of 39. Since $n > 1$, $n = 13$ or $n = 3$. But $n = 13$ is impossible because then Carol's total score would be at least 13 instead of 9 if she got the lowest positive integer score of 1 in each exam. Thus $n = 3$. Let's assume that the three exams were algebra (A), combinatorics (C), and geometry (G). Now we have

$$3(x + y + z) = 39, \quad x + y + z = 13.$$

Since Alice's total score was at most $3x$, we have $3x \geq 20$. So $x \geq 7$. Since Betty's total score was at least $x + 1 + 1$, we have $x + 1 + 1 \leq 10$, $x \leq 8$. Therefore $x = 7$ or $x = 8$.

If $x = 7$, then Betty's three test scores would be $A = 7$ and $C + G = 3$. But then $x + y + z = 7 + 2 + 1 < 13$, a contradiction. Therefore $x = 8$. So Betty's scores were: $A = 8$, $C = G = 1$. Thus $z = 1$ and $y = 13 - x - y = 4$. Since $4 + 4 + 8 < 20$, Alice's scores must be: $A = 4$, $C = G = 8$. Finally we see that Carol's scores must be: $A = 1$, $C = G = 4$. Therefore $\boxed{\text{Carol}}$ placed second in both the combinatorics and geometry exams.

	algebra (A)	combinatorics (C)	geometry (G)
Alice	4	8	8
Betty	8	1	1
Carol	1	4	4

Problems for Chapter 3

Problem 3.1. Solution Y is 30 percent liquid X and 70 percent water. If 2 kilograms of water evaporate from 8 kilograms of solution Y and 2 kilograms of solution Y are added to the remaining 6 kilograms of liquid, what percent of this new liquid solution is liquid X? (GMAT)

Problem 3.2. A particular online vendor offers discounts for orders of 11 or more shirts, as the table shows. For how many different quantities of shirts would the cost exceed the cost of buying the least number of shirts at the next discount level? (MathCounts)

Number of Shirts	Discount
1-10	no discount
11-25	10% off
26-50	15% off
51-100	20% off
101-250	30% off
251 or more	35% off

Problem 3.3. Alice leaves Denver, driving at a constant speed. After a while, she passes a mile marker displaying a two-digit number. One hour later, she passes a second marker with the same two digits in reverse order. In another hour she passes a third marker with the same two digits separated by a zero. What is the rate of Alice's car in miles per hour? (MathCounts)

Problem 3.4. If 330 people are required to construct 30 km of railway track in 9 months, how many months will it take 275 people, working at the same rate, to construct 150 km of track? (MathCounts)

Problem 3.5. Three players play 4 rounds of a game and end with a tie score of 80. A different player wins each of the final three rounds. Starting from round 2, when a player wins, he or she doubles his or her points, and the two losers each must subtract the amount the winner gains from his or her score. What was the highest score at the end of round 1? (MathCounts)

Problem 3.6. The combined weight of two airline passengers' checked luggage is 105 kilograms. The airline's checked-luggage policy allows each passenger a maximum weight at no charge, and charges a constant, per-kilogram rate for any extra weight. One passenger pays $12.00 for the total extra weight of her luggage, and the other passenger pays $18.00 for the total extra weight of his luggage. If all of the luggage had belonged to one of the passengers, the over-weight charge would have been $78.00. How many kilograms of luggage is one person permitted without charge by the airline? (MathCounts)

Problem 3.7. Abe can paint the room in 15 hours, Bea can paint 50 percent faster than Abe, and Coe can paint twice as fast as Abe. Abe begins to paint the room and works alone for the first hour and a half. Then Bea joins Abe, and they work together until half the room is painted. Then Coe joins Abe and Bea, and they work together until the entire room is painted. Find the number of minutes after Abe begins for the three of them to finish painting the room. (AIME)

Problem 3.8. A consumer report revealed the following information about three tubes of toothpaste. Bright is 60% more expensive than Fresh and has 25% less volume than Glow. Glow is 25% less expensive than Bright and has $33\frac{1}{3}$% more volume than Fresh. Fresh costs $1.00 per unit of volume. What is the number of cents per unit of volume of Glow? (MathCounts)

Problem 3.9. There are two boats that start out on opposite sides of a river at the same time. Each one is heading across the river to the other side at a constant speed. The current of the river can be ignored. The first time they pass, they are 700 yards from one of the banks of the river. The second time they pass, they have each turned around after reaching their respective opposite shores and have started back toward where they each began. When they pass the second time, they are 300 yards from the other bank of the river. How wide is the river?

Problem 3.10. Lupe went to the store and paid for her purchase with a $10 bill. She found that the digits making the amount of her purchase could be rearranged to make the amount she received back in change. If her purchase amount and her change amount were different and each amount was at least $1, how many possible amounts of change could she have received? (MathCounts)

Problem 3.11. There are three treasure chests. One chest is plated with silver, one with gold, and one with bronze. One of the three chests is filled with great treasure, whereas the other two chests both house man-eating pythons. Faced with a dilemma, you then notice that there are inscriptions on the chests:

Silver Chest: The treasure is in this chest.
Gold Chest: Treasure is not in this chest.
Bronze Chest: Treasure is not in the Gold Chest.

If at least one statement is true and at least one statement is false, which chest contains the treasure? (Waterloo)

Problem 3.12. Jon and Steve ride their bicycles on a path that parallels two side-by-side train tracks running in the east/west direction. Jon rides east at 20 miles per hour, and Steve rides west at 20 miles per hour. Two trains of equal length traveling in opposite directions at constant but different speeds, each passes the two riders. Each train takes exactly 1 minute to go past Jon. The westbound train takes 10 times as long as the eastbound train to go past Steve. What is the length of each train? (AIME)

Problems for Chapter 3

Problem 3.13. An escalator of n steps descends at constant speed. Ann and Zoe walk down the escalator steadily as it moves. Ann goes twice as many escalator steps per minute as Zoe. Ann reaches the bottom after taking 27 steps while Zoe reaches the bottom after taking 18 steps. What is n? (AHSME)

Problem 3.14. Four friends took a multiple-choice test. Their papers are shown below. Each of them has exactly two correct answers. Using their answers, what are the correct answers to questions 1, 2, 3, and 4, in that order? (MathCounts)

Jerry: 1. A   2. B   3. A   4. C
Jim: 1. B   2. A   3. D   4. B
John: 1. B   2. A   3. A   4. C
Jeremy: 1. A   2. C   3. D   4. A

Problem 3.15. Four friends Alice, Bobby, Cathy, and Doug, come to a bridge. They have one flashlight. It's dark, so nobody can walk without the flashlight. Anyone can walk either alone, or together with someone else, but the bridge can't hold more than two people at a time. It takes 1 minute for Alice to cross the bridge, 2 minutes for Bobby, 5 minutes for Cathy, and 10 minutes for Doug. Any two of them together must walk at the speed of the slower one. What is the smallest amount of time needed for all four friends to end up on the other side of the bridge? (Mathworks)

Problem 3.16. A contest challenges you to build a soft-landing device for eggs dropped out of a building. You may make the following assumptions:

- All eggs are identical.
- If an egg survives a drop from some height, it would survive a drop from any lower height.
- If an egg does not survive a drop from some height, it would not survive a drop from any higher height.
- An egg might not even survive a fall from the first floor.

If you have only one egg, to see how good your device is, you must start at the first floor, and test from successive floors until the egg breaks. If you had started at a higher floor and your egg broke on the first drop, you would have no way to determine from which, if any, of the lower floors your device would have worked. What is the tallest building for which you can test every floor with only ten drops and two eggs? (Chicago ARML)

Problem 3.17. The Chateau family has two cupboards for its wine bottles, a small cupboard and one much larger. Being very fussy, they do not like their wine exposed to the light more than 12 times, including both the time they buy it and the time they drink it and each time they open the cupboard. If they drink one bottle each day, how often does the Chateau family need to buy wine? (Francis Xavier)

Problem 3.18. The only people living in an island are knights and liars. The knights always tell the truth, while the liars always lie. A traveler met three islanders and asked each one of them: "How many of the other two islanders are knights?" The first one said: "None." The second one said: "One." What did the third one say? (Moscow)

Problem 3.19. Ben's clock reads 5:37. When is the next time the angle between the hour hand and the minute hand will be the same as it is now?

Problem 3.20. As Kyle walked along a street at a constant speed, he noticed that every 12 minutes, a bus passed him traveling in the same direction as Kyle, and every 4 minutes, a bus passed him traveling in the opposite direction as Kyle. If all the buses travel at a constant speed and leave the terminals at each end of the street at equally spaced intervals, how many minutes long is that interval? (MathCounts)

Problem 3.21. In a mathematics contest, 100 students had to solve four problems. No student solved all four problems. The first problem was solved by 90 students, the second problem was solved by 80 students, the third problem was solved by 70 students, and the fourth problem was solved by 60 students. How many students solved both the third and fourth problems? (PMWC)

Problem 3.22. Rooster, Raven, and Cuckoo took part in a singing contest. Each judge voted for one of the three participants. Woodpecker counted 59 judges, with 15 judges voting for Rooster or Raven, 18 voting for Raven or Cuckoo, and 20 voting for Cuckoo or Rooster. Woodpecker counted poorly. However, each of the four numbers he counted above differed from reality by no more than 13. How many judges voted for Raven? (Moscow)

Problem 3.23. Al walks down to the bottom of an escalator that is moving up and he counts 150 steps. Bob walks up to the top of the escalator and he counts 75 steps. If Al's speed of walking (in steps per unit time) is three times Bob's walking speed, how many steps are visible on the escalator at a given time? (AIME)

Chapter 4

Polynomials

A *polynomial* is a function $p(x)$ in the form of $p(x) = a_n x^n + a_{n-1} x^{n-1} + \cdots + a_1 x + a_0$, where $a_n, a_{n-1}, \ldots, a_1, a_0$ are complex numbers. The highest power in a polynomial is called its *degree*. In arithmetic, when a natural number a is divided by another natural number d, we get a quotient q and a remainder r where $0 \leq r < d$. That is, $a = q \cdot d + r$. Similarly, when a polynomial $p(x)$ is divided by another polynomial $d(x)$ with degree n, we get a quotient polynomial $q(x)$ and a remainder polynomial $r(x)$ where the degree of $r(x)$ is less than n. That is,

$$p(x) = q(x) \cdot d(x) + r(x), \quad 0 \leq \deg(r(x)) < \deg(d(x)).$$

For example, when $x^4 + 1$ is divided by $x^2 + x + 1$, we get a quotient $x^2 - x$ and a remainder $x + 1$. That is, $x^4 + 1 = (x^2 - x)(x^2 + x + 1) + x + 1$.

4.1 Remainder and Factor Theorems

Polynomial division can be carried out using *long division*. However, sometimes the following two theorems can help us solve problems more efficiently.

Theorem 4.1. (Remainder Theorem) *When a polynomial $p(x)$ is divided by $x - a$, the remainder is $p(a)$.*

Theorem 4.2. (Factor Theorem) *$x - a$ is a factor of polynomial $p(x)$ if and only if $p(a) = 0$.*

Let's look at an example.

Example 4.1. The polynomial $p(x)$ satisfies $p(-x) = -p(x)$. When $p(x)$ is divided by $x - 3$, the remainder is 6. Find the remainder when $p(x)$ is divided by $x^2 - 9$.

Answer: $2x$

Solution: Let $ax + b$ be the remainder when $p(x)$ is divided by $x^2 - 9$. That is,

$$p(x) = p_1(x)(x^2 - 9) + ax + b,$$

for some polynomial $p_1(x)$. By the Remainder Theorem, $p(3) = 6$. So $3a + b = 6$. Since $p(-x) = -p(x)$, $p(-3) = -p(3) = -6$. So $-3a + b = -6$. Thus,

$$3a + b = 6,$$
$$-3a + b = -6.$$

Solving the system of equations, we get $a = 2$ and $b = 0$. Therefore the remainder is $ax + b = \boxed{2x}$.

4.2 Roots of a Polynomial

A *root*, or *zero*, of the polynomial $p(x)$ is a number a such that $p(a) = 0$. The Fundamental Theorem of Algebra states that every nonconstant polynomial has a root. In other words, a nonconstant polynomial with degree n has n roots (not necessarily distinct). Although it's good to know how many roots a polynomial should have, the Fundamental Theorem of Algebra does not tell us what the roots are. So we need other tools to find the roots of a polynomial.

Given a quadratic polynomial equation $ax^2 + bx + c = 0$, we can use the quadratic formula to find its roots:
$$x = \frac{-b \pm \sqrt{b^2 - 4ac}}{2a}.$$
Here the expression $b^2 - 4ac$ is called the *discriminant* of the quadratic equation $ax^2 + bx + c = 0$. There are also formulas for the roots of third and fourth degree polynomials, but they are too long to be worth memorizing. French mathematician Evariste Galois proved that there are no general formulas for the roots of polynomials of fifth and higher degrees. Thus, to find the roots of a polynomial of degree 3 or higher, we often need to use some clever substitution to change the polynomial to one we can manage: a quadratic. Let's look at an HMMT problem.

Example 4.2. Find all real roots of

$$(2x+1)(3x+1)(5x+1)(30x+1) = 10.$$

Answer: $\dfrac{-4 \pm \sqrt{31}}{15}$

4.2 Roots of a Polynomial

Solution: Note that
$$(3x+1)(5x+1) = 15x^2 + 8x + 1,$$
and
$$(2x+1)(30x+1) = 60x^2 + 32x + 1 = 4(15x^2 + 8x) + 1.$$
So we let $y = 15x^2 + 8x$ and convert the original fourth degree polynomial to a quadratic polynomial.

$$(y+1)(4y+1) = 10, \quad 4y^2 + 5y - 9 = 0, \quad (4y+9)(y-1) = 0, \quad y = 1 \text{ or } y = -\frac{9}{4}.$$

When $y = 1$, we have $15x^2 + 8x - 1 = 0$. Using the quadratic formula, we get
$$x = \frac{-8 \pm \sqrt{124}}{30} = \frac{-4 \pm \sqrt{31}}{15}.$$

When $y = -\frac{9}{4}$, we have $60x^2 + 32x + 9 = 0$. Since the discriminant $32^2 - 4 \cdot 60 \cdot 9 < 0$, it has no real roots. Therefore, the real roots of our equation are $\boxed{\dfrac{-4 \pm \sqrt{31}}{15}}$.

Our next example comes from Purple Comet.

Example 4.3. There are positive integers m and n so that $x = m + \sqrt{n}$ is a solution to the equation
$$x^2 - 10x + 1 = \sqrt{x}(x+1).$$
Find $m + n$.

Answer: 55

Solution: We divide both sides by x and get
$$x + \frac{1}{x} - 10 = \sqrt{x} + \frac{1}{\sqrt{x}}.$$

Letting $y = \sqrt{x} + \frac{1}{\sqrt{x}}$, we get $y^2 = x + \frac{1}{x} + 2$. Plugging it into our equation, we have
$$y^2 - 2 - 10 = y, \quad y^2 - y - 12 = 0, \quad y = 4 \text{ or } y = -3.$$

Since $\sqrt{x} + \frac{1}{\sqrt{x}}$ is nonnegative, $y = -3$ does not work. So $y = 4$ and
$$\left(\sqrt{x} + \frac{1}{\sqrt{x}}\right) = 4^2, \quad x + \frac{1}{x} + 2 = 16, \quad x^2 - 14x + 1 = 0, \quad x = 7 \pm \sqrt{48}.$$

Since the required solution is of the form $x = m + \sqrt{n}$ for positive integers m and n, we have $m = 7$ and $n = 48$. Therefore, $m + n = 7 + 48 = \boxed{55}$.

4.3 Vieta's Formulas

Given a polynomial $p(x) = a_n x^n + a_{n-1} x^{n-1} + \cdots + a_1 x + a_0$, the Fundamental Theorem of Algebra tells us that $p(x)$ has exactly n roots $r_1, r_2, \ldots, r_n$. Therefore,

$$a_n x^n + a_{n-1} x^{n-1} + \cdots + a_1 x + a_0 = a_n (x - r_1)(x - r_2) \cdots (x - r_n). \qquad (*)$$

Let σ_k be the sum of the roots taken k at a time. That is,

$$\sigma_1 = r_1 + r_2 + \cdots + r_n,$$
$$\sigma_2 = r_1 r_2 + r_1 r_3 + \cdots + r_{n-1} r_n,$$
$$\sigma_3 = r_1 r_2 r_3 + r_1 r_2 r_4 + \cdots + r_{n-2} r_{n-1} r_n,$$
$$\vdots$$
$$\sigma_n = r_1 r_2 r_3 \cdots r_n.$$

In $(*)$, if we expand its right hand side and compare the coefficients of both sides, we get Vieta's Formulas

$$\sigma_1 = -\frac{a_{n-1}}{a_n},$$
$$\sigma_2 = \frac{a_{n-2}}{a_n},$$
$$\vdots$$
$$\sigma_n = (-1)^n \frac{a_0}{a_n}.$$

Vieta's Formulas are useful when we try to find the roots of higher degree polynomials, as we will see in the next two examples.

Example 4.4. The solutions of $x^3 - 3x^2 + kx + 15 = 0$ form an arithmetic sequence. What is the value of k? (MathCounts)

Answer: -13

Solution: Since the three roots of the polynomial $x^3 - 3x^2 + kx + 15$ form an arithmetic sequence, there exist two numbers a and d such that the three roots are $a - d$, a, and $a + d$. By Vieta's Formulas,

$$(a - d) + a + (a + d) = 3, \qquad a = 1.$$

Therefore, $x = 1$ is a root of the polynomial. Thus,

$$1^3 - 3 \cdot 1^2 + k \cdot 1 + 15 = 0, \qquad k = \boxed{-13}.$$

Example 4.5. Find all real roots of $x^4 + (2-x)^4 = 34$. (HMMT)

Answer: $1 \pm \sqrt{2}$

Solution: First we note that if x is a root of the equation, then so is $2-x$. We also note that x and $2-x$ are two distinct roots. So we can let a, $2-a$, b, and $2-b$ be the four roots of the equation. Expanding $x^4 + (2-x)^4 = 34$, we get

$$x^4 - 4x^3 + 12x^2 - 16x - 9 = 0.$$

By Vieta's Formulas, we have

$$a(2-a)b(2-b) = -9, \qquad (**)$$
$$a(2-a) + ab + a(2-b) + (2-a)b + (2-a)(2-b) + b(2-b) = 12.$$

Simplifying the last equation, we get $a(2-a) + b(2-b) = 8$. Letting $c = a(2-a)$, from $(**)$, we get

$$c\bigl(b(2-b)\bigr) = -9, \qquad b(2-b) = \frac{-9}{c}.$$

Since $a(2-a) + b(2-b) = 8$, we have

$$c + \frac{-9}{c} = 8, \qquad c^2 - 8c - 9 = 0, \qquad c = 9, \text{ or } c = -1.$$

When $c = 9$, $a^2 - 2a + 9 = 0$. Since its discriminant $2^2 - 4 \cdot 9 < 0$, it has no real roots. When $c = -1$, $a^2 - 2a - 1 = 0$. $a = \frac{2 \pm \sqrt{8}}{2} = 1 \pm \sqrt{2}$. So the real roots of the equation are $\boxed{1 \pm \sqrt{2}}$.

4.4 Newton's Sums

Given a polynomial $p(x) = a_n x^n + a_{n-1} x^{n-1} + \cdots + a_1 x_1 + a_0$ with roots $r_1, r_2, ..., r_n$, we defined σ_k as the sum of the roots of the polynomial taken k at a time in Section 4.3. Here, we define s_k as $r_1^k + r_2^k + \cdots + r_n^k$. That is,

$$s_1 = r_1 + r_2 + \cdots + r_n, \qquad s_2 = r_1^2 + r_2^2 + \cdots + r_n^2, \qquad s_3 = r_1^3 + r_2^3 + \cdots + r_n^3, \qquad \cdots$$

Newton's Sums state that

$$s_1 = \sigma_1,$$
$$s_2 = \sigma_1 s_1 - 2\sigma_2,$$
$$s_3 = \sigma_1 s_2 - \sigma_2 s_1 + 3\sigma_3,$$
$$\vdots$$

The combination of Vieta's Formulas and Newton's Sums is a powerful tool when we need to work with symmetric polynomials, as we will see in the following examples.

Example 4.6. Let x, y, and z be three distinct complex numbers satisfying

$$x^3 + 5y + 5z = y^3 + 5x + 5z = z^3 + 5x + 5y = 5.$$

What is $x^2 + y^2 + z^2$?

Answer: 10

Solution: Let $x + y + z = \sigma$. We see that $x^3 - 5x + 5\sigma = 5$. Similarly, $y^3 - 5y + 5\sigma = 5$ and $z^3 - 5z + 5\sigma = 5$. So x, y, and z are the roots of the polynomial $t^3 - 5t + 5\sigma - 5 = 0$. By Vieta's Formulas, $x + y + z = 0$. So $t^3 - 5t - 5 = 0$. Thus, $xy + yz + zx = -5$. By Newton's Sums,

$$x^2 + y^2 + z^2 = (x + y + z)^2 - 2(xy + yz + zx) = 0 - 2(-5) = \boxed{10}.$$

Example 4.7. (USAMO) Determine all the roots, real or complex, of the system of simultaneous equations

$$x + y + z = 3,$$
$$x^2 + y^2 + z^2 = 3,$$
$$x^3 + y^3 + z^3 = 3.$$

Answer: $x = y = z = 1$

Solution: Let x, y, and z be the roots of the cubic equation $t^3 + at^2 + bt + c = 0$. By Vieta's Formulas,

$$a = -(x + y + z), \qquad b = xy + yz + zx, \qquad c = -xyz.$$

Since $x + y + z = 3$, we have $a = -3$. Since

$$x^2 + y^2 + z^2 = (x + y + z)^2 - 2(xy + yz + zx), \qquad 3 = 3^2 - 2b,$$

we have $b = 3$. By Newton's Sums,

$$x^3 + y^3 + z^3 = (x + y + z)(x^2 + y^2 + z^2 - xy - yz - zx) + 3xyz, \qquad 3 = 3 \cdot (3 - 3) - 3c.$$

Therefore, $c = -1$. Thus, x, y, and z are the roots of the cubic equation $t^3 - 3t^2 + 3t - 1 = (t - 1)^3 = 0$. Since this cubic equation has three repeated roots which are all equal to 1, we have $\boxed{x = y = z = 1}$.

Problems for Chapter 4

Problem 4.1. If $P(x)$ is a polynomial in x, and
$$x^{23} + 23x^{17} - 18x^{16} - 24x^{15} + 108x^{14} = (x^4 - 3x^2 - 2x + 9) \cdot P(x)$$
for all values of x, compute the sum of the coefficients of $P(x)$. (ARML)

Problem 4.2. Find the remainder when $x^{51} + 51$ is divided by $x + 1$. (AHSME)

Problem 4.3. The polynomial $P(x)$ has remainder 99 when divided by $x - 19$ and remainder 19 when divided by $x - 99$. What is the remainder when $P(x)$ is divided by $(x - 19)(x - 99)$? (AHSME)

Problem 4.4. The polynomial $P(x) = x^3 + ax^2 + bx + c$ has the property that the mean of its zeros, the product of its zeros, and the sum of its coefficients are all equal. The y-intercept of the graph of $y = P(x)$ is 2. What is b? (AMC 12)

Problem 4.5. Suppose that $P(\frac{x}{3}) = x^2 + x + 1$. What is the sum of all values of x for which $P(3x) = 7$? (AMC 10)

Problem 4.6. For nonzero constants c and d, the equation
$$4x^3 - 12x^2 + cx + d = 0$$
has two real roots which add to 0. Find $\frac{d}{c}$. (MAΘ)

Problem 4.7. (MAΘ) Let r, s, t be the roots of $x^3 - 6x^2 + 5x - 7 = 0$. Find
$$\frac{1}{r^2} + \frac{1}{s^2} + \frac{1}{t^2}.$$

Problem 4.8. Suppose that a and b are integers such that $x^2 - x - 1$ is a factor of $ax^3 + bx^2 + 1$. What is b? (AHSME)

Problem 4.9. Find the remainder when $x^{81} + x^{49} + x^{25} + x^9 + x$ is divided by $x^3 - x$.

Problem 4.10. Let r, s, and t be the roots of the polynomial $x^3 + ax^2 + bx + c$. What is the product of $rs + t$, $st + r$, and $tr + s$ in terms of a, b, and c?

Problem 4.11. The product of two of the four zeros of the quartic equation
$$x^4 - 18x^3 + kx^2 + 200x - 1984 = 0$$
is -32. Find k. (USAMO)

Problem 4.12. The roots of $x^4 - x^3 - x^2 - 1 = 0$ are a, b, c, and d. Find
$$p(a) + p(b) + p(c) + p(d),$$
where $p(x) = x^6 - x^5 - x^3 - x^2 - x$. (AIME)

Problem 4.13. (MAΘ) If the roots of $3x^3 - 14x^2 + x + 62 = 0$ are a, b, and c, determine
$$\frac{1}{a+3} + \frac{1}{b+3} + \frac{1}{c+3}.$$

Problem 4.14. Let a and b be complex numbers satisfying the following two equations
$$a^2 + b^2 = 5,$$
$$a^3 + b^3 = 7.$$
What is the greatest possible value for $a + b$? (Purple Comet)

Problem 4.15. Let $f(x) = x^4 + x^3 + x^2 + x + 1$. Find the remainder when $f(x^5)$ is divided by $f(x)$.

Problem 4.16. Find the remainder when $x^{60} - 1$ is divided by $x^3 - 2$.

Problem 4.17. There exists an 11th degree polynomial $p(x)$ such that
$$(x+1)p(x) = (x-10)p(x+1).$$
Find the sum of the roots of $p(x)$.

Problem 4.18. What is the remainder when $x^{44} + x^{33} + x^{22} + x^{11} + 1$ is divided by $x^4 + x^3 + x^2 + x + 1$? (PMO)

Problem 4.19. Let $p(x)$ be a polynomial with degree n and
$$p(k) = \frac{k}{k+1}, \qquad k = 0, 1, ..., n.$$
What is $p(n+1)$? (USAMO)

Problem 4.20. Let x and y be real numbers satisfying
$$(x^2 + x - 1)(x^2 - x + 1) = 2(y^3 - 2\sqrt{5} - 1)$$
and
$$(y^2 + y - 1)(y^2 - y + 1) = 2(x^3 + 2\sqrt{5} - 1).$$
Find $8x^2 + 4y^3$. (Purple Comet)

Chapter 5

Sequences and Series

A *sequence* is an ordered list of numbers. Sometimes, a sequence is called a *progression*. We often use a_n to denote the nth term of a sequence. When we add all the numbers of a sequence, the sum is called an *infinite series*, or just a *series*. We use $\sum_{n=1}^{\infty} a_n$ to denote the infinite sum $a_1 + a_2 + a_3 + a_4 + \cdots$, and $\prod_{n=1}^{\infty} a_n$ to denote the infinite product $a_1 \cdot a_2 \cdot a_3 \cdot a_4 \cdots$.

5.1 Arithmetic and Geometric Sequences

Given $\{a_1, a_2, a_3, \ldots\}$, we call the sequence $\{a_2 - a_1, a_3 - a_2, a_4 - a_3, \ldots\}$ its *sequence of first differences*, and the sequence $\{(a_3 - a_2) - (a_2 - a_1), (a_4 - a_3) - (a_3 - a_2), \ldots\}$ its *sequence of second differences*, and so on. If every term in its sequence of first differences is the same, then the original sequence is called an *arithmetic sequence*, or an *arithmetic progression*. The difference is called the *common difference*. In an arithmetic sequence with common difference d, we have

$$a_n = a_1 + (n-1)d, \qquad 2a_{n+1} = a_n + a_{n+2}, \quad \text{for all } n \geq 1.$$

If the ratio between any two consecutive terms of a sequence is a constant, the sequence is called a *geometric sequence* or a *geometric progression*. The ratio is called the *common ratio*. In a geometric sequence with common ratio r, we have

$$a_n = a_1 r^{n-1}, \qquad a_{n+1}^2 = a_n \cdot a_{n+2}, \quad \text{for all } n \geq 1.$$

Example 5.1. A sequence of three real numbers forms an arithmetic progression with a first term of 9. If 2 is added to the 2nd term and 20 is added to the 3rd term, the three resulting numbers form a geometric progression. What is the smallest possible value for the 3rd term of the geometric progression? (AMC 12)

Answer: 1

Solution: Let d be the common difference of the arithmetic progression. The original sequence is: $\{9, 9+d, 9+2d\}$. Since $\{9, 9+d+2, 9+2d+20\}$ is a geometric progression, we have

$$(d+11)^2 = 9(2d+29),$$
$$d^2 + 22d + 121 = 18d + 261.$$

Therefore,
$$d^2 + 4d - 140 = 0, \qquad (d+14)(d-10) = 0.$$

So $d = -14$, or $d = 10$. When $d = -14$, the third term $2d + 29$ is 1. When $d = 10$, $2d + 29 = 49$. Thus the smallest possible value for the third term of the geometric progression is $\boxed{1}$.

Sometimes we are given a sequence whose n^{th} term is the product of the nth term of an arithmetic sequence $\{a_1, a_2, a_3, ...\}$ and the nth term of a geometric sequence $\{b_1, b_2, b_3, ...\}$. Then the sequence $\{a_1 b_1, a_2 b_2, a_3 b_3, ...\}$ is called an *arithmetico-geometric sequence*. The sum of its consecutive terms is called an *arithmetico-geometric series*. There is a standard way to compute an arithmetico-geometric series. We introduce this method by working through an ARML problem.

Example 5.2. Compute the unique positive integer n such that

$$2 \cdot 2^2 + 3 \cdot 2^3 + 4 \cdot 2^4 + \cdots + n \cdot 2^n = 2^{n+10}.$$

Answer: 513

Solution: We see that $\{2, 3, 4, ...\}$ is an arithmetic sequence and $\{2^2, 2^3, 2^4, ...\}$ is a geometric sequence. So we need to compute an arithmetico-geometric series. First, we write down this series:

$$2 \cdot 2^2 + 3 \cdot 2^3 + 4 \cdot 2^4 + \cdots + n \cdot 2^n = 2^{n+10}. \qquad (*)$$

Next, we multiply both sides of $(*)$ by 2, the common ratio of the geometric sequence, and get

$$2 \cdot 2^2 + 3 \cdot 2^3 + 4 \cdot 2^4 + \cdots + n \cdot 2^n = 2^{n+10},$$
$$2 \cdot 2^3 + 3 \cdot 2^4 + 4 \cdot 2^5 + \cdots + n \cdot 2^{n+1} = 2^{n+11}.$$

Finally, subtracting these two equations, we get

$$2 \cdot 2^2 + 2^3 + 2^4 + \cdots + 2^n - n \cdot 2^{n+1} = -2^{n+10},$$
$$n \cdot 2^{n+1} - 2 \cdot 2^2 - 2^3(1 + 2 + 2^2 + \cdots + 2^{n-3}) = 2^{n+10}.$$

5.2 Telescoping Sums

Thus,

$$n \cdot 2^{n+1} - 8 - 8\left(\frac{1-2^{n-2}}{1-2}\right) = 2^{n+10}, \qquad n \cdot 2^{n+1} - 8 - 8(2^{n-2} - 1) = 2^{n+10}.$$

Therefore,

$$(n-1) \cdot 2^{n+1} = 2^{n+10}, \qquad n - 1 = 2^9, \qquad n = 2^9 + 1 = \boxed{513}.$$

5.2 Telescoping Sums

A telescoping sum is an infinite or finite sum in which most terms cancel each other, leaving only a fixed number of terms. For example,

$$\sum_{n=1}^{\infty} \frac{1}{n(n+1)} = \sum_{n=1}^{\infty} \left(\frac{1}{n} - \frac{1}{n+1}\right) = \left(1 - \frac{1}{2}\right) + \left(\frac{1}{2} - \frac{1}{3}\right) + \left(\frac{1}{3} - \frac{1}{4}\right) + \cdots = 1.$$

When using this technique, we write the general term of the series as the difference of two expressions and see if the terms can cancel. If the general term is a fraction, we use *partial fraction decomposition* to rewrite it as the sum of several fractions with simpler denominators. For example, to decompose $\frac{2x-2}{x^2+2x}$, we write

$$\frac{2x-2}{x^2+2x} = \frac{A}{x} + \frac{B}{x+2}.$$

Then we get

$$2x - 2 = (A+B)x + 2A.$$

Comparing the coefficients of both sides, we get $A + B = 2$ and $2A = -2$. Therefore, $A = -1$ and $B = 3$. Thus,

$$\frac{2x-2}{x^2+2x} = -\frac{1}{x} + \frac{3}{x+2}.$$

Example 5.3. Evaluate $\sum_{n=3}^{\infty} \frac{1}{n^5 - 5n^3 + 4n}$. (Purple Comet)

Answer: $\frac{1}{96}$

Solution:

$$\sum_{n=3}^{\infty} \frac{1}{n^5 - 5n^3 + 4n} = \sum_{n=3}^{\infty} \frac{1}{n(n^4 - 5n^2 + 4)} = \sum_{n=3}^{\infty} \frac{1}{n(n^2-4)(n^2-1)}$$

$$= \sum_{n=3}^{\infty} \frac{1}{(n-2)(n-1)n(n+1)(n+2)} = \frac{1}{4}\sum_{n=3}^{\infty} \frac{(n+2)-(n-2)}{(n-2)(n-1)n(n+1)(n+2)}$$

$$= \frac{1}{4}\sum_{n=3}^{\infty} \left(\frac{1}{(n-2)(n-1)n(n+1)} - \frac{1}{(n-1)n(n+1)(n+2)} \right)$$

$$= \frac{1}{4} \cdot \frac{1}{(3-2)(3-1)3(3+1)} = \boxed{\frac{1}{96}}.$$

5.3 Recurrence Relations

When we define a term of a sequence as a function of the preceding terms, we get a *recurrence relation*. In other words, given the values of the initial terms, we define the sequence recursively. To solve a recurrence relation is to find a *closed form* of the function. That is, we would like to get rid of recursion from the definition of the function. Let's look at an AIME problem.

Example 5.4. You have 8 cubes of size 1 through 8. A tower is to be built using all 8 cubes according to the following rules: a) Any cube may be the bottom cube in the tower. b) The cube immediately on top of a cube with size k must have size at most $k+2$. How many different towers can be constructed?

Answer: 1458

Solution: Let a_n be the number of different towers that can be constructed using n cubes. We see that $a_1 = 1$ and $a_2 = 2$. We would like to find a recurrence relation for a_n. Given a tower with $n-1$ cubes of size 1 to $n-1$, where $n \geq 3$, we can put the nth cube with size n at the bottom, or above the cube with size $n-1$, or above the cube with size $n-2$. Each of these three placements gives us a distinct configuration of the cubes. Therefore, $a_n = 3a_{n-1}$. So we have

$$a_3 = 2 \cdot 3, \quad a_4 = 2 \cdot 3^2, \quad \cdots, \quad a_8 = 2 \cdot 3^6 = \boxed{1458}.$$

5.4 Characteristic Equations

In math competitions, often we are asked to solve recurrence relations such as

$$a_n = Aa_{n-1} + Ba_{n-2},$$

where A and B are real numbers. A systematic way to solve this type of problems is to find the roots of its characteristic equation

5.4 Characteristic Equations

$$\lambda^2 - A\lambda - B = 0.$$

If the characteristic equation of the recurrence relation has two distinct real roots λ_1 and λ_2, then for some real numbers α and β, we have

$$a_n = \alpha \lambda_1^n + \beta \lambda_2^n.$$

If the characteristic equation has two identical roots $\lambda_1 = \lambda_2 = \lambda$, then

$$a_n = \alpha \lambda^n + \beta n \lambda^n,$$

for some real numbers α and β.

Example 5.5. The numbers in the sequence 1, 6, 15, 28, 45, ... are called the hexagonal numbers. What is the 11th hexagonal number?

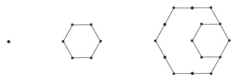

Answer: 231

Solution: Let h_n be the nth hexagonal number. Let's compute its sequence of first differences. We get the sequence $5, 9, 13, 17, \ldots$. Next, let's find its sequence of second differences. We get the sequence $4, 4, 4, \ldots$. Therefore, for all $n \geq 1$,

$$(h_{n+3} - h_{n+2}) - (h_{n+2} - h_{n+1}) = (h_{n+2} - h_{n+1}) - (h_{n+1} - h_n).$$

That is, $h_{n+3} - 3h_{n+2} + 3h_{n+1} - h_n = 0$ for all $n \geq 1$.

The characteristic equation of this recurrence relation is

$$\lambda^3 - 3\lambda^2 + 3\lambda - 1 = 0, \qquad (\lambda - 1)^3 = 0.$$

Since it has three repeated roots, there are real numbers A, B, and C, such that

$$h(n) = A(1)^n + Bn(1)^n + Cn^2(1)^n = A + Bn + Cn^2.$$

Plugging in the first three hexagonal numbers, we get

$$A + B + C = 1,$$
$$A + 2B + 4C = 6,$$
$$A + 3B + 9C = 15.$$

Solving the system of equations, we get $A = 0$, $B = -1$ and $C = 2$. Therefore, $h_n = 2n^2 - n$. Thus the 11th hexagonal number is $2 \cdot 11^2 - 11 = \boxed{231}$.

A recurrence relation such as $a_n = Aa_{n-1} + Ba_{n-2}$ is called *homogeneous* because a_n can be expressed in terms of and only in terms of constant multiples of preceding terms. Sometimes we also need to solve *non-homogeneous* recurrence relations like

$$a_n = Aa_{n-1} + Ba_{n-2} + f(n),$$

where $f(n) \neq 0$ is a function of n. Trying to eliminate the non-homogeneous part is a good way to approach non-homogeneous recurrence relations. For example, to solve $a_{n+2} = 2a_{n+1} - a_n + 1$, we write

$$a_{n+2} = 2a_{n+1} - a_n + 1,$$
$$a_{n+3} = 2a_{n+2} - a_{n+1} + 1.$$

Subtracting the two equations, we get $a_{n+3} = 3a_{n+2} - 3a_{n+1} + a_n$, a homogeneous recurrence relation. Let's look at a classic computer science problem.

Example 5.6. A computer system considers a string of decimal digits a valid codeword if it contains an even number of 0s. Find a closed form for a_n, the number of valid n-digit codewords.

Answer: $\frac{1}{2}(8^n + 10^n)$

Solution: We see that $a_1 = 9$. A valid 2-digit codeword either contains two zeros or no zeros. So $a_2 = 9 \cdot 9 + 1 = 82$. For any $n-1$ digits, we have a_{n-1} valid strings and $10^{n-1} - a_{n-1}$ invalid strings. Now an n-digit codeword can start with either 0 or some other digit. The number of valid codewords starting with 0 is $10^{n-1} - a_{n-1}$ because one more 0 makes an invalid string valid. The number of valid codewords starting with some other digit is $9a_{n-1}$. Therefore,

$$a_n = 10^{n-1} - a_{n-1} + 9a_{n-1} = 8a_{n-1} + 10^{n-1}.$$

Thus,

$$10a_n = 80a_{n-1} + 10^n,$$
$$a_{n+1} = 8a_n + 10^n.$$

Subtracting the two equations, we eliminate the non-homogeneous part and get $a_{n+1} = 18a_n - 80a_{n-1}$. Solving its characteristic equation $\lambda^2 - 18\lambda + 80 = 0$, we get $\lambda_1 = 8$ and $\lambda_2 = 10$. Thus,

$$a_n = A \cdot 8^n + B \cdot 10^n,$$

for some real numbers A and B. Plugging a_1 and a_2 into the equation, we have,

$$8A + 10B = 9, \quad \text{and} \quad 64A + 100B = 82.$$

So $A = \frac{1}{2}$ and $B = \frac{1}{2}$. Therefore, $a_n = \boxed{\frac{1}{2}(8^n + 10^n)}$.

Problems for Chapter 5

Problem 5.1. The sequence

$$3, 4, 13, 15, 30, 33, 54, 58, 85, 90, \ldots$$

contains, in increasing order, all the positive integers that yield a triangular number when multiplied by 7. What is the 100th term of this sequence? (MathCounts)

Problem 5.2. In order, the first four terms of a sequence are 2, 6, 12, and 72, where each term, beginning with the third term, is the product of the two preceding terms. If the ninth term is $2^a 3^b$, what is the value of $a + b$? (MathCounts)

Problem 5.3. The sequence $a_1, a_2, a_3, \ldots$ satisfies $a_1 = 19$, $a_9 = 99$, and for all $n \geq 3$, a_n is the arithmetic mean of the first $n - 1$ terms. Find a_2. (AHSME)

Problem 5.4. Suppose that the sequence $\{a_n\}$ is defined by $a_1 = 2$, and

$$a_{n+1} = a_n + 2n,$$

for $n \geq 1$. What is a_{100}? (AHSME)

Problem 5.5. The increasing sequence of positive integers $a_1, a_2, a_3, \ldots$ has the property that $a_{n+2} = a_n + a_{n+1}$ for all $n \geq 1$. Suppose that $a_7 = 120$, what is a_8? (AHSME)

Problem 5.6. Let 1, 4, ... and 9, 16, ... be two arithmetic sequences. The set S is the union of the first 2004 terms of each sequence. How many distinct numbers are in S? (AMC 10)

Problem 5.7. Let $f(n) = 3f(n-2) - 2f(n-1)$, where $f(2) = 3$ and $f(1) = -1$. What is the value of $f(9)$? (MathCounts)

Problem 5.8. A sequence is defined by $a_1 = 0$, $a_2 = 4$, and $a_n = 4(a_{n-1} - a_{n-2})$ for $n > 2$. What is the greatest value of n such that $n < 100$ and a_n is a power of 2?

Problem 5.9. For any sequence of real numbers $A = a_1, a_2, a_3, \ldots$, define ΔA as the sequence of numbers $a_2 - a_1, a_3 - a_2, a_4 - a_3, \ldots$, whose n^{th} term is $a_{n+1} - a_n$. Suppose that all of the terms of the sequence $\Delta(\Delta A)$ are 1, and that $a_{19} = a_{92} = 0$. Find a_1. (AIME)

Problem 5.10. Find the eighth term of the sequence 1440, 1716, 1848, ..., whose terms are formed by multiplying the corresponding terms of two arithmetic sequences. (AIME)

Problem 5.11. Consider the sequence 1, 2, 3, 4, 5, 6, 7, 8, 9, 19, 29, ..., where the sum of the digits of a_n, the nth term, is equal to n, and a_{n+1} is the smallest positive integer such that $a_{n+1} > a_n$. How many digits are in the 100th term of this sequence? (MathCounts)

Problem 5.12. Evaluate the infinite product $\prod_{n=2}^{\infty} \frac{n^3 - 1}{n^3 + 1}$. (Putnam)

Problem 5.13. The increasing sequence 1, 3, 4, 9, 10, 12, 13, ... consists of all those positive integers which are powers of 3 or sums of distinct powers of 3. Find the 100th term of this sequence. (AIME)

Problem 5.14. Consider the sequence of numbers: 4, 7, 1, 8, 9, 7, 6, ... For $n > 2$, the nth term of the sequence is the units digit of the sum of the two previous terms. Let S_n denote the sum of the first n terms of this sequence. What is the smallest value of n for which $S_n > 10,000$? (AMC 12)

Problem 5.15. Find the units digit of the number

$$\left(2 + \sqrt{3}\right)^{2016} + \left(2 - \sqrt{3}\right)^{2016}.$$

Problem 5.16. In the decimal representation of the number $(2 + \sqrt{3})^{2016}$, what is the digit immediately to the right of the decimal point?

Problem 5.17. (USAMTS) Evaluate the value of

$$S = \sqrt{1 + \frac{1}{1^2} + \frac{1}{2^2}} + \sqrt{1 + \frac{1}{2^2} + \frac{1}{3^2}} + \cdots + \sqrt{1 + \frac{1}{1999^2} + \frac{1}{2000^2}}.$$

Problem 5.18. Let $a_1, a_2, a_3, \ldots$ be a sequence of positive real numbers such that $a_k a_{k+2} = a_{k+1} + 1$ for all positive integers k. If a_1 and a_2 are positive integers, find the maximum possible value of a_{2014}. (USAMTS)

Problem 5.19. Find the value of $S = \frac{1}{3^2 + 1} + \frac{1}{4^2 + 2} + \frac{1}{5^2 + 3} + \cdots$. (HMMT)

Problem 5.20. (AIME) A sequence is defined over non-negative integral indices in the following way: $a_0 = a_1 = 3$, $a_{n+1} a_{n-1} = a_n^2 + 2016$. Find the greatest integer that does not exceed

$$\frac{a_{2015}^2 + a_{2016}^2}{a_{2015} \cdot a_{2016}}.$$

Chapter 6

Functional Equations

When solving ordinary equations, we need to find unknown numbers that satisfy the given equations. Sometimes the unknowns are functions, instead of numbers. In that case, the given equations are called *functional equations*. For example, a recurrence relation such as $f(n) = 3f(n-2) - 2f(n-1)$ is a functional equation. Do we need to know functional equations for MathCounts? Absolutely. Just take a look at the 2015 MathCounts Chapter Competition Target Round.

6.1 Evaluating Functional Equations

Problems involving functional equations are usually hard because there are no fixed methods to deal with them. To get a feel of how to solve them, we need a lot of practice. Let's look at an example.

Example 6.1. The function $f : \mathbb{R} \to \mathbb{R}$ satisfies $2f(x) + f(1-x) = x^2$ for all $x \in \mathbb{R}$. Find $f(5)$.

Answer: $\dfrac{34}{3}$

Solution: We try to get $f(x)$ and $f(1-x)$ in terms of x. Currently we have one equation and two unknowns. To get a second equation, we can replace x with $1 - x$ in the original equation. Then we have

$$2f(x) + f(1-x) = x^2,$$
$$2f(1-x) + f(x) = (1-x)^2.$$

Multiplying the first equation by 2 and subtracting the second equation, we get

$$3f(x) = 2x^2 - (1-x)^2 = x^2 + 2x - 1,$$

$$f(x) = \frac{x^2 + 2x - 1}{3}. \quad \text{Thus,} \quad f(5) = \frac{25 + 10 - 1}{3} = \boxed{\frac{34}{3}}.$$

Before we move on to the next example, let us define some terms. A function that satisfies $f(x) = f(-x)$ is called an *even* function. Likewise, a function that satisfies $f(x) = -f(-x)$ is an *odd* function. A function $f(x)$ is an *increasing* function or *non-decreasing* function if $f(a) \le f(b)$ whenever $a < b$. A function $f(x)$ is a *strictly increasing* function if $f(a) < f(b)$ whenever $a < b$. Similarly, a function $f(x)$ is a *decreasing* function or *non-increasing* function if $f(a) \ge f(b)$ whenever $a < b$. A function $f(x)$ is a *strictly decreasing* function if $f(a) > f(b)$ whenever $a < b$. An increasing or a decreasing function is also called a *monotonic* function.

Example 6.2. Let $f : \mathbb{Z}^+ \to \mathbb{Z}^+$ be a strictly increasing function such that for all $m, n \in \mathbb{Z}^+$,

$$f(n + f(m)) = f(n) + m + 1.$$

Find all possible values of $f(2016)$.

Answer: 2017

Solution: Since f is a strictly increasing function, for all $n \in \mathbb{Z}^+$, $f(n+1) > f(n)$. Since f is a function from positive integers to positive integers, we have $f(n) \ge n$ for all n. First we prove that $f(1) \ne 1$. Suppose to the contrary that $f(1) = 1$. Then

$$f(2) = f(1 + f(1)) = f(1) + 1 + 1 = 3,$$
$$f(4) = f(1 + f(2)) = f(1) + 2 + 1 = 4.$$

But this is impossible, because $f(3)$ should be an integer between $f(2)$ and $f(4)$ but there is no integer between 3 and 4. Thus, there is a positive integer $a \ne 1$ such that $f(1) = a$. Now

$$f(1) = a,$$
$$f(1 + a) = f(1 + f(1)) = f(1) + 1 + 1 = a + 2.$$

Since $a \ne 1$ and there is only one integer between a and $a+2$, we must have $f(2) = a+1$ and $1+a = 3$. So $f(1) = a = 2$ and $f(2) = a+1 = 3$. Next, we use induction to prove that $f(n) = n+1$ for all $n \in \mathbb{Z}^+$. We have shown that the base case is true. If $f(k) = k+1$ for all $k \le n$, then $f(n-1) = n$ and

$$f(n+1) = f(1 + f(n-1)) = f(1) + n - 1 + 1 = n + 2.$$

Thus, $f(n) = n+1$ for all $n \in \mathbb{Z}^+$. In particular, $f(2016) = 1 + 2016 = \boxed{2017}$.

6.2 Properties of Functions and Polynomial Equations

Properties of functions such as one-to-one, onto, and one-to-one correspondence play a key role in solving functional equations. Here we will give a formal definition for each of them.

Definition 6.1. Let X and Y be two sets. A function $f : X \to Y$ is *injective* or *one-to-one*, if for any $x_1, x_2 \in X$ such that $x_1 \neq x_2$, we have $f(x_1) \neq f(x_2)$. An injective function is an *injection*. Note that if f is an injection, then for any $x_1, x_2 \in X$, $f(x_1) = f(x_2)$ implies $x_1 = x_2$.

Definition 6.2. Let X and Y be two sets. A function $f : X \to Y$ is *surjective* or *onto*, if for any $y \in Y$, there is an $x \in X$ such that $f(x) = y$. A surjective function is a *surjection*.

Definition 6.3. Let X and Y be two sets. A function $f : X \to Y$ is *bijective* or a *one-to-one correspondence*, if it is both injective and surjective. A bijective function is a *bijection*. Note that a strictly monotonic function is a bijection.

If a polynomial has two or more distinct roots, then clearly it is not one-to-one. However, when the given functional equation is a polynomial, we can apply properties of a polynomial to solve the problem. In our next example from AwesomeMath, we solve the problem by using the fact that any nonconstant polynomial of degree n has at most n roots.

Example 6.3. Find all polynomials satisfying the functional equation

$$xP(x-1) = (x-15)P(x).$$

Answer: $P(x) = a(x-14)(x-13)\cdots(x-1)(x)$, for some constant a.

Solution: Plugging $x = 15$ in the original equation, we get $15P(14) = 0$. Therefore, $x = 14$ is a root of $P(x)$. So there is a polynomial $P_1(x)$ such that $P(x) = (x-14)P_1(x)$. Thus $P(x-1) = (x-15)P_1(x-1)$. Now the original equation can be written as

$$x(x-15)P_1(x-1) = (x-15)(x-14)P_1(x).$$

Plugging $x = 14$ in the equation above, we get $14 \cdot (-1) \cdot P_1(13) = 0$. So $x = 13$ is a root of $P(x)$ and there is a polynomial $P_2(x)$ such that $P_1(x) = (x-13)P_2(x)$. Repeating the process, we see that $P(x)$ has 14, 13, ..., 2, 1, 0 as its roots. So there is a polynomial $Q(x)$ such that

$$P(x) = Q(x)(x-14)(x-13)\cdots(x-1)(x).$$

Plugging this into the original equation, we get

$$xQ(x-1)(x-15)(x-14)\cdots(x-2)(x-1) = (x-15)Q(x)(x-14)(x-13)\cdots(x-1)(x).$$

So $Q(x-1) = Q(x)$ for all but finitely many x. That is, the polynomial $Q(x)-Q(x-1)$ has infinitely many zeros. But the degree of $Q(x)$ is finite, so $Q(x)$ is a constant a. Thus,

$$\boxed{P(x) = a(x-14)(x-13)\cdots(x-1)(x) \text{ for some constant } a}.$$

6.3 Solving Single Variable Functional Equations

Functional equations with one variable are relatively easier to solve than their multi-variable counterparts. The most common method of solving such an equation is substitution. We try to replace one expression with another and get a system of equations that we can solve. Let's look at an AwesomeMath problem.

Example 6.4. Find all functions $f : \mathbb{R}\setminus\{0,1\} \to \mathbb{R}$ such that

$$f(x) + f\left(\frac{1}{1-x}\right) = 1 + \frac{1}{x(1-x)}.$$

Answer: $f(x) = x + \dfrac{1}{x}$

Solution: Since we have one equation and two unknowns $f(x)$ and $f\left(\frac{1}{1-x}\right)$, we replace x with $\dfrac{1}{1-x}$ in our equation. We get

$$f\left(\frac{1}{1-x}\right) + f\left(\frac{1}{1-\frac{1}{1-x}}\right) = 1 + \frac{1}{\frac{1}{1-x} \cdot \frac{x}{x-1}},$$

$$f\left(\frac{1}{1-x}\right) + f\left(1 - \frac{1}{x}\right) = 3 - x - \frac{1}{x}.$$

Now we get a third unknown $f\left(1 - \frac{1}{x}\right)$. We replace x with $1 - \frac{1}{x}$ in our original equation and get

$$f\left(1 - \frac{1}{x}\right) + f\left(\frac{1}{\frac{1}{x}}\right) = 1 + \frac{1}{\frac{1}{x}(1 - \frac{1}{x})},$$

$$f\left(1 - \frac{1}{x}\right) + f(x) = 2 + x - \frac{1}{1-x}.$$

Now we have a system of three unknowns and three equations:

6.4 Solving Multi-Variable Functional Equations

$$f(x) + f\left(\frac{1}{1-x}\right) = 1 + \frac{1}{x(1-x)},$$
$$f\left(\frac{1}{1-x}\right) + f\left(1 - \frac{1}{x}\right) = 3 - x - \frac{1}{x},$$
$$f\left(1 - \frac{1}{x}\right) + f(x) = 2 + x - \frac{1}{1-x}.$$

Adding these three equations together, we get

$$2f(x) + 2f\left(\frac{1}{1-x}\right) + 2f\left(1 - \frac{1}{x}\right) = 1 + \frac{1}{x(1-x)} + 3 - x - \frac{1}{x} + 2 + x - \frac{1}{1-x},$$
$$f(x) + f\left(\frac{1}{1-x}\right) + f\left(1 - \frac{1}{x}\right) = 3.$$

Since $f\left(\frac{1}{1-x}\right) + f\left(1 - \frac{1}{x}\right) = 3 - x - \frac{1}{x}$, we have

$$f(x) = 3 - \left(3 - x - \frac{1}{x}\right). \quad \text{So} \quad \boxed{f(x) = x + \frac{1}{x}}.$$

6.4 Solving Multi-Variable Functional Equations

When we solve a functional equation with more than one variable, it is often beneficial to reduce it to a single variable functional equation by setting other variables equal to constants. Let's look at an AHSME problem.

Example 6.5. The function f satisfies the functional equation

$$f(x) + f(y) = f(x+y) - xy - 1$$

for every pair of real numbers x and y. If $f(1) = 1$, how many integers $n \neq 1$ satisfy $f(n) = n$?

Answer: 1 integer

Solution: For any integer n, letting $x = n$ and $y = 1$, we get $f(n+1) - f(n) = n+2$. Similarly, letting $x = n+1$ and $y = 1$, we get $f(n+2) - f(n+1) = (n+1)+1+1 = n+3$. Therefore, the second difference

$$(f(n+2) - f(n+1)) - (f(n+1) - f(n)) = 1.$$

From the solution of Example 5.5, we know that if the second differences are all the same, then the recurrence relation is a quadratic function. Therefore, there are real numbers a, b, and c such that $f(n) = an^2 + bn + c$. In the original equation, when we let $x = y = 0$, we get $2f(0) = f(0) - 1$. So, $f(0) = -1$. Similarly, letting $x = y = 1$, we get $f(2) = 2f(1) + 1 + 1 = 4$. Plugging in $f(0)$, $f(1)$, and $f(2)$, we get

$$a \cdot 0^2 + b \cdot 0 + c = -1,$$
$$a \cdot 1^2 + b \cdot 1 + c = 1,$$
$$a \cdot 2^2 + b \cdot 2 + c = 4.$$

Solving the system, we get $a = \frac{1}{2}$, $b = \frac{3}{2}$, and $c = -1$. Thus $f(n) = \frac{n^2+3n-2}{2}$ for all integers n. To find those n such that $f(n) = n$, we have

$$\frac{n^2 + 3n - 2}{2} = n, \quad n^2 + n - 2 = 0, \quad n = 1, \text{ or } n = -2.$$

Thus, there is $\boxed{1 \text{ integer}}$ $n \neq 1$ such that $f(n) = n$, namely, -2.

Example 6.6. (EGMO) Find all functions $f : \mathbb{R} \to \mathbb{R}$ such that for all $x, y \in \mathbb{R}$,

$$f(yf(x+y) + f(x)) = 4x + 2yf(x+y).$$

Answer: $f(x) = 2x$

Solution: Letting $y = 0$, we get $f(f(x)) = 4x$. For any $t_1, t_2 \in \mathbb{R}$ such that $t_1 \neq t_2$, we have

$$f(f(t_1)) = 4t_1 \neq 4t_2 = f(f(t_2)).$$

So $f(t_1) \neq f(t_2)$. That is, f is injective. Plugging $x = 0$ into $f(f(x)) = 4x$, we have $f(f(0)) = 4 \cdot 0$, $f(f(f(0))) = f(4 \cdot 0) = f(0)$. But $f(f(f(0))) = 4f(0)$, so $f(0) = 4f(0)$.

Therefore, $f(0) = 0$. Plugging $x = 0$ and $y = 1$ into the original equation, we get $f(f(1)) = 2f(1)$. Since $f(f(x)) = 4x$, $2f(1) = 4$. So $f(1) = 2$. Now plugging $y = 1 - x$ into the original equation, we get

$$f(2(1-x) + f(x)) = 4x + 2(1-x)f(1) = 4 = f(f(1)).$$

Since f is injective, we have

$$2(1-x) + f(x) = f(1) = 2, \quad \boxed{f(x) = 2x}.$$

This concludes our study of algebra. We will start to explore geometry in the next chapter. Some mathletes can bash their way through an algebra problem, but sit on their hands staring at the diagram when they deal with geometry. While blind algebraic manipulation might not be the best approach to a math problem, getting your hands dirty is nevertheless a good problem solving strategy. After all, intuition is inseparable from toil, even for geometry.

Problems for Chapter 6

Problem 6.1. A function f satisfies $f(x+y) = 4f(x) \cdot f(y)$ for all real numbers x and y. If $f(3) = 32$, determine the value of $f(1)$.

Problem 6.2. If $f\left(\dfrac{x+1}{x}\right) = \dfrac{x^2-1}{x} + \dfrac{x}{x+1}$, find $f(x)$.

Problem 6.3. The function f has the property that whenever a, b, and n are positive integers such that $a+b = 2^n$, then $f(a) + f(b) = n^2$. What is $f(2002)$? (HMMT)

Problem 6.4. A function $f(x, y)$ of two variables has the property that
$$f(x, y) = x + f(x-1, x-y).$$
If $f(1, 0) = 5$, then what is the value of $f(5, 2)$? (Mandelbrot)

Problem 6.5. Find all functions $f : \mathbb{Q} \to \mathbb{Q}$ such that $f(2x) = 2f(x)$ and $f(x) + f(\dfrac{1}{x}) = 1$. (AoPS)

Problem 6.6. Let $P(x)$ be a polynomial with real coefficients and $P(-x) = -P(x)$. If the sum of the coefficients of $P(x)$ is 1988, what is the remainder when $P(x)$ is divided by $x^3 - x$? (AwesomeMath)

Problem 6.7. (AHSME) How many polynomial functions f of degree greater than or equal to 1 satisfy
$$f(x^2) = (f(x))^2 = f(f(x))?$$

Problem 6.8. Find all polynomials $P(x)$ with real coefficients satisfying the following functional equation
$$P(x+1) - P(x) = 3x^2 + 3x + 1.$$

Problem 6.9. The function f has the property that, for each real number x,
$$f(x) + f(x-1) = x^2.$$
If $f(19) = 94$, what is the remainder when $f(94)$ is divided by 1000? (AIME)

Problem 6.10. A nonconstant polynomial $P(x)$ satisfies
$$P(x-1) + P(x+1) = 2P(x)$$
for all real numbers x. What is the degree of $P(x)$?

Problem 6.11. Find $f(x)$ if
$$f(x) + f\left(\frac{x-1}{x}\right) = 1 - x.$$

Problem 6.12. (AwesomeMath) Find all polynomials $f(x)$ such that for all real numbers x,
$$xf(x-1) = (x+1)f(x).$$

Problem 6.13. Find all strictly increasing functions $f : \mathbb{Z}^+ \to \mathbb{Z}^+$ such that $f(2) = 2$ and $f(mn) = f(m)f(n)$ for all m and n. (CMO)

Problem 6.14. Let $P_0(x) = x^3 + 313x^2 - 77x - 8$. For integers $n \geq 1$, define
$$P_n(x) = P_{n-1}(x - n).$$
What is the coefficient of x in $P_{20}(x)$? (AIME)

Problem 6.15. The function f, defined on the set of ordered pairs of positive integers, satisfies the following properties:
$$f(x, x) = x,$$
$$f(x, y) = f(y, x),$$
$$(x + y)f(x, y) = yf(x, x + y).$$
What is $f(14, 52)$? (AIME)

Problem 6.16. Find all functions $f : \mathbb{R} \to \mathbb{R}$ such that $f(xy) = xf(x) + yf(y)$ for all $x, y \in \mathbb{R}$. (AwesomeMath)

Problem 6.17. Find all functions $f : \mathbb{Z}^+ \to \mathbb{Z}^+$ for which $f(0) = 0$ and
$$f(2n + 1) = f(2n) + 1 = f(n) + 1$$
for all $n \in \mathbb{Z}^+$. (AwesomeMath)

Problem 6.18. Find all functions $f : \mathbb{Z} \to \mathbb{Z}$ such that
$$3f(n) - 2f(f(n)) = n$$
for all $n \in \mathbb{Z}$. (Bulgaria)

Problem 6.19. Find all functions $f : \mathbb{Z}^+ \to \mathbb{Z}^+$ such that $f(n+1) > f(f(n))$. (IMO)

Problem 6.20. Find all functions $f : \mathbb{N} \to \mathbb{N}$ such that $f(f(n)) = n + 1987$. (IMO)

Chapter 7

Triangles and Polygons

To study polygons, we start with triangles because they are the simplest polygons. Naturally, trigonometry comes to our aid since we need to study the relationships between the lengths and angles of a triangle. While it is true that MathCounts does not require trigonometry, MathCounts also tests a mathlete's speed. If trigonometry can save us a few precious seconds, why don't we use it?

7.1 MathCounts Trigonometry

Just a little trigonometry goes a long way in MathCounts. The Law of Sines and the Law of Cosines are essential.

Theorem 7.1. (Law of Sines) *Let R be the radius of the circumcircle of triangle ABC. Then*
$$\frac{a}{\sin \angle A} = \frac{b}{\sin \angle B} = \frac{c}{\sin \angle C} = 2R.$$

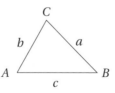

Theorem 7.2. (Law of Cosines) *In any triangle ABC,*
$$c^2 = a^2 + b^2 - 2ab \cos \angle C.$$

In addition to sine and cosine values of common angles such as 0°, 30°, 45°, 60°, and 90°, the sine and cosine values of 15° and 75° are also useful in MathCounts.

$$\sin 15° = \cos 75° = \frac{\sqrt{6} - \sqrt{2}}{4}, \quad \sin 75° = \cos 15° = \frac{\sqrt{6} + \sqrt{2}}{4}.$$

In our first example, we will solve the problem using a double-angle formula:

$$\tan 2\alpha = \frac{2\tan\alpha}{1 - \tan^2\alpha}.$$

Example 7.1. In square $ABCD$, each vertex is connected to the midpoints of its two opposite sides, as shown. What is $\dfrac{QR}{PQ}$? (MathCounts)

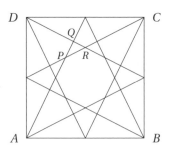

Answer: $\dfrac{3}{4}$

Solution: Let E and F be the midpoints of BC and DA, respectively. Since $CE = FA$ and $CE \parallel FA$, $AECF$ is a parallelogram. Thus $PR \parallel AE$ and $\frac{QR}{PQ} = \frac{QE}{AQ}$. Letting $\alpha = \angle BAE$, we have $\tan\alpha = \frac{1}{2}$. In $\triangle AEQ$, $m\angle EAQ = 90° - 2\alpha$, $m\angle AEQ = 180° - 2(90° - \alpha) = 2\alpha$. Thus $\triangle AEQ$ is a right triangle with $m\angle AQE = 90°$. Therefore,

$$\frac{QR}{PQ} = \frac{QE}{AQ} = \tan\angle EAQ = \tan(90° - 2\alpha) = \frac{1}{\tan 2\alpha} = \frac{1 - \tan^2\alpha}{2\tan\alpha} = 1 - \frac{1}{4} = \boxed{\frac{3}{4}}.$$

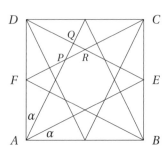

Some other useful trigonometry identities are the angle addition formulas.

$$\sin(\alpha + \beta) = \sin\alpha\cos\beta + \cos\alpha\sin\beta,$$
$$\cos(\alpha + \beta) = \cos\alpha\cos\beta - \sin\alpha\sin\beta.$$

7.2 Area Formulas and Theorems

When we let $\alpha = \beta$, we get two more double-angle formulas.

$$\sin 2\alpha = 2\sin\alpha\cos\alpha, \qquad \cos 2\alpha = \cos^2\alpha - \sin^2\alpha.$$

Example 7.2. In $\triangle ABC$, D, E, and F are points on BC such that $AD \perp BC$, AE is the angle bisector of $\angle BAC$, and $BF = FC$. If $m\angle BAD = m\angle DAE = m\angle EAF = m\angle FAC = \alpha$, what is $m\angle BCA$?

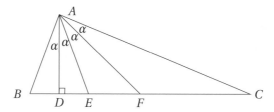

Answer: $22.5°$

Solution: We see that $m\angle ABF = 90° - \alpha$. Using the Law of Sines in $\triangle ABF$, we get

$$\frac{\sin 3\alpha}{BF} = \frac{\sin(90° - \alpha)}{AF}.$$

We see that $m\angle ACF = 90° - 3\alpha$. Using the Law of Sines in $\triangle AFC$, we get

$$\frac{\sin\alpha}{FC} = \frac{\sin(90° - 3\alpha)}{AF}.$$

Since $BF = FC$, we have

$$\frac{\sin 3\alpha}{\sin\alpha} = \frac{\sin(90° - \alpha)}{\sin(90° - 3\alpha)} = \frac{\cos\alpha}{\cos 3\alpha}.$$

Therefore, $\sin 3\alpha \cos 3\alpha = \sin\alpha \cos\alpha$. Using the double-angle formula for sine, we get $\sin 6\alpha = \sin 2\alpha$. Since $\alpha \neq 0°$ and $3\alpha < 90°$, we must have

$$180° - 6\alpha = 2\alpha, \qquad \alpha = \frac{180°}{8} = 22.5°.$$

Therefore, $m\angle BCA = 90° - 3\alpha = \boxed{22.5°}$.

7.2 Area Formulas and Theorems

Given $\triangle ABC$ with three sides a, b, and c, $s = \frac{1}{2}(a+b+c)$ is called its *semiperimeter*. The area of $\triangle ABC$ is equal to one-half the base times the height. Equivalently,

$$[ABC] = \frac{1}{2}ab\sin\angle C = rs = \frac{abc}{4R},$$

where r is the radius of its inscribed circle and R the radius of its circumcircle. Another useful triangle area formula is Heron's Formula.

Theorem 7.3. (Heron's Formula) *Let s be the semiperimeter of $\triangle ABC$. Then*

$$[ABC] = \sqrt{s(s-a)(s-b)(s-c)}.$$

When we know the coordinates of the vertices of a polygon, we can use the Shoelace Theorem to calculate its area.

Theorem 7.4. (Shoelace Theorem) *Let $P_1(x_1, y_1), P_2(x_2, y_2), ..., P_n(x_n, y_n)$ be the vertices of an n-gon $P_1 P_2 ... P_n$. Then*

$$[P_1 P_2 ... P_n] = \frac{1}{2}|(x_1 y_2 + x_2 y_3 + \cdots + x_n y_1) - (x_2 y_1 + x_3 y_2 + \cdots + x_1 y_n)|.$$

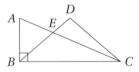

Example 7.3. Both right triangle ABC and isosceles triangle BCD, as shown, have height 5 cm from base $BC = 12$ cm. What is the area of $\triangle BCE$? (MathCounts)

Answer: $20\,\text{cm}^2$

Solution: Imposing a coordinate system upon a diagram is a common geometry method. We use this method here. Let B be the origin $(0,0)$. We see that the coordinates of A, C, and D are $(0,5)$, $(12,0)$, and $(6,5)$, respectively. The equation of the line BD is $y = \frac{5}{6}x$. The equation of the line AC is $y = -\frac{5}{12}(x-12)$. Since E is the intersection of BD and AC, we have

$$\frac{5}{6}x = -\frac{5}{12}(x-12).$$

So $x = 4$ and $y = \frac{10}{3}$. Therefore, the height of $\triangle BCE$ is $\frac{10}{3}$ and $[BCE] = \frac{1}{2} \cdot \frac{10}{3} \cdot 12 = \boxed{20\,\text{cm}^2}$.

7.3 Other Useful Theorems

A *lattice polygon* is a polygon whose vertices are points on a lattice. When we need to calculate the area of a lattice polygon, Pick's Theorem is quite useful.

Theorem 7.5. (Pick's Theorem) $A = \frac{1}{2}B + I - 1$. *The area (A) of a lattice polygon $= \frac{1}{2}$ the number of fenceposts (B) + the number of interior horses (I) -1 cowboy.*

Here "horses" are all the lattice points inside the polygon (I) and "fenceposts" are points on the polygon boundary that coincide with the lattice points (B). Note that when we apply Pick's Theorem to calculate the area, all the vertices of the polygon must be lattice points. Let's look at an example.

Example 7.4. The grid below contains six rows with six points in each row. Points that are adjacent either horizontally or vertically are a distance two apart. Find the area of the irregularly shaped ten sided figure shown. (Purple Comet)

Answer: 66

Solution: First we assume that grid points that are horizontally or vertically adjacent are a distance one apart. Using Pick's Theorem, we see that there are 12 horses and 11 fenceposts. So the area is $\frac{1}{2} \cdot 11 + 12 - 1 = \frac{33}{2}$. But, since the adjacent grid points are a distance two apart, the area of the polygon is $4 \cdot \frac{33}{2} = \boxed{66}$.

7.3 Other Useful Theorems

The distance from a point to a line is the shortest distance from the point to the line.

Theorem 7.6. (Point-Line Distance Formula) *Given a point $P(x_1, y_1)$ and a line l with equation $ax + by + c = 0$, the distance from P to l is:*

$$\frac{|ax_1 + by_1 + c|}{\sqrt{a^2 + b^2}}.$$

Theorem 7.7. (Angle Bisector Theorem) *Given $\triangle ABC$ and angle bisector AD, where D is on BC, we have $\frac{AB}{AC} = \frac{BD}{DC}$.*

The converse of the Angle Bisector Theorem is true as well.

Theorem 7.8. (Stewart's Theorem) *Given* $\triangle ABC$ *and cevian AD, where D is on BC, AD = d, BD = m, DC = n, and a = m + n, we have*

$$man + dad = bmb + cnc.$$

"A man and his dad put a bomb in the sink."

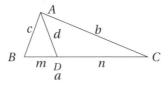

Theorem 7.9. (Ceva's Theorem) *In* $\triangle ABC$, *three cevians AD, BE, and CF are concurrent if and only if the following identity holds:*

$$\frac{AF}{FB} \cdot \frac{BD}{DC} \cdot \frac{CE}{EA} = 1$$

Example 7.5. In the triangle shown, $AD = 9$ and $DC = 7$. DM is the perpendicular bisector of BC and BD bisects $\angle ABC$. Find the area of $\triangle ABD$. (AMC 12)

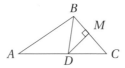

Answer: $14\sqrt{5}$

Solution: Since DM is the perpendicular bisector of BC, $\triangle BMD \cong \triangle CMD$. Therefore $BD = DC = 7$. Since BD is the angle bisector of $\angle ABC$, $AB : BC = 9 : 7$. Letting $AB = 9x$, we have $BC = 7x$. We use Stewart's Theorem in triangle ABC and get:
$$(9x)^2 \cdot 7 + (7x)^2 \cdot 9 = 7^2 \cdot 16 + 16 \cdot 9 \cdot 7.$$
Solving the equation, we get $x = \frac{4}{3}$. So $AB = 12$. The semiperimeter of $\triangle ABD$ is $\frac{1}{2}(12 + 9 + 7) = 14$. Next we use Heron's Formula to find the area of $\triangle ABD$.

$$[ABD] = \sqrt{14(14-12)(14-9)(14-7)} = \boxed{14\sqrt{5}}.$$

7.4 The Triangle Inequality

The sum of the lengths of any two sides of a triangle is greater than the length of the third side. Equivalently, the absolute difference of the lengths of any two sides of a triangle is less than the length of the third side. The extension of this triangle inequality to polygons is the key to the solution of our next example, which comes from a KJHS MathCounts Team Selection Test.

Example 7.6. The bases of a trapezoid have lengths 10 and x, and the legs have lengths 4 and 5. What is the sum of the four positive integers less than 19 which cannot be a value of x?

Answer: 31

Solution: Let $ABCD$ be the given trapezoid with $AD = 4$, $BC = 5$, base $CD = x$, and base $AB = 10$. Clearly $x \neq 10$ because otherwise the trapezoid would be a parallelogram. But $AD \neq BC$, a contradiction. We construct a semicircle with center A and radius 4. We see that AD is a radius of this circle. Similarly, we construct a semicircle with center B and radius 5. We see that BC is a radius of this larger circle. Letting the two rays $\overrightarrow{AD}$ and $\overrightarrow{BC}$ point towards each other, we see that CD cannot have a length of 1 because $4 + 1 + 5 = 10$. It can have lengths from 2 to 7. The figure below shows that CD reaches the length of 7 when $AD \perp AB$ and $\sin \angle ABC = \frac{4}{5}$.

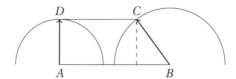

When the two rays both point to the left, we see that CD can have a length of 8 but it cannot have a length of 9 because $4 + 10 - 5 = 9$. When the two rays both point to the right, we see that CD can have a length of 12 or 13 but it cannot have a length of 11 because $5 + 10 - 4 = 11$. The figure below shows that CD reaches the length of 13 when $AD \perp AB$ and $\sin \angle BCD = \frac{4}{5}$.

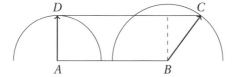

When the left ray points to the left and the right ray points to the right, we see that CD can have lengths from 14 to 18 but it cannot have a length of 19 because $4 + 10 + 5 = 19$. Therefore, the positive integer values less than 19 that we are looking for are 1, 9, 10, and 11. Their sum is $\boxed{31}$.

Problems for Chapter 7

Problem 7.1. Four equilateral triangles $\triangle ADG$, $\triangle ABH$, $\triangle BCE$, and $\triangle CDF$ are constructed inside square $ABCD$, as shown. Points E, F, G, and H are the vertices of the triangles that lie within square $ABCD$. What is the ratio of the area of square $EFGH$ to the area of square $ABCD$? (MathCounts)

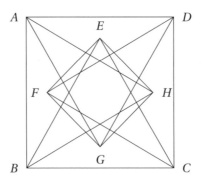

Problem 7.2. Right triangle ABC has $AB = 3$, $BC = 4$, and $AC = 5$. Square $XYZW$ is inscribed in $\triangle ABC$ with X and Y on AC, W on AB, and Z on BC. What is the side length of the square? (AMC 10)

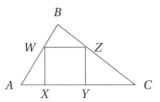

Problem 7.3. In the diagram below, square $ABCD$ with side length 23 is cut into nine rectangles by two lines parallel to AB and two lines parallel to BC. The area of four of these rectangles are indicated in the diagram. Compute the largest possible value for the area of the central rectangle. (NIMO)

Problem 7.4. Three lines are drawn parallel to each of the sides of triangle ABC so that they intersect in the interior of $\triangle ABC$. The resulting three smaller triangles have areas 1, 4, and 9. Find the area of triangle ABC. (Purple Comet)

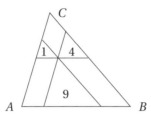

Problem 7.5. Triangle ABC has area 240. Points X, Y, and Z lie on sides AB, BC, and CA, respectively. Given that

$$\frac{AX}{BX} = 3, \quad \frac{BY}{CY} = 4, \quad \frac{CZ}{AZ} = 5,$$

find the area of $\triangle XYZ$. (Purple Comet)

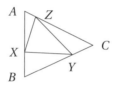

Problem 7.6. The vertices of quadrilateral $ABCD$ are: $A = (0,0)$, $B = (1,2)$, $C = (3,3)$ and $D = (4,0)$. The quadrilateral is cut into equal area pieces by a line passing through A. This line intersects CD at point $E = \left(\frac{p}{q}, \frac{r}{s}\right)$, where these fractions are in the lowest terms. What is $p + q + r + s$? (AMC 12)

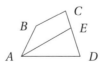

Problem 7.7. Triangle ABC is isosceles with point A at $(2,7)$, point B at $(-2,0)$, and point C at $(3,-1)$. Triangle ABC is reflected over BC to form $\triangle A'BC$. Triangle $A'BC$ is reflected over $A'C$ to form $\triangle A'B'C$. Triangle $A'B'C$ is reflected over $B'C$ to form $\triangle A''B'C$. What is the slope of $A''A$? (MathCounts)

Problem 7.8. The coordinates of the vertices of a trapezoid $ABCD$ are $(1,7)$, $(1,11)$, $(8,4)$, and $(4,4)$. What is the area of the trapezoid? (MathCounts)

Problem 7.9. In acute, scalene triangle ABC, $AB = 9$, $AC = 6$. What is the sum of all possible positive integer lengths of side BC? (German Problems)

Problem 7.10. In rectangle $ABCD$, $AB = 20$ and $BC = 10$. Let E be a point on CD such that $m\angle CBE = 15°$. What is AE? (AMC 10)

Problem 7.11. In trapezoid $ABCD$, BC is perpendicular to bases AB and CD, and the diagonals AC and BD are perpendicular. Given that $AB = \sqrt{11}$ and $AD = \sqrt{1001}$, find BC^2. (AIME)

Problem 7.12. Find the length of the shortest path that begins at point $A = (0,0)$, touches the line $y = 5$, then touches the line $x = 6$, and finally ends at the point $B = (4,-5)$. (MathPath)

Problem 7.13. An angle is drawn on a set of equally spaced parallel lines as shown. The ratio of the area of quadrilateral region C to the area of quadrilateral region B is $\frac{11}{5}$. Find the ratio of quadrilateral region D to the area of triangle region A. (AIME)

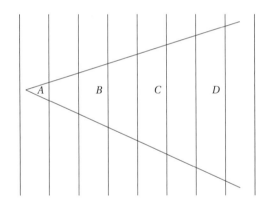

Problem 7.14. Two villages A and B lie on opposite sides of a straight river in the positions shown. The perpendicular distance from A to the river is 1 km and that from B to the river is 3 km. The river is 1 km wide and village B is 3 km down the river from village A. If we build a bridge in an optimal position across and perpendicular to the river, what is the shortest distance from A to the bridge, across the bridge, and onward to B? (Berkeley)

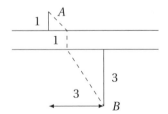

Problem 7.15. Let $ABCDE$ be a convex pentagon with $AB = BC$ and $CD = DE$. If $m\angle ABC = 120°$, $m\angle CDE = 60°$, and $BD = 2$, find the area of $ABCDE$. (Berkeley)

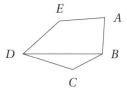

Problem 7.16. Point P is inside the square $ABCD$ such that $PA = 7$, $PB = 5$, and $PC = 1$. What is the area of the square?

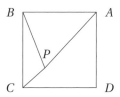

Problem 7.17. Trapezoid $ABCD$ has height 4 and $DC \parallel AB$. The diagonals DB and AC are perpendicular to each other, and $AC = 5$. What is the area of the trapezoid? (Prasolov)

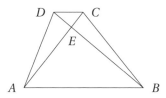

Problem 7.18. Triangle ABC is isosceles with $AB = AC$. D is the midpoint of BC. E is on AC such that $DE \perp AC$. F is the midpoint of DE. The intersection of AF and BE is G. What is $m\angle AGE$? (Prasolov)

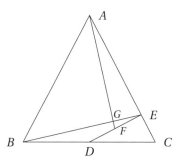

Problem 7.19. In triangle ABC, point E is the midpoint of side BC, point D lies on side AC. Given that $AC = 1$, $m\angle BAC = 60°$, $m\angle ACB = 20°$, and $m\angle DEC = 80°$, find $[ABC] + 2[CDE]$. (Prasolov)

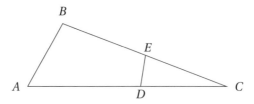

Problem 7.20. In trapezoid $ABCD$ with $AB \parallel CD$, $m\angle DAB + m\angle CBA = 90°$, $AB = 20$, and $CD = 8$. E and F are midpoints of AB and CD, respectively. What is the length of EF? (Prasolov)

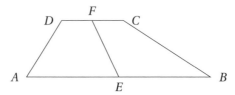

Problem 7.21. In regular pentagon $ABCDE$, point M is the midpoint of side AE, and segments AC and BM intersect at point Z. If $ZA = 3$, what is the value of AB? (MathCounts)

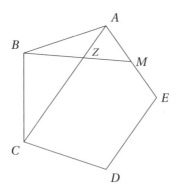

Chapter 8
Circles

When circles meet with straight lines, we get a fascinating area of study in plane geometry. We are especially interested in cyclic quadrilaterals. As a matter of fact, circles and lines are very similar. We can say that a line is a circle with infinite radius. This concept is studied in inversive geometry.

8.1 Areas in a Circle

In MathCounts, we are oftentimes asked to calculate the area of a shaded region. The key is to divide and conquer. The solution to such an area problem usually requires us to partition the region into simpler parts where the area of each part is calculable. Let's look at an example.

Example 8.1. In the figure below, a semicircle of radius 5 is on top of two semicircles with the same radius. What is the area of the shaded region? (German Problems)

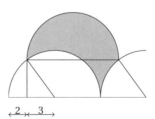

Answer: 40

Solution: We have a 3-4-5 triangle here, making the vertical leg 4. The region bounded by the two vertical lines can be divided into one semicircle of radius 5 plus one 4 × 10 rectangle. Note also that region *A* is identical to region *B*. Thus the area of the unshaded region between the two vertical lines is equal to the area of the semicircle. Therefore, the area of the shaded region is the same as the area of the 4 × 10 rectangle, which is $\boxed{40}$.

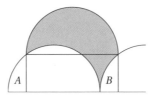

Let's look at another German problem.

Example 8.2. Find the area of the shaded region below.

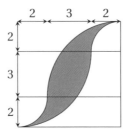

Answer: $\dfrac{21}{2}\pi - 21$

Solution: First let's calculate the area of the lightly shaded region in the left diagram below. It is equivalent to the area of a 5 × 7 rectangle minus the area of a quarter-circle of radius 5. So, the area is

$$5 \cdot 7 - \frac{1}{4}\pi \cdot 5^2.$$

Adding a quarter-circle of radius 2, we see that the lightly shaded region in the right diagram is

$$5 \cdot 7 - \frac{1}{4}\pi \cdot 5^2 + \frac{1}{4}\pi \cdot 2^2 = 35 - \frac{1}{4}\pi \cdot 21.$$

The desired area is the area of the 7 × 7 square minus twice the area of the lightly shaded region in the right diagram. So it is

$$49 - 2\left(35 - \frac{1}{4}\pi \cdot 21\right) = \boxed{\frac{21}{2}\pi - 21}.$$

Example 8.3. In trapezoid $ABCD$ we have $AD \parallel BC$ and $m\angle ABC = 90°$. A circle is inscribed in the trapezoid so that it is tangent to each side of $ABCD$. Given that it is tangent to DC at point E with $DE = 4$ and $EC = 16$, what is the area of $ABCD$? (MathCounts)

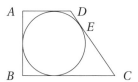

Answer: 288

Solution: Let O be the center of the inscribed circle and r be its radius. Let G be the point of tangency of the circle with AD and H the point of tangency of the circle with BC. Since DG and DE are the two tangent lines from D to circle O, $\triangle ODG \cong \triangle ODE$. Thus DO bisects $\angle ADC$ and $GD = ED$. Similarly, we see that CO bisects $\angle BCD$ and $HC = EC$. Since $AD \parallel BC$ and $m\angle ABC = 90°$, we have

$$m\angle ADC + m\angle BCD = 180°, \qquad m\angle ODC + m\angle OCD = 90°.$$

Thus $\triangle DOC$ is a right triangle. Since $OE \perp DC$, right triangles $\triangle DEO$ and $\triangle OEC$ are similar. Thus,

$$\frac{DE}{OE} = \frac{OE}{CE}, \qquad \frac{4}{r} = \frac{r}{16}, \qquad r = 8.$$

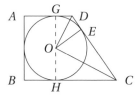

Since $AB \perp BC$, $ABHG$ is a rectangle with dimensions $r \times 2r$. So the height of the trapezoid is $8 + 8 = 16$, $AD = r + 4 = 12$, and $BC = r + 16 = 24$. Therefore,

$$[ABCD] = \frac{1}{2}(12 + 24) \cdot 16 = \boxed{288}.$$

8.2 Cyclic quadrilaterals

When the given problem involves a quadrilateral and we can show that the quadrilateral is cyclic, then we get a lot of information about the problem because there are special relationships among the angles and lengths of a cyclic quadrilateral. Even if the statement of the problem does not mention any circle at all, chasing a phantom circle often leads to the solution of the problem. Cyclic quadrilaterals have many properties, as we will see in the theorem below.

Theorem 8.1. (Properties of a Cyclic Quadrilateral) *A quadrilateral ABCD is cyclic if and only if any of the statements below is true:*

1) *its four perpendicular bisectors to the sides are concurrent,*
2) $m\angle ABD = m\angle ACD$,
3) *the measures of its opposite angles sum to* $180°$,
4) $AP \cdot PC = BP \cdot PD$, *where P is the intersection of the diagonals AC and BD,*
5) $AB \cdot CD + BC \cdot DA = AC \cdot BD$. *(Ptolemy's Theorem)*

Example 8.4. Triangle ABC has incircle centered at I and circumcircle centered at O. The extension of ray AI intersects the circumcircle at point X. Given $AI = 7$ and $IX = 5$, what is CX?

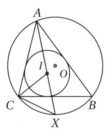

Answer: 5

Solution: Since I is the incenter of $\triangle ABC$, AI is the angle bisector of $\angle CAB$ and CI is the angle bisector of $\angle ACB$. So the measure of the exterior angle

$$m\angle CIX = \frac{1}{2}(m\angle CAB + m\angle ACB).$$

Since quadrilateral $ABXC$ is cyclic, $m\angle XCB = m\angle XAB = \frac{1}{2}m\angle CAB$. So

$$m\angle XCI = m\angle XCB + m\angle BCI$$
$$= \frac{1}{2}m\angle CAB + \frac{1}{2}m\angle ACB = m\angle CIX.$$

Thus triangle XCI is isosceles and $CX = IX = \boxed{5}$.

8.3 Power of a Point

Given a circle O and a point P that is not on the circle, let l be any line that goes through P and intersects circle O at points A and B. Then the product of the two lengths $PA \cdot PB$ is a constant, independent of our choice of l. This constant is called the *power of a point*. The term was first used by Swiss mathematician Jakob Steiner in 1826. Power of a point has three possible cases depending on whether P is inside or outside the circle and whether l is tangent to the circle or not.

Theorem 8.2. *Let P be a point outside circle O. One line goes through P and intersects circle O at points A and B. A second line goes through P and is tangent to circle O at point C. Then $PA \cdot PB = PC^2$.*

Theorem 8.3. *Let P be a point outside circle O. One line goes through P and intersects circle O at points A and B. A second line goes through P and intersects circle O at points C and D. Then $PA \cdot PB = PC \cdot PD$.*

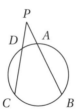

Theorem 8.4. *Let P be a point inside circle O. One line goes through P and intersects circle O at points A and B. A second line goes through P and intersects circle O at points C and D. Then $PA \cdot PB = PC \cdot PD$.*

We see from Theorem 8.3 and Theorem 8.4 that whether P is outside or inside the circle, the four points on the circle form a cyclic quadrilateral. So, cyclic quadrilaterals and power of a point go hand in hand.

Example 8.5. Triangle ABC has incircle with center I and radius 8. Its circumcircle has center O and radius 25. What is the length of IO?

Answer: 15

Solution: As in Example 8.4, we extend AI and let it meet the circumcircle O again at X. Let R and r be the radii of circles O and I, respectively. Let $IO = x$. Extend line IO and let P and Q be the intersection points of the extended line with circle O. We see that $IQ = R - x$ and $IP = R + x$. Since I is the intersection of AX and PQ,

$$IQ \cdot IP = (R-x)(R+x) = R^2 - x^2 = IA \cdot IX \qquad (*)$$

by Power of a Point. Let Y be the point of tangency of AB with circle I. We see that

$$IY = r = IA \cdot \sin(\tfrac{1}{2}\angle CAB), \quad \text{so} \quad IA = \frac{r}{\sin(\tfrac{1}{2}\angle CAB)}.$$

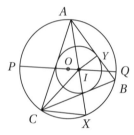

Triangle ACX is circumscribed by circle O as well. By the Law of Sines,

$$\frac{CX}{\sin(\tfrac{1}{2}\angle CAB)} = 2R.$$

By Example 8.4, $IX = CX$. So $IX = CX = 2R\sin(\tfrac{1}{2}\angle CAB)$. Back to our Power of a Point equation $(*)$:

$$IQ \cdot IP = R^2 - x^2 = IA \cdot IX = \frac{r}{\sin(\tfrac{1}{2}\angle CAB)} \cdot 2R\sin(\tfrac{1}{2}\angle CAB) = 2Rr.$$

So $x^2 = R^2 - 2Rr$. Therefore, $IO = x = \sqrt{R^2 - 2Rr} = \sqrt{25^2 - 2 \cdot 25 \cdot 8} = \boxed{15}$.

8.4 Ptolemy's Theorem

In Theorem 8.1, we learned five if and only if conditions of cyclic quadrilaterals. The fifth is called *Ptolemy's Theorem* and we restate it here.

8.4 Ptolemy's Theorem

Theorem 8.5. (Ptolemy's Theorem) *A quadrilateral ABCD is cyclic if and only if the sum of the products of the two pairs of opposite sides is equal to the product of the diagonals. That is, if and only if $AB \cdot CD + BC \cdot DA = AC \cdot BD$.*

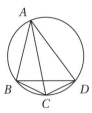

Ptolemy's Theorem is very useful when we need to find relationships between sides and diagonals of a cyclic polygon. Let's look at an AIME problem.

Example 8.6. Hexagon $ABCDEF$ is inscribed in a circle such that $AB = BC = CD = DE = EF = 81$ and $AF = 31$. What is $AC + AD + AE$?

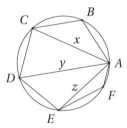

Answer: 384

Solution: Let $AC = x$, $AD = y$, and $AE = z$. We see that $BD = CE = DF = AC = x$ and $BE = AD = y$. Applying Ptolemy's Theorem to quadrilateral $ABCD$, we have

$$x^2 = 81^2 + 81 \cdot y.$$

Applying Ptolemy's Theorem to quadrilateral $ADEF$, we have

$$x \cdot z = 31 \cdot 81 + 81 \cdot y.$$

Applying Ptolemy's Theorem to quadrilateral $ABDE$, we have

$$y^2 = 81^2 + x \cdot z.$$

From the last two equations, we get $xz = y^2 - 81^2 = 31 \cdot 81 + 81y$. Thus, $y^2 - 81y - 81 \cdot 112 = 0$. That is, $(y - 144)(y + 63) = 0$. So, $y = 144$. Plugging the y value into the first equation, we get $x = 135$. Plugging the x and y values into the second equation, we get $z = 105$. Therefore, the sum of the lengths of the three diagonals is $135 + 144 + 105 = \boxed{384}$.

Problems for Chapter 8

Problem 8.1. In circle P with radius 2, $m\angle NPR = 100°$. What is the area of the shaded region? (MathCounts)

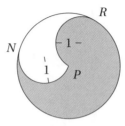

Problem 8.2. In the figure, arc $\widehat{AFD}$ has its center at C, arc $\widehat{AED}$ has its center at B, $AD = DB = 20$ inches and $m\angle ACD = 2(m\angle ABD)$. What is the area of the shaded region between the two arcs to the nearest whole number? (MathCounts)

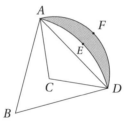

Problem 8.3. Circles A, B, and C are externally tangent to each other and internally tangent to circle O. Circles B and C are congruent. Circle A has a radius of 1 and passes through the center of circle O. What is the radius of circle B? (AMC 12)

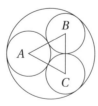

Problem 8.4. In triangle ABC, we have $AB = 7$, $AC = 8$, and $BC = 9$. Point D is on the circumscribed circle of the triangle so that AD bisects $\angle BAC$. What is the value of $\dfrac{AD}{CD}$? (AMC 10)

Problem 8.5. Rosario wants to cut out five circles, each 2 cm in diameter, from a rectangular piece of cardboard that is 6 cm long. What must be the minimum width of the rectangular cardboard? (MathCounts)

Problems for Chapter 8

Problem 8.6. A circle passes through two diagonally opposite vertices of a 3-inch by 4-inch rectangle. What is the least possible distance between the center of the circle and a vertex of the rectangle? (MathCounts)

Problem 8.7. Triangle ABC is inscribed in circle O. The radius of circle O is 12 and $m\angle ABC = 30°$. A circle with center B is drawn tangent to line AC. Let R be the region within $\triangle ABC$ but outside circle B. What is the maximum area of R? (ARML)

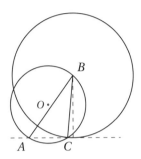

Problem 8.8. Points A, B, C, and D lie on the given circle. If $AB = 8$, $AP = 2$, and $PC = 4$, determine the ratio of the area of quadrilateral $PAEC$ to the area of $\triangle ABE$. (ARML)

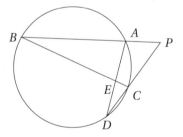

Problem 8.9. In the diagram, we have two circles with radii 8 and 6, respectively. The distance between the centers of the circles is 12. At P, one of the points of intersection, a line is drawn in such a way that chords PQ and PR are of equal length. Compute the length PQ. (AIME)

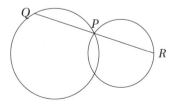

Problem 8.10. Let $ABCD$ be a cyclic quadrilateral where $AB = 4$, $BC = 11$, $CD = 8$, and $DA = 5$. If BC and DA intersect at X, find the area of triangle XAB.

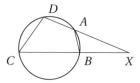

Problem 8.11. The figure below shows a quarter-circle of radius 1, with A on the arc $\widehat{BD}$ such that $m\angle AOD = 30°$. What must the distance OX be such that the region bounded by AX, BX, and the arc $\widehat{AB}$ occupies half the area of the quarter-circle?

Problem 8.12. On sides BC and CD of square $ABCD$, points E and F are taken so that $m\angle EAF = 45°$. AE and AF intersect diagonal BD at points P and Q, respectively. What is $\dfrac{[AEF]}{[APQ]}$? (Prasolov)

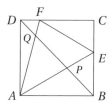

Problem 8.13. AC and BD, the diagonals of cyclic quadrilateral $ABCD$, are perpendicular to each other and intersect at point P. E and F are points on AD and BC, respectively, such that EF goes through P and is perpendicular to BC. Given that $AD = 6$ and $BC = 10$, what is the length of AE? (Prasolov)

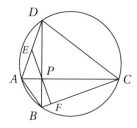

Problems for Chapter 8

Problem 8.14. Let O be the circumcircle of isosceles triangle ABC with $AB = BC = 17$. Let the tangents at A and B intersect at D. Line CD meets circle O again at point E. Let F be the intersection of BD and the extension of AE. Given that $AD = 24$, what is the length of BF? (Yufei Zhao)

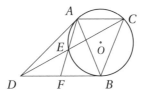

Problem 8.15. In triangle ABC, $m\angle ABC = 60°$. Angle bisectors AD and CE intersect at point O. Given that $AB = 16$ and $OD = 5$, what is the length of OE? (Prasolov)

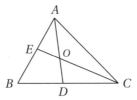

Problem 8.16. In isosceles triangle ABC, we have $m\angle ABC = m\angle ACB = 40°$, $AB = AC = x$ and $BC = y$. BD is the angle bisector of $\angle ABC$ and $BD = z$. What is the length of AD in terms of x, y, and z? (Prasolov)

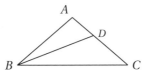

Problem 8.17. Triangle ABC has area 150, $m\angle BAC = 90°$, $AB > AC$, and $BC = 25$. Circle I is inscribed in $\triangle ABC$ and touches AC at M. Line BM meets circle I again at L. What is the length of BL? (HMMT)

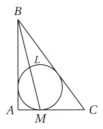

Problem 8.18. Cyclic quadrilateral $ABCD$ has an incircle. Its sides are $AB = 130$, $BC = 110$, $CD = 70$, and $DA = 90$. The point of tangency of the incircle to AB divides AB into segments of lengths x and y. What is the positive difference of x and y? (AMC 12)

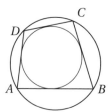

Problem 8.19. Let P be a point on arc $\overset{\frown}{BC}$ of the circumcircle of equilateral triangle ABC such that $PB = 3$ and $PC = 5$. AP intersects BC at Q. What is the length of PQ?

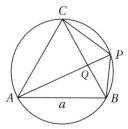

Problem 8.20. Let $ABCD$ be a rectangle. Point P is inside the rectangle so that $m\angle APD + m\angle CPB = 180°$. What is $m\angle ADP + m\angle PBC$? (CMO)

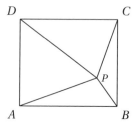

Chapter 9

Three-Dimensional Geometry

Just as a circle and a straight line have very similar properties, a 3D object also has a lot in common with its two-dimensional and higher-dimensional cousins. Because of this relationship, sometimes we will project a three-dimensional object onto a plane or render it in four-dimensional space when we need to solve a 3D geometry problem.

9.1 Three Views of a 3D Object

Architects and artists often need to represent 3D objects using 2D drawings. As we all know, a 3-dimensional shape can look different from different angles. To get a relatively accurate picture of a 3D object, we need to view it from multiple perspectives. One way to represent a 3D figure is using the front view, right side view, and top view. The following MathCounts problem asks us to identify the correct view of a building.

Example 9.1. A building modeled after the Chicago Willis Tower consists of 9 square towers arranged in a 3 by 3 grid. They have congruent bases, and the heights, in units, are indicated in the grid below. Which of the following is a side view of the building, and from which direction?

	back		
	1	2	1
left	3	1	2	right
	2	2	1
	front		

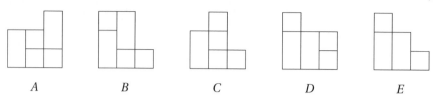

| A | B | C | D | E |

Answer: *D*, front

Solution: We can view the building from four sides. When we look at it from the back side, we will see the left diagram below; when we look at it from the right side, we will see the right diagram below.

When we look at it from the left side, we will see the left diagram below; when we look at it from the front side, we will see the right diagram below.

Therefore, $\boxed{D \text{ is the front view of the building}}$.

Example 9.2. In Example 9.1, if each tower has congruent 1-unit by 1-unit base, how many square units would be in the surface area (including the base) of the building?

Answer: 50 square units

Solution: The surface area of the top and bottom of the building will be 9 square units each. When one tower is taller than its neighbor, the exposed part of the taller tower counts toward the surface area. So, we will measure the height of each tower relative to its neighbors. The result is as follows:

```
       ┌─1─┬─2─┬─1─┐
       1 1 │ 2 │ 1 1
       ├─2─┼─1─┼─1─┤
       3 3 │ 2 │ 1 1 │ 2 2
       ├─1─┼─1─┼─1─┤
       2 2 │ 0 │ 2 │ 1 1
       └─2─┴─2─┴─1─┘
```

By adding the four rows, we get the total surface area of the front and back sides: $1+2+1+2+1+1+1+1+1+2+2+1 = 16$. By adding the four columns, we get the total surface area of the left and right sides: $1+3+2+1+2+0+1+1+1+1+2+1 = 16$.

Therefore, the surface area of the building is $9 + 9 + 16 + 16 = \boxed{50 \text{ square units}}$.

9.2 Folding and Cutting

In addition to the three views we discussed in Section 9.1, another common 2D representation of a 3D object is a *net*. A net is a two-dimensional pattern that can be folded to form a 3D shape. Our next example also comes from MathCounts.

Example 9.3. A regular octahedron is folded from the net shown. What number shows on the top when the face numbered 1 is on the bottom?

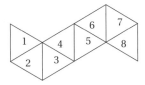

Answer: 8

Solution: Let's mark the three vertices surrounding face 1 as A, B, and C. In an octahedron, each vertex is associated with four faces. We see that vertex A is associated with faces 1, 2, 3, and 4. So vertices B and B' are the same vertex. So we can glue side AB to side AB'. Now we see that vertex B is associated with faces 1, 4, 5, and 6. Thus, vertices C and C' must be the same vertex and we can glue BC to $B'C'$.

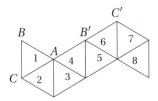

Therefore, each of the faces 1, 2, 3, 4, 5, 6, and 7 is associated with at least one vertex of face 1. The only face that is on the opposite side of face 1 is face 8. Thus, the number $\boxed{8}$ shows on the top.

Since folding and cutting go hand in hand, let's look at a cutting problem from AHSME.

Example 9.4. A cube of cheese $C = \{(x, y, z) \mid 0 \le x, y, z \le 1\}$ is cut along the planes $x = y$, $y = z$, and $z = x$. How many pieces are there? (No cheese is moved until all three cuts are made.)

Answer: 6

Solution: Note that each cut is a separation of points in C. For example, the plane of $x = y$ separates points with $x \leq y$ from those with $x > y$. So, depending on the order of x, y, and z, any point $(x, y, z) \in C$ is in one of the following regions.

Region 1: $\quad 0 \leq x \leq y \leq z \leq 1$, $\qquad$ Region 2: $\quad 0 \leq x \leq z < y \leq 1$,
Region 3: $\quad 0 \leq z < x \leq y \leq 1$, $\qquad$ Region 4: $\quad 0 \leq y < x \leq z \leq 1$,
Region 5: $\quad 0 \leq y \leq z < x \leq 1$, $\qquad$ Region 6: $\quad 0 \leq z < y < x \leq 1$.

Therefore, there are $\boxed{6}$ pieces.

9.3 Angles and Distances

A *dihedral angle* is the angle α between two planes. When α is zero, the two planes are called *coplanar*.

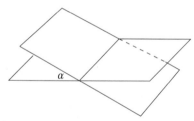

Theorem 9.1. *If line l is perpendicular to two intersecting lines l_1 and l_2 of a plane at their point of intersection, then line l is perpendicular to the plane.*

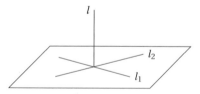

Theorem 9.2. *If plane p_l contains line l that is perpendicular to another plane p, then the planes p_l and p are perpendicular to each other.*

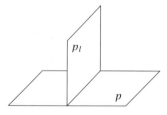

9.3 Angles and Distances

Our next example is an SAT question from many years ago.

Example 9.5. Take a regular tetrahedron and a square based pyramid, with all sides equal, and glue two triangular faces together so that they coincide exactly. How many faces does the resulting solid have?[1]

Answer: 5

Solution: Let's place two copies of the square based pyramid with equal side lengths next to each other, as shown in the diagram. We connect their apexes and see that the space between the two pyramids is a tetrahedron with all sides equal. Since the only tetrahedron with all equal side lengths is the regular tetrahedron, our tetrahedron fits perfectly between the two square based pyramids. That is, the front face of the pyramid and the front face of the tetrahedron are coplanar. So are the two back faces. Therefore, the resulting solid of our problem has $\boxed{5}$ faces.

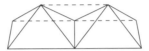

In Theorem 7.6, we learned how to calculate the distance between a point and a line using the Point-Line Distance Formula. Similarly, in three-dimensional geometry, we can calculate the distance between a point and a plane using the Point-Plane Distance Formula.

Theorem 9.3. (Point-Plane Distance Formula) *Given a point* (x_1, y_1, z_1) *and a plane with equation* $ax + by + cz + d = 0$, *the distance between the point and the plane is:*

$$\frac{|ax_1 + by_1 + cz_1 + d|}{\sqrt{a^2 + b^2 + c^2}}.$$

If we have two lines in space that are non-parallel and non-intersecting, then we call them a pair of *skew lines*. The distance between a pair of skew lines is the shortest distance between them. So, it is the length of a line segment that is perpendicular to both lines. Let's look at an AIME problem that uses this concept.

Example 9.6. Given that the shortest distances between an interior diagonal of a rectangular parallelepiped, P, and the edges it does not meet are $2\sqrt{5}$, $\frac{30}{\sqrt{13}}$, and $\frac{15}{\sqrt{10}}$, determine the volume of P.

Answer: 750

---

[1] When this problem first appeared in an SAT test, the problem writer intended the answer to be 7. One test-taker found out the error and the news made its way to the *New York Times*.

Solution: Let $d(A_1A_2, B_1B_2)$ represent the distance between the lines A_1A_2 and B_1B_2. Without loss of generality, let's assume that the three dimensions of P are: $AB = x$, $AD = y$, and $AE = z$. Furthermore, let's assume that $d(AG, BC) = 2\sqrt{5}$, $d(AG, BF) = \dfrac{30}{\sqrt{13}}$, and $d(AG, DC) = \dfrac{15}{\sqrt{10}}$.

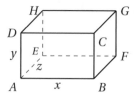

In plane $CGHD$, let K be the foot of the perpendicular from point C to line DG. Similarly, in plane $BFEA$, let K' be the foot of the perpendicular from point B to line AF. We see that $BCKK'$ is a rectangle. Since $CK \perp DG$ and $CK \perp KK'$, CK is perpendicular to the plane $AFGD$. Since BC is not in the plane $AFGD$ and $BC \parallel AD$, BC is parallel to the plane $AFGD$. So, the distance between BC and AG is the same as the distance between BC and the plane $AFGD$, which is the same as CK, the distance from point C to line DG. This is because $CK \perp BC$, and CK is perpendicular to the plane $AFGD$.

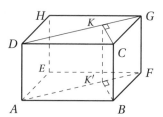

Since $CK \cdot DG = DC \cdot CG$, we have

$$CK = \frac{DC \cdot CG}{DG} = \frac{xz}{\sqrt{x^2+z^2}} = 2\sqrt{5}.$$

Similarly, we see that

$$d(AG, BF) = \frac{xy}{\sqrt{x^2+y^2}} = \frac{30}{\sqrt{13}}, \quad \text{and} \quad d(AG, DC) = \frac{yz}{\sqrt{y^2+z^2}} = \frac{15}{\sqrt{10}}.$$

Squaring the three equations and taking the reciprocals, we get

$$\frac{1}{x^2} + \frac{1}{z^2} = \frac{1}{20},$$
$$\frac{1}{x^2} + \frac{1}{y^2} = \frac{13}{900},$$
$$\frac{1}{y^2} + \frac{1}{z^2} = \frac{2}{45}.$$

Adding these three equations and dividing by two, we get

$$\frac{1}{x^2} + \frac{1}{y^2} + \frac{1}{z^2} = \frac{49}{900}.$$

Subtracting each of the previous three equations from the last equation, we get $\frac{1}{x^2} = \frac{1}{100}$, $\frac{1}{y^2} = \frac{1}{225}$, and $\frac{1}{z^2} = \frac{1}{25}$. So $x = 10$, $y = 15$, and $z = 5$. Therefore, the volume of P is $xyz = 10 \cdot 15 \cdot 5 = \boxed{750}$.

9.4 Higher Dimensions

In previous sections, we learned that 2D representations (such as the three views and the net) can help us study 3D shapes. In general, reducing a complicated object to something simpler is a powerful technique. However, sometimes the opposite is also true, and it's beneficial to render a shape in higher dimensions. For example, sometimes it's useful to represent an equilateral triangle in three dimensions to simplify calculation.

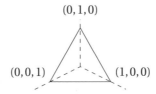

When the coordinates of the three vertices of an equilateral triangle are $(1,0,0)$, $(0,1,0)$, and $(0,0,1)$, the center of the triangle, that is, its centroid, has coordinates $(\frac{1}{3}, \frac{1}{3}, \frac{1}{3})$. We will use this fact in our next example.

Example 9.7. In a regular tetrahedron, the centers of the four faces are the vertices of a smaller tetrahedron. The ratio of the volume of the smaller tetrahedron to that of the larger one is $\frac{m}{n}$, where m and n are relatively prime positive integers. Find $m + n$. (AIME)

Answer: 28

Solution: We render the tetrahedron in 4D. Let the coordinates of the four vertices of the tetrahedron be $(1,0,0,0)$, $(0,1,0,0)$, $(0,0,1,0)$, and $(0,0,0,1)$. The side length of the tetrahedron is $\sqrt{2}$ for all sides. The coordinates of the centers of the four faces are $(\frac{1}{3}, \frac{1}{3}, \frac{1}{3}, 0)$, $(0, \frac{1}{3}, \frac{1}{3}, \frac{1}{3})$, $(\frac{1}{3}, 0, \frac{1}{3}, \frac{1}{3})$, and $(\frac{1}{3}, \frac{1}{3}, 0, \frac{1}{3})$. The distance between any two centers is $\sqrt{2}/3$. So the ratio of the side length of the smaller tetrahedron to that of the larger one is $1 : 3$. Thus the ratio of the volumes is $1 : 27$. Therefore, $m + n = 1 + 27 = \boxed{28}$.

Problems for Chapter 9

Problem 9.1. The diagram shown is the net of a regular dodecahedron. In a regular dodecahedron, every vertex is associated with three faces and we call the sum of the numbers on these three faces the number of the vertex. What is the minimum number any vertex of this dodecahedron could have?

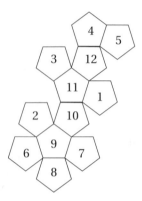

Problem 9.2. The front view and right side view of some arrangement of unit cubes are shown here. Let N denote the largest number of possible unit cubes in an arrangement with the two views shown, and let n denote the least number of possible unit cubes. What is the value of $N - n$? Note that when two cubes are glued together, we see two unit cubes instead of one $1 \times 1 \times 2$ rectangular prism. (MathCounts)

Front View   Right Side View

Problem 9.3. A solid with a square base is formed with identical 1 by 1 by 1 cubic blocks. The number of blocks in each grid in shown below. If all the surfaces except for the 3 by 3 base are painted, how many blocks have exactly two sides painted?

3	2	2
2	1	1
1	2	3

Problem 9.4. A sphere is inscribed in a tetrahedron whose vertices are $A = (6,0,0)$, $B = (0,4,0)$, $C = (0,0,2)$, and $D = (0,0,0)$. The radius of the sphere is $\frac{m}{n}$, where m and n are relatively prime positive integers. Find $m + n$. (AIME)

Problems for Chapter 9

Problem 9.5. A net with 5 square faces and 10 equilateral triangular faces, each with unit side length, is folded into a 15-faced polyhedron. A gecko on vertex A spots a fly on vertex B. What is the length of the shortest path the gecko can take to reach the fly assuming that it does not jump and can only walk across the surfaces of the polyhedron?

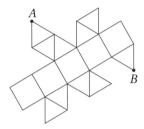

Problem 9.6. A rectangular solid made of unit cubes has front view, top view, and right side view as shown. What is the maximum number of unit cubes that can be removed from the top layer of this solid so that the resulting solid has the same front, top, and right side views as the original solid?

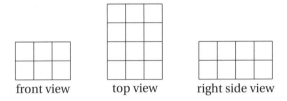

Problem 9.7. Consider the paper triangle whose vertices are $(0,0)$, $(34,0)$, and $(16,24)$. The vertices of its midpoint triangle are the midpoints of its sides. A triangular pyramid is formed by folding the triangle along the sides of its midpoint triangle. What is the volume of this pyramid? (AIME)

Problem 9.8. The pattern, as shown, is folded along the dashed lines to make a right triangular prism. What is the volume, in cubic units, of the triangular prism? (MathCounts)

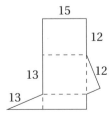

Problem 9.9. Take a regular octahedron and a regular tetrahedron, with all sides equal, and glue two triangular faces together so that they coincide exactly. How many faces does the resulting solid have?

Problem 9.10. The shape below can be folded along the dashed lines and taped together along the edges to form a three-dimensional polyhedron. All lengths in the diagram are given in inches. What is the volume of the resulting polyhedron? (MathCounts)

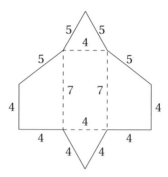

Problem 9.11. Let $ABCD$ be a regular tetrahedron with side length 2. The plane parallel to edges AB and CD and lying halfway between them cuts $ABCD$ into two pieces. Find the surface area of one of these pieces. (HMMT)

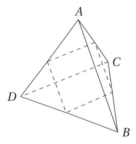

Problem 9.12. A spiral staircase turns $270°$ as it rises 10 feet. The radius of the staircase is $\dfrac{7}{\pi}$ feet. What is the length of the handrail? (MathCounts)

Problem 9.13. The solid shown has a square base of side length s, the upper edge is parallel to the base and has length $2s$. All other edges have length s. Given that $s = 6\sqrt{2}$, what is the volume of the solid? (AIME)

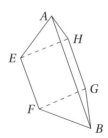

Problem 9.14. In the figure, A, E, and F are isosceles right triangles; B, C, and D are squares with sides of length 1; and G is an equilateral triangle. The figure can be folded along its edges to form a polyhedron. What is the volume of this polyhedron? (AHSME)

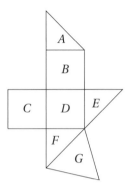

Problem 9.15. On a $4 \times 4 \times 3$ rectangular parallelepiped, vertices A, B, and C are adjacent to vertex D. Consider the plane containing the points A, B, and C. What is the perpendicular distance from D to this plane? (AHSME)

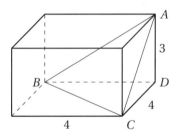

Problem 9.16. Let $ABCD$ be a tetrahedron with $AB = 41$, $AC = 7$, $AD = 18$, $BC = 36$, $BD = 27$, and $CD = 13$, as shown in the figure. Let d be the distance between the midpoints of edges AB and CD. Find d^2. (AIME)

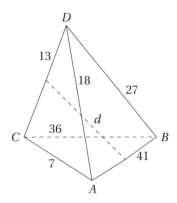

Problem 9.17. Consider two solid spherical balls, one centered at $(0, 0, \frac{21}{2})$ with radius 6, and the other centered at $(0, 0, 1)$ with radius $\frac{9}{2}$. How many points (x, y, z) with only integer coordinates (lattice points) are there in the intersection of the balls? (AHSME)

Problem 9.18. A container in the shape of a right circular cone is 12 inches tall and its base has a 5-inch radius. The liquid that is sealed inside is 9 inches deep when the cone is held with its point down and its base horizontal. When the liquid is held with its point up and its base horizontal, what is the height of the liquid from the base? (AIME)

Problem 9.19. A convex polyhedron has 12 squares, 8 regular hexagons, and 6 regular octagons for its faces. At each vertex of the polyhedron one square, one hexagon, and one octagon meet. How many segments joining vertices of the polyhedron lie in the interior of the polyhedron rather than along an edge or a face? (AIME)

Problem 9.20. A regular icosahedron consists of 20 equilateral triangles of side length 1. What is the length of the shortest path on the surface of the icosahedron between the opposite vertices S and N? (AMC 12)

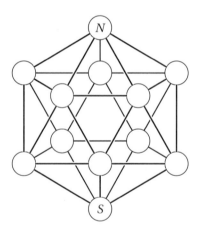

Problem 9.21. A bubble in the shape of a hemisphere of radius 1 is on a tabletop. Inside the bubble are five congruent spherical marbles, four of which are sitting on the table and one rests atop the others. All marbles are tangent to the bubble, and their centers can be connected to form a pyramid with volume V and with a square base. Compute V. (ARML)

Chapter 10

Angle Chasing

Using information in a geometric diagram to find the degree measure of a particular angle is called *angle chasing*. Angle chasing problems can be daunting and annoying if we don't get the right answer at first. However, we can take comfort in the fact that, if the problem is in a test, it must be solvable. Usually such a problem has an elegant solution.

10.1 Angles in a Polygon

A triangle with two equal sides is a triangle with two equal angles, and vice versa. We will use this simple fact again and again, because isosceles and equilateral triangles provide us a lot of useful information and thus are our friends in our angle chasing quest. Of course, a typical angle chasing problem usually involves more than angle chasing alone. We have to combine angle chasing with other geometric observations. A large and accurate diagram is especially helpful. Let's first look at a GMAT problem.

Example 10.1. In the figure shown, what is $v + x + y + z + w$?

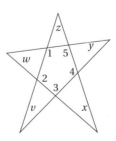

Answer: $180°$

Solution: We see that ∠1, ∠2, ∠3, ∠4, and ∠5 are interior angles of a pentagon. Since the sum of the interior angles of an n-gon is $(n-2) \cdot 180°$, we have

$$m\angle 1 + m\angle 2 + m\angle 3 + m\angle 4 + m\angle 5 = 540°.$$

Since ∠1, v, and y are interior angles of a triangle, $m\angle 1 + y + v = 180°$. Similarly,

$$m\angle 2 + x + z = 180°, \quad m\angle 3 + y + w = 180°, \quad m\angle 4 + v + z = 180°, \quad m\angle 5 + x + w = 180°.$$

So
$$m\angle 1 + m\angle 2 + m\angle 3 + m\angle 4 + m\angle 5 + 2v + 2x + 2y + 2z + 2w = 5 \cdot 180°.$$

Therefore, $v + x + y + z + w = \dfrac{5 \cdot 180 - 540}{2} = \boxed{180°}$.

Our next example is especially interesting because it introduces a special type of triangles.

Example 10.2. Trapezoid $ABCD$ is isosceles, with $AD \parallel BC$ and $AB = BC = CD$. If $AC = AD$, what is the degree measure of $\angle ADC$?

Answer: 72°

Solution: Let $m\angle BAC = x$. Since $AB = BC$, $m\angle ACB = x$. Since AD and BC are parallel, $m\angle CAD = x$. Since trapezoid $ABCD$ is isosceles, $m\angle CDA = m\angle BAD = 2x$. Since $AC = AD$, in triangle ACD, we have $m\angle CAD = x$, $m\angle ADC = \angle ACD = 2x$. So $x + 2x + 2x = 180°$. Therefore, $m\angle ADC = 2x = \boxed{72°}$.

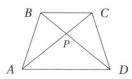

In Example 10.2, triangle ADC is a $36° - 72° - 72°$ triangle. Such a triangle is called a *Golden Triangle*. Letting P be the intersection of AC and BD, we see that $\triangle APB$ and $\triangle DPC$ are also golden triangles. Note that trapezoid $ABCD$ is a part of a regular pentagon. From the solution of Problem 7.21, we see that, in a regular pentagon, the ratio of the length of a diagonal to that of a side is $\frac{1+\sqrt{5}}{2}$. This ratio is called the *Golden Ratio*. In a $36° - 72° - 72°$ triangle, the ratio of the length of a side to that of the base is the golden ratio. That's why it is called a golden triangle.

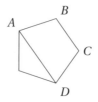

10.2 Angles in a Circle

Sometimes auxiliary lines and extra constructions are needed to solve an angle chasing problem, as we will see in the next example.

Example 10.3. Quadrilateral $ABCD$ has $AB = BC = CD$, $m\angle ABC = 70°$ and $m\angle BCD = 170°$. What is the degree measure of $\angle BAD$? (AMC 10)

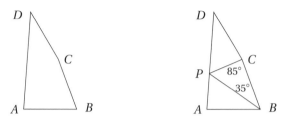

Answer: 85°

Solution: Let P be the intersection of angle bisector of $\angle ABC$ and angle bisector of $\angle DCB$. We connect P with D and P with A. Since $BA = BC$, $\triangle ABP \cong \triangle CBP$. Similarly, since $DC = BC$, $\triangle PBC \cong PDC$. Since $m\angle BPC = 180° - 85° - 35° = 60°$, we have $m\angle APB = m\angle BPC = m\angle CPD = 60°$. Because these three angles add to 180°, AP and PD are collinear. So, $m\angle BAD = m\angle BAP = m\angle BCP = \boxed{85°}$.

10.2 Angles in a Circle

In Theorem 8.1, we gave five if and only if conditions for cyclic quadrilaterals. Among these five conditions, the following two are most relevant to angle chasing in a circle. A quadrilateral is cyclic if and only if:

1. the measures of its opposite angles add to 180°,
2. the measure of an angle between a side and a diagonal is equal to that of the angle between the opposite side and the other diagonal.

For example, in the figure shown, quadrilateral $ABCD$ is cyclic if and only if $m\angle ACB = m\angle ADB$.

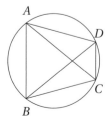

Given a quadrilateral, we need to check if it is cyclic, or if we can construct a cyclic quadrilateral from it. That is, we try to get a *phantom circle* out of a quadrilateral.

Example 10.4. Let $ABCD$ be a convex quadrilateral with $m\angle DAC = m\angle BDC = 36°$, $m\angle CBD = 18°$ and $m\angle BAC = 72°$. The diagonals intersect at point P. Determine the degree measure of $\angle APD$. (JBMO)

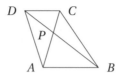

Answer: 108°

Solution: Let E be a point on BD such that AE is the angle bisector of $\angle PAB$. We see that AP and AE trisect $\angle DAB$. Since $m\angle CDE = m\angle CAE = 36°$, quadrilateral $AECD$ is cyclic. So $m\angle DEC = m\angle DAC = 36°$. Since $m\angle DBC = 18°$, $m\angle ECB = 36° - 18° = 18°$. So triangle EBC is isosceles and $EB = CE$.

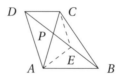

Note that $\triangle PAD \sim \triangle PEC$, so

$$\frac{CE}{DA} = \frac{PE}{PA}.$$

Using the Angle Bisector Theorem in triangle PAB, we have

$$\frac{PE}{PA} = \frac{EB}{AB}.$$

That is,

$$\frac{CE}{DA} = \frac{PE}{PA} = \frac{EB}{AB}.$$

Since $EB = CE$, we have $DA = AB$. So triangle DAB is isosceles and $m\angle ADP = \frac{1}{2}(180° - 36° - 72°) = 36°$. Therefore, $m\angle APD = 180° - 36° - 36° = \boxed{108°}$.

10.3 Trigonometric Form of Ceva's Theorem

We learned Ceva's Theorem in Theorem 7.9. The trigonometric form of Ceva's Theorem, Trig Ceva, for short, is a useful tool in solving angle chasing problems.

10.3 Trigonometric Form of Ceva's Theorem

Theorem 10.1. (Trig Ceva) *In $\triangle ABC$, three cevians AD, BE, and CF are concurrent if and only if the following identity holds:*

$$\frac{\sin \angle BAD}{\sin \angle DAC} \cdot \frac{\sin \angle CBE}{\sin \angle EBA} \cdot \frac{\sin \angle ACF}{\sin \angle FCB} = 1.$$

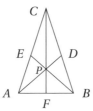

Example 10.5. Triangle ABC is isosceles with $AC = BC$ and $m\angle ACB = 106°$. Point M is in the interior of the triangle so that $m\angle MAC = 7°$ and $m\angle MCA = 23°$. Find the number of degrees in $\angle CMB$. (AIME)

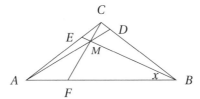

Answer: 83°

Solution: We see that $m\angle CAB = m\angle CBA = \frac{1}{2}(180° - 106°) = 37°$. We see that $m\angle FCB = 106° - 23° = 83°$ and $m\angle BAD = 37° - 7° = 30°$. Let $m\angle ABE = x$. By Trig Ceva, we have

$$\frac{\sin 30°}{\sin 7°} \cdot \frac{\sin(37° - x)}{\sin x} \cdot \frac{\sin 23°}{\sin 83°} = 1,$$

Since $\sin 30° = \frac{1}{2}$, we have

$$\frac{\sin(37° - x)}{\sin x} = \frac{2\sin 7° \cdot \sin 83°}{\sin 23°}.$$

Since $\sin \alpha \sin \beta = \frac{1}{2}\big(\cos(\alpha - \beta) - (\cos(\alpha + \beta)\big)$,

$$2\sin 7° \cdot \sin 83° = \cos(-76°) - \cos 90° = \cos 76° - 0 = \sin 14°.$$

Therefore

$$\frac{\sin(37° - x)}{\sin x} = \frac{\sin 14°}{\sin 23°}.$$

So $x = 23°$. Therefore,

$$m\angle CMB = m\angle CFB + m\angle FBM = m\angle CAF + m\angle ACF + m\angle FBM = 37° + 2 \cdot 23° = \boxed{83°}.$$

10.4 Langley's Adventitious Angles

Langley's Adventitious Angles is a famous angle chasing problem first posed in 1922 by E. M. Langley in the *Mathematical Gazette*, Volume 11, p. 173. We use it here as an example to illustrate that constructing an equilateral triangle helps in solving angle chasing problems. This technique is a powerful tool that we can use to tackle other geometry problems.

Example 10.6. (Langley's Adventitious Angles) Let ABC be an isosceles triangle with $m\angle BAC = 20°$ and $AB = AC$. Point D is on side AC such that $m\angle DBC = 60°$. Point E is on side AB such that $m\angle ECB = 50°$. What is the degree measure of $\angle EDB$?

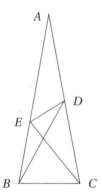 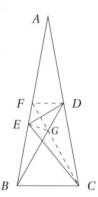

Answer: 30°.

Solution: We see that $\triangle ABC$ is a $20°-80°-80°$ triangle. Let F be on AB such that $FD \parallel BC$. Let G be the intersection of BD and CF. We see that $FB = DC$, $m\angle BFD = m\angle CDF$. Thus, $\triangle BDF \cong \triangle CFD$ by SAS. So $m\angle BCF = m\angle DBC = 60°$. Thus both $\triangle GBC$ and $\triangle FGD$ are equilateral triangles. Since

$$m\angle BEC = 180° - 80° - 50° = 50°,$$

$BE = BC = BG$. So $\triangle BGE$ is an isosceles triangle. Therefore,

$$m\angle BGE = \frac{1}{2}\left(180° - (80° - 60°)\right) = 80°.$$

Thus
$$m\angle EGF = 180° - 80° - 60° = 40°.$$

In $\triangle BCF$, we see that $m\angle BFC = 180° - 80° - 60° = 40°$. So $\triangle FEG$ is an isosceles triangle and $FE = GE$. Therefore, $\triangle FDE \cong \triangle GDE$ by SSS. Thus,

$$m\angle EDB = m\angle FDE = \frac{1}{2} \cdot 60° = \boxed{30°}.$$

Problems for Chapter 10

Problem 10.1. In $\triangle ABC$, $AX = XY = YB = BC$, and $m\angle ABC = 120°$. What is $m\angle BAC$?

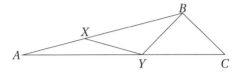

Problem 10.2. The trisectors of two angles of scalene triangle ABC meet at points P and Q as shown. The third angle of the triangle, $\angle A$, measures $30°$. Find the number of degrees in $\angle BPC$. (MathCounts)

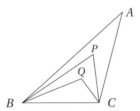

Problem 10.3. Triangles ABC and ADC are isosceles with $AB = BC$ and $AD = DC$. Point D is inside triangle ABC, $m\angle ABC = 40°$ and $m\angle ADC = 140°$. What is the degree measure of $\angle BAD$? (AMC 12)

Problem 10.4. Find the number of degrees in the positive difference between the sum of the measures of the five acute interior angles and the sum of the measures of the five obtuse exterior angles of the five-pointed star. (MathCounts)

Problem 10.5. In triangle ABC, $m\angle A = 60°$ and $m\angle B = 45°$. The bisector of $\angle A$ intersects BC at T and $AT = 24$. The area of triangle ABC can be written in the form $a + b\sqrt{c}$, where a, b, and c are positive integers, and c is not divisible by the square of any prime. Find $a + b + c$. (AIME)

Problem 10.6. Triangle ABC is isosceles with $m\angle A = 100°$ and $AB = AC$. A point D is constructed outside the triangle such that $BD = AC$ and $m\angle DBC = 20°$. What is the degree measure of $\angle BCD$?

Problem 10.7. In the figure below, $m\angle R = 36°$, and $m\angle T = 42°$. Find the number of degrees in $\angle RQV$. (MathCounts)

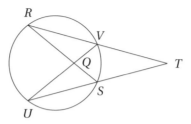

Problem 10.8. In isosceles triangle ABC with $AB = AC$ and $m\angle BAC = 82°$, a point P is located inside the triangle such that $BP = BA$ and $m\angle ABP = 38°$. Find the degree measure of $\angle PCA$.

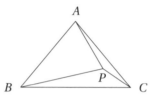

Problem 10.9. In $\triangle ABC$, $AB = 2AC$. Let D and E be on AB and BC, respectively, such that $m\angle BAE = m\angle ACD$. Let F be the intersection of AE and CD, and suppose that $\triangle CEF$ is equilateral. What is $m\angle ACB$? (AMC 10)

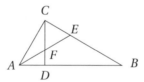

Problem 10.10. In the figure below, $m\angle CAB = m\angle ADB = m\angle DEB = 90°$. If the degree measure of $\angle ABC$ is $27°$, what is $m\angle ADE$? (Mandelbrot)

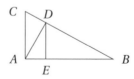

Problem 10.11. Square $ABCD$ has a point E inside such that

$$m\angle EBC = m\angle ECB = 15°.$$

What is $m\angle EDA$?

Problem 10.12. There is a semicircle with diameter AB and point D is outside the circle such that $AB = AD$. AD intersects the semicircle at point E. Let F be a point on the chord AE such that $DE = EF$. The extension of BF intersects the semicircle at point C. If $m\angle CAE = 20°$, what is the degree measure of $\angle BAD$?

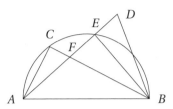

Problem 10.13. $ABCDE$ is a regular pentagon and P is a point in its interior such that $m\angle PBA = m\angle PEA = 42°$. What is the degree measure of $\angle CPD$? (Andreescu)

Problem 10.14. In the figure shown, $AB = BC = AC = CD = 10$, $AD = 13$. What is $m\angle ADB$? (Mandelbrot)

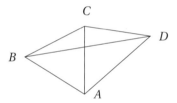

Problem 10.15. In the figure, $m\angle E = 40°$ and $\overset{\frown}{AB}$, $\overset{\frown}{BC}$, and $\overset{\frown}{CD}$ have the same length. What is $m\angle ACD$? (AHSME)

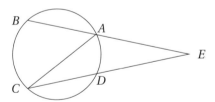

Problem 10.16. In the figure below, $AB \parallel CD$. $m\angle BXY = 45°$, $m\angle DZY = 25°$, and $XY = YZ$. What is the degree measure of $\angle YXZ$? (Purple Comet)

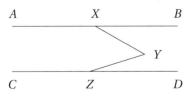

Problem 10.17. $ABCD$ is a convex quadrilateral such that $AB < AD$. The diagonal AC bisects $\angle BAD$, and $m\angle ABC = 130°$. Let E be a point on the interior of AD. Given that $m\angle BAD = 40°$ and $BC = CD = DE$, what is the degree measure of $\angle ACE$? (HMMT)

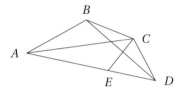

Problem 10.18. Point P is inside triangle ABC such that $m\angle PAB = m\angle PAC = 22°$, $m\angle PBA = 8°$, and $m\angle PBC = 30°$. What is the degree measure of $\angle PCA$?

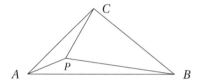

Problem 10.19. In $\triangle ABC$, $m\angle A = 84°$, $m\angle C = 78°$. Points D and E are taken on the sides AB and BC, so that $m\angle ACD = 48°$ and $m\angle CAE = 63°$. What is the degree measure of $\angle CDE$? (Calvin Lin)

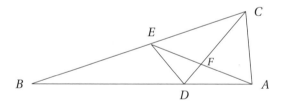

Problem 10.20. Point D lies inside triangle ABC such that $m\angle DAC = m\angle DCA = 30°$ and $m\angle DBA = 60°$. Point E is the midpoint of segment BC. Point F lies on AC with $AF = 2FC$. What is $m\angle DEF$? (CGMO)

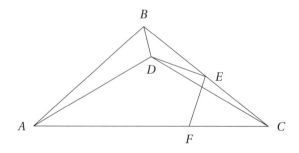

Chapter 11

Mass Points

A *mass point* is a point assigned a mass. We use mP to denote a point P with mass m. Here, m can be a positive or negative real number. The mass points technique is fascinating because it is so powerful. However, it could backfire if you do not fully understand the principles of mass points.

Theorem 11.1. (Principles of Mass Points)

1. *A system of mass points has a center of mass. This center is unique.*

2. *Given mass points mP and nQ, their center R has a mass of $m + n$. We say that $mP + nQ = (m + n)R$. R lies on line segment PQ if m and n are both positive or both negative. R is on the extension of line segment PQ if one of m and n is positive and the other is negative. Furthermore, $|m| : |n| = RQ : PR$.*

3. *Commutativity: $mP + nQ = nQ + mP$.*

4. *Associativity: The center of mass of a system of mass points does not change if a subsystem of mass points is replaced by its center with its total mass. That is,*

$$mP + nQ + kR = mP + (nQ + kR) = (mP + nQ) + kR.$$

For example, if we have two mass points $1P$ and $1Q$, then R, the midpoint of line segment PQ, is the center of these two mass points. We say that

$$1P + 1Q = 2R.$$

We can also rewrite it as

$$1P = 2R + (-1)Q,$$

and say that P is the center of mass of $2R$ and $(-1)Q$. Note that P is on the extension of line segment QR. As we will see in Section 11.4, negative mass points can be quite useful in solving complicated geometry problems. Throughout this chapter, we will use "mass" and "weight" interchangeably.

11.1 Mass Points and Cevians

A *cevian* is a line segment from a vertex of a triangle to the other side. The simplest mass points problems are those that involve only cevians. Let's look at an example.

Example 11.1. In $\triangle ABC$, points E and D are selected on sides AB and BC, respectively, such that $AE:EB = 2:3$ and $CD:DB = 7:4$. Line segment CE intersects AD at F. Find $AF:FD$.

Answer: $22:21$

Solution: In order to use E to balance AB, we assign a weight of 3 to A and a weight of 2 to B. To use D as a balance point of BC, we assign a weight of $\frac{8}{7}$ to C.

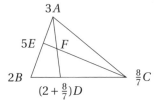

Since the three mass points $3A$, $2B$, and $\frac{8}{7}C$ can be balanced by $3A$ and $(2+\frac{8}{7})D$, the center of mass is on AD. These three mass points can also be balanced by $\frac{8}{7}C$ and $5E$. So, the center of mass is on CE. Therefore, the center of mass is on the intersection of AD and CE, namely, point F. Thus,

$$3AF = (2+\frac{8}{7})FD,$$
$$AF:FD = \boxed{22:21}.$$

Now let's look at a MathCounts problem.

Example 11.2. In rectangle $ABCD$, point M is the midpoint of side BC, and point N lies on CD such that $DN:NC = 1:4$. Line segment BN intersects AM and AC at points R and S, respectively. If $NS:SR:RB = x:y:z$, where x, y, and z are positive integers, what is the minimum possible value of $x+y+z$?

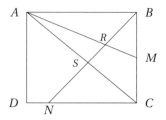

Answer: 126

Solution: We see that $NC : AB = 4 : 5$. Since $\triangle NSC$ and $\triangle BSA$ are similar, $NS : SB = 4 : 5 = CS : SA$. So $NS = \frac{4}{5}SB$. Now let's use mass points in $\triangle ABC$ to find the ratio $SR : SB$. To use S to balance AC, we assign a mass of 5 to C and a mass of 4 to A. To use M to balance CB, we assign a mass of 5 to B. We see that the three mass points $4A$, $5C$, and $5B$ can be balanced by $9S$ and $5B$. They can also be balanced by $4A$ and $10M$. So, the center of mass is the intersection of SB and AM. That is, R is the center of mass of $\triangle ABC$.

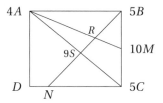

Therefore, $9SR = 5RB$, and so $SR = \frac{5}{9}RB = \frac{5}{5+9}SB = \frac{5}{14}SB$ and $RB = \frac{9}{14}SB$. So,

$$NS : SR : RB = \frac{4}{5} : \frac{5}{14} : \frac{9}{14} = 56 : 25 : 45.$$

Since $\gcd(56, 25, 45) = 1$, $x + y + z$ has a minimum value of $56 + 25 + 45 = \boxed{126}$.

11.2 Mass Points and Transversals

A *transversal* is a line that intersects two other distinct lines. Mass points problems involving transversals in addition to cevians are more complicated than those in Section 11.1. The vertex that is associated with both sides of a transversal will have a *split mass*. For example, in the figure shown, vertex A will have a split mass. To understand this, just imagine that A is actually two points, A_1 and A_2, glued together with A_1B on the left side and A_2C on the right side. If A_1 is assigned a weight of m and A_2 is assigned a weight of n, then $(m+n)A = mA_1 + nA_2$. So $A = \frac{m}{m+n}A_1 + \frac{n}{m+n}A_2$.

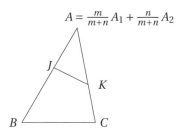

Let's look at the following example.

Example 11.3. In $\triangle ABC$, D is the midpoint of BC. Point E lies on line segment AC such that $AE:EC = 11:9$. Point F lies on cevian AD such that $AF:FD = 2:3$. The extension of line segment EF intersects AB at G. What is $GF:FE$?

Answer: $4:7$

Solution: Since GE is a transversal, we treat vertex A as two vertices, A_1 and A_2, glued together with A_1B on the left side and A_2C on the right side. In order to use E to balance A_2C, we assign a weight of 11 to C and a weight of 9 to A_2. To use D to balance BC, we assign a weight of 11 to B. So D has a weight of 22. To use F to balance AD, A must have a total weight of 33 because $AF:FD = 2:3$.

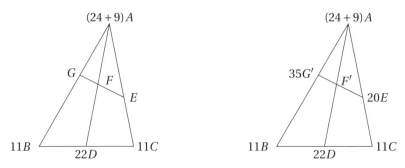

We see that $55F$ is the center of mass of three mass points $33A$, $11B$, and $11C$ because it is the balance point of AD and D is the balance point of BC. Since A_2 has a weight of 9, A_1 must have a weight of 24. Next we pick the point G' on AB such that $AG':G'B = 11:24$. We see that G' is the balance point of A_1 and B. We then connect G' with E and let F' be the intersection of AD and $G'E$.

We see that $24A_1$ and $11B$ are balanced by $35G'$, and $9A_2$ and $11C$ are balanced by $20E$. So $33A$, $11B$, and $11C$ are balanced by $35G'$ and $20E$. Since these three mass points are also balanced by $33A$ and $22D$, the intersection of $G'E$ and AD, namely, F', is the center of mass. Therefore F and F' are the same point. Thus, G and G' are also the same point. So F is the balance point of GE and $GF:FE = 20:35 = \boxed{4:7}$.

11.3 Multiple Mass Points Systems

Sometimes problems are so involved that it's not enough to assign mass to each vertex once. In such situations, we need to set up mass points systems multiple times. Before we go on to our next example, let's prove the following theorem.

11.3 Multiple Mass Points Systems

Theorem 11.2. *Let D be a point on side BC of triangle ABC. Let m, n, and k be masses assigned to A, B, and C, respectively. Let F be the center of mass of mA, nB, and kC. Then D is the balance point of nB and kC if and only if F is on AD.*

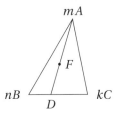

Proof. If D is the balance point of nB and kC, then the three mass points mA, nB, and kC are balanced by mA and $(n+k)D$. So the center of mass must be on AD. Thus F is on AD.

To show that the other direction of the statement is true, we use proof by contradiction. Suppose that F, the center of mass, is on AD. If point D', different from D, is on BC and is the balance point of nB and kC. Then the center of three mass points mA, nB, and kC are balanced by mA and $(n+k)D'$. So F, the center of mass, is on AD'. Since $D \neq D'$, F is not on AD. This is a contradiction. □

Theorem 11.2 comes in handy, as we will see in our next example.

Example 11.4. In $\triangle ABC$, BB_1 and CC_1 are medians. D is on BC such that L, the intersection of AD and BB_1, is the midpoint of BB_1. K is the intersection of AD and CC_1. What is $C_1K : KC$?

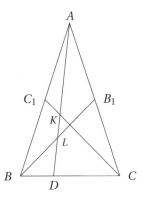

Answer: $\dfrac{1}{4}$

Solution: To solve this problem, we will first use L as the center of mass of triangle ABC to find the ratio $BD : DC$. Next we will use K as the center of mass to get the ratio $C_1K : KC$.

We assign masses to make L the center of mass of triangle ABC. To use B_1 to balance AC, we let A and C each have a weight of 1. Then B_1 has a weight of 2. To use L to balance BB_1, we assign a weight of 2 to B. We see that L is the center of mass of $1A$, $2B$, and $1C$. By Theorem 11.2, D is the balance point of $2B$ and $1C$ and $BD:DC = 1:2$.

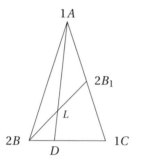 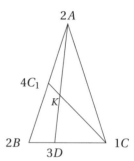

Next we assign masses to make K the center of mass. Since $BD:DC = 1:2$, we assign a weight of 2 to B and a weight of 1 to C. So D has a weight of 3. Since C_1 is the midpoint of AB, we assign a weight of 2 to A. We see that the three mass points $2A$, $2B$, and $1C$ are balanced by $2A$ and $3D$. Also they are balanced by $4C_1$ and $1C$. So K, the intersection of CC_1 and AD, is the center of mass. So $4C_1K = 1KC$. Therefore, $\dfrac{C_1K}{KC} = \boxed{\dfrac{1}{4}}$.

11.4 Mass Points in Space

The application of mass points technique is not limited to points in a plane. The principles of mass points apply to mass points in space as well. Negative mass points comes in handy when we try to solve 3-dimensional geometry problems.

Theorem 11.3. *Let $ABCD$ be a parallelogram. A, B, and C are assigned with masses m, $-m$, and m, respectively. Then D is the center of mass of the three mass points mA, $(-m)B$, and mC. That is, $mA + (-m)B + mC = mD$.*

Proof. Let E be the intersection of AC and BD. Since the diagonals of a parallelogram bisect each other, E is the midpoint of AC. So $2mE$ is the balance point of mA and mC.

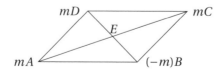

11.4 Mass Points in Space

Since E is also the midpoint of DB, $2mE = mD + mB$. So

$$mD = 2mE + (-m)B = mA + mC + (-m)B = mA + (-m)B + mC. \qquad \square$$

The following example shows how negative mass points can be used to simplify calculations.

Example 11.5. The base $ABCD$ of a pyramid $FABCD$ is a parallelogram. The plane α intersects AF, BF, CF, and DF at points A_1, B_1, C_1, and D_1, respectively. Given that

$$\frac{AA_1}{A_1F} = 2, \qquad \frac{BB_1}{B_1F} = 5, \qquad \frac{CC_1}{C_1F} = 10,$$

find the ratio $\dfrac{DD_1}{D_1F}$.

Answer: 7

Solution: We would like to use A_1 to balance AF, B_1 to balance BF, and C_1 to balance CF. To make D the center of mass of A, B, and C, we assign a weight of 1 to A, a weight of -1 to B, and a weight of 1 to C. Thus F will have a split mass because $1A$, $(-1)B$, and $1C$ each imposes a weight of 2, -5, and 10 on F, respectively.

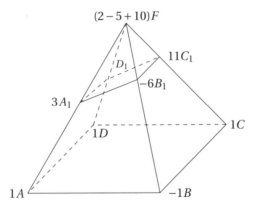

Now $3A_1$ is the balance point of AF; $-6B_1$ is the balance point of BF; and $11C_1$ is the balance point of CF. We see that the four mass points, $1A$, $-1B$, $1C$, and $(2-5+10)F$, are balanced by $3A_1$, $-6B_1$, and $11C_1$. So the center of mass is on the plane α. By Theorem 11.3, $1D$ is the center of mass of $1A$, $-1B$, and $1C$. So the center of mass of $1A$, $-1B$, $1C$, and $(2-5+10)F$ is on DF. Thus, D_1, the intersection of DF and the plane α, is the center of mass. Therefore,

$$\frac{DD_1}{D_1F} = \frac{2-5+10}{1} = \boxed{7}.$$

Problems for Chapter 11

Problem 11.1. In $\triangle ABC$, point D is on AC with $AD:DC = 2:1$, and point E is on AB with $AE:EB = 2:3$. Line segments EC and DB intersect at point K. What is $DK:KB$? (MathCounts)

Problem 11.2. In right triangle ABC, $AC = 4$ and $CB = 7$. E is the midpoint of AC. Point F lies on CB such that $CF:FB = 3:4$. D is the intersection of AF and EB. What is the area of $\triangle ABD$? (MathCounts)

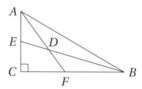

Problem 11.3. Let M and P be points on the sides AC and BC of $\triangle ABC$, respectively, so that $AM:MC = 3:1$ and $BP:PC = 1:2$. Let Q be the intersection of AP and BM. Given that the area of $\triangle BPQ$ is equal to 1 square inch, find the area of $\triangle ABC$.

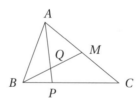

Problem 11.4. In rectangle $ABCD$, point E lies on BC so that $\dfrac{BE}{EC} = 2$ and point F lies on DC so that $\dfrac{CF}{FD} = 2$. Line segments AE and AC intersect BF at points X and Y, respectively. Given that $FY:YX:XB = a:b:c$, where a, b, and c are relatively prime positive integers, what is the value of $a+b+c$? (MathCounts)

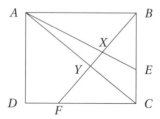

Problems for Chapter 11

Problem 11.5. Triangle ABC has sides $AB = 39$, $BC = 57$, and $CA = 70$ as shown. Median AD is divided into three congruent segments by points E and F. Lines BE and BF intersect side AC at points G and H, respectively. Find the distance from G to H. (Purple Comet)

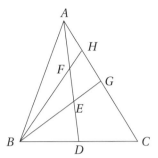

Problem 11.6. The sides of $\triangle ABC$ are $AB = 13$, $BC = 15$, and $AC = 14$. Let BD be an altitude of the triangle. The angle bisector of $\angle C$ intersects side AB at F and altitude BD at E. Find $CE : EF$.

Problem 11.7. Let $ABCD$ be a quadrilateral with an inscribed circle. Let M on AB, N on BC, P on CD, and Q on DA be the points of tangency of the quadrilateral with the circle. Suppose that $AM = a$, $BN = b$, $CP = c$, and $DQ = d$. Let Z be the intersection of MP and NQ. Find the ratio $MZ : ZP$.

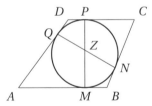

Problem 11.8. In $\triangle ABC$, the bisector of $\angle B$ intersects AC at D and intersects median AM at E. If $\sin \angle A = 4/5$ and $\sin \angle C = 24/25$, find $AE : EM$.

Problem 11.9. In $\triangle ABC$, angle bisectors AD and BE intersect at P. The sides of the triangle are $BC = 3$, $CA = 5$, $AB = 7$. If $BP = x$ and $PE = y$, compute the ratio $x : y$. (ARML)

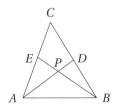

Problem 11.10. In $\triangle ABC$, cevians AD, BE, and CF intersect at point P. The areas of $\triangle PAF$, $\triangle PFB$, $\triangle PBD$, and $\triangle PCE$ are 40, 30, 35, and 84, respectively. Find the area of $\triangle ABC$. (AIME)

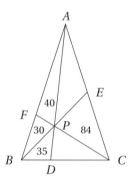

Problem 11.11. In $\triangle ABC$, $m\angle CBA = 72°$. E is the midpoint of side AC and D is a point on side BC such that $2BD = DC$; AD and BE intersect at F. Find the ratio of the area of $\triangle BDF$ to the area of quadrilateral $FDCE$. (AHSME)

Problem 11.12. In parallelogram $ABCD$, point M is on AB so that $\dfrac{AM}{AB} = \dfrac{17}{1000}$ and point N is on AD so that $\dfrac{AN}{AD} = \dfrac{17}{2009}$. Let P be the point of intersection of AC and MN. Find $\dfrac{AC}{AP}$. (AIME)

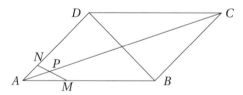

Problem 11.13. In $\triangle ABC$, D is on AB such that $AD:DB = 3:2$ and E is on BC such that $BE:EC = 3:2$. If ray DE and ray AC intersect at F, find $DE:EF$.

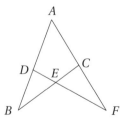

Problem 11.14. In $\triangle ABC$, A', B', and C' are on the sides BC, CA, and AB, respectively. Given that AA', BB', and CC' are concurrent at the point O, and that

$$\frac{AO}{OA'} + \frac{BO}{OB'} + \frac{CO}{OC'} = 92, \quad \text{find} \quad \frac{AO}{OA'} \cdot \frac{BO}{OB'} \cdot \frac{CO}{OC'}. \quad \text{(AIME)}$$

Problem 11.15. Let P be an interior point of $\triangle ABC$ and extend lines from the vertices through P to the opposite sides. Given that $AP = a$, $BP = b$, $CP = c$, $PF = PE = PD = d$, find the product abc if $a + b + c = 43$ and $d = 3$. (AIME)

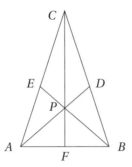

Problem 11.16. $\triangle ABC$ has $AB = 21$, $AC = 22$, and $BC = 20$. Points D and E are located on AB and AC, respectively, such that DE is parallel to BC and contains the center of the inscribed circle of $\triangle ABC$. DE can be expressed as $\frac{m}{n}$, where m and n are relatively prime positive integers. Find $m + n$. (AIME)

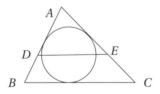

Problem 11.17. Point P is inside $\triangle ABC$. Line segments APD, BPE, and CPF are drawn with D on BC, E on AC, and F on AB. Given that $AP = 6$, $BP = 9$, $PD = 6$, $PE = 3$, and $CF = 20$, find the area of $\triangle ABC$. (AIME)

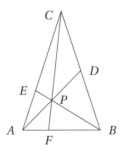

Problem 11.18. Let $PABC$ be a *right triangular pyramid*. That is, the pyramid's base $\triangle ABC$ is an equilateral triangle, and the altitude from P goes through the centroid M of $\triangle ABC$. A plane α intersects PA, PB, PC, and PM at points A_1, B_1, C_1, and M_1, respectively. If $PA_1 : A_1A = 2:3$, $PB_1 : B_1B = 3:2$, and $PC_1 : C_1C = 4:1$, find the ratio $PM_1 : M_1M$.

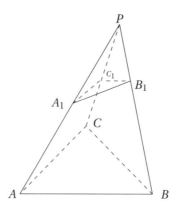

Problem 11.19. The base of a pyramid $SABCD$ is a parallelogram $ABCD$. A plane α intersects the sides SA, SB, SC, and SD at points A_1, B_1, C_1, and D_1, respectively. Given that

$$SA_1 = \frac{1}{3}SA, \ SB_1 = \frac{1}{5}SB, \text{ and } SC_1 = \frac{1}{4}SC,$$

find the ratio $\dfrac{SD_1}{SD}$.

Problem 11.20. Let A_1, B_1, C_1 be points on the sides of triangle ABC such that

$$\frac{BA_1}{BC} = \frac{CB_1}{CA} = \frac{AC_1}{AB} = \frac{1}{4}.$$

Let S be the area of triangle ABC. Find the area of the triangle PQR bounded by the lines AA_1, BB_1, and CC_1 in terms of S.

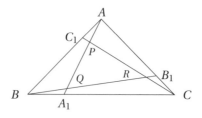

Chapter 12

Number Sense

Number theory conjectures usually have simple statements. For example, Fermat's Last Theorem states that if $n > 2$, then there is no solution to the equation $x^n + y^n = z^n$, where x, y, and z are positive integers. This famous conjecture in mathematics was neither proved nor disproved for more than 350 years. It was not until 1993 that Andrew Wiles of Princeton University solved the mystery. For its "magical charm" and "inexhaustible wealth," German mathematician Carl Friedrich Gauss called number theory the "Queen of Mathematics."

12.1 Prime Factorization

Number theory's main focus is the properties of whole numbers. Prime numbers, natural numbers that are greater than 1 and have no positive divisors other than 1 and itself, play a major role in number theory because of the following Fundamental Theorem of Arithmetic.

Theorem 12.1. (Fundamental Theorem of Arithmetic) *Every positive integer $n > 1$ can be uniquely represented as a product of prime powers.*

$$n = p_1^{e_1} p_2^{e_2} \cdots p_k^{e_k},$$

where $p_1 < p_2 < \cdots < p_k$ are primes and $e_1, e_2, ..., e_k$ are positive integers.

From the Fundamental Theorem of Arithmetic, we see that a natural number $p_1^{e_1} p_2^{e_2} ... p_k^{e_k}$ has

$$(1 + e_1)(1 + e_2) \cdots (1 + e_k)$$

positive divisors and the sum of all its positive divisors is

$$(1 + p_1 + p_1^2 + \cdots + p_1^{e_1})(1 + p_2 + p_2^2 + \cdots + p_2^{e_2}) \cdots (1 + p_k + p_k^2 + \cdots + p_k^{e_k}).$$

We will use this fact in our next example.

Example 12.1. There are 100 lightbulbs. The light switches are conveniently labeled with the numbers 1 to 100. First, you turn on all the lightbulbs. Then you flip the switches of any lightbulbs labeled with a number that is a multiple of 2. Next you flip the switches of any lightbulbs labeled with a number that is a multiple of 3. Then you flip multiples of 4, 5, 6, etc., all the way to 100. When you finish, how many lightbulbs are lit? (Putnam)

Answer: 10 lightbulbs

Solution: We see that a lightbulb is lit if and only if it is flipped an odd number of times. Given any n, $1 \leq n \leq 100$, the number of times the switch $n = p_1^{e_1} p_2^{e_2} \cdots p_k^{e_k}$ is flipped is equal to the number of factors of n. Since n has

$$(1+e_1)(1+e_2)\cdots(1+e_k)$$

factors, it has an even number of factors if and only if one of $e_1, e_2, ..., e_k$ is odd. In other words, n has an odd number of factors if and only if all of $e_1, e_2, ..., e_k$ are even. That is, if and only if n is a perfect square. Thus the number of lightbulbs that are lit is the same as the number of perfect squares from 1 to 100. Therefore, $\boxed{10 \text{ lightbulbs}}$ are lit.

The *greatest common divisor* (gcd) of two natural numbers a and b is the largest natural number that divides both a and b. We can use the Euclidean algorithm to find $\gcd(a,b)$. For example, to find $\gcd(154, 242)$, we have:

$$242 = 1 \cdot 154 + 88,$$
$$154 = 1 \cdot 88 + 66,$$
$$88 = 1 \cdot 66 + 22,$$
$$66 = 3 \cdot 22 + 0.$$

Therefore, $\gcd(242, 154) = 22$. Furthermore, we see that

$$22 = 88 - 66 = 88 - (154 - 88) = 2 \cdot 88 - 154 = 2 \cdot (242 - 154) - 154 = 2 \cdot 242 - 3 \cdot 154.$$

That is, the greatest common divisor of any two integers can be expressed as a linear combination of those two integers.

Theorem 12.2. (Bézout's Identity) *For any positive integers a and b, there are integers m and n such that*

$$\gcd(a,b) = ma + nb.$$

Bézout's Identity is important not only for its own sake, but also for providing an interesting contrast with the Chicken McNugget Theorem that we will study later in this chapter.

12.2 Number Bases

The *least common multiple* of two natural numbers a and b, denoted as $\text{lcm}(a, b)$, is the smallest natural number which is a multiple of both a and b. We see that

$$\gcd(a, b) \cdot \text{lcm}(a, b) = a \cdot b.$$

12.2 Number Bases

In our decimal or base-10 system, the number 312 means $3 \times 10^2 + 1 \times 10^1 + 2 \times 10^0$. Similarly, in a base-$b$ number system, the number $(a_n a_{n-1} a_{n-2}..a_1 a_0)_b$ means

$$a_n b^n + a_{n-1} b^{n-1} + a_{n-2} b^{n-2} + \cdots + a_1 b^1 + a_0 b^0.$$

Oftentimes it is beneficial to represent numbers in bases other than 10. For example, binary system is used in computer science. So we need to know how to convert from one base to another. Let's look at a base conversion problem.

Example 12.2. Express 224 in base (-3) number system. (Mathworks)

Answer: $1,201,112_{(-3)}$

Solution: We find its base (-3) expression by repeated division by -3 and recording nonnegative remainders.

$$
\begin{aligned}
224/-3 &= -74, &\quad \text{remainder 2,} \\
-74/-3 &= 25, &\quad \text{remainder 1,} \\
25/-3 &= -8, &\quad \text{remainder 1,} \\
-8/-3 &= 3, &\quad \text{remainder 1,} \\
3/-3 &= -1, &\quad \text{remainder 0,} \\
-1/-3 &= 1, &\quad \text{remainder 2,} \\
1/-3 &= 0, &\quad \text{remainder 1.}
\end{aligned}
$$

Therefore, 224_{10} is $\boxed{1,201,112_{(-3)}}$.

Example 12.3. Mady has an infinite number of balls and empty boxes available to her. The empty boxes, each capable of holding four balls, are arranged in a row from left to right. At the first step, she places a ball in the first box of the row. At each subsequent step, she places a ball in the first box of the row that still has room for a ball and empties any previous boxes. How many balls in total are in the boxes as a result of Mady's 2010th step? (MathCounts)

Answer: 6 balls

Solution: Let's try some small numbers. After the first step, one ball is in the first box. After the 4th step, four balls are in the first box. After the 5th step, the first box is empty and one ball is in the second box. After the 9th step, four balls are in the first box and one ball is in the second box. After the 10th step, the first box is empty and two balls are in the second box. We see that this is just the base-5 representation of the numbers. Since $2010_{10} = 31020_5$, after the 2010th step, there are in total $3 + 1 + 2 = \boxed{6 \text{ balls}}$ in the boxes.

12.3 Chicken McNugget Theorem

Number theorists don't just study abstract conjectures such as Fermat's Last Theorem, they also wonder about mundane moments of daily life. The classic Chicken McNugget problem goes like this:

> Chicken McNuggets can be purchased in quantities of 6, 9, and 20 pieces. You can buy exactly 15 pieces by purchasing a 6 and a 9, but you can't buy exactly 10 McNuggets. What is the largest number of McNuggets that can NOT be purchased?

This Chicken McNugget problem (Problem 12.1) can be solved with the help of the following theorem.

Theorem 12.3. (Chicken McNugget Theorem) *Let a and b be two natural numbers. If $\gcd(a, b) = 1$, then*

1. *The greatest positive integer that cannot be written in the form $ma + nb$ for nonnegative integers m and n is $ab - a - b$.*

2. *If integers x and y satisfy $0 \le x, y \le ab - a - b$ and $x + y = ab - a - b$, then exactly one of x and y cannot be written in the form $ma + nb$ for nonnegative integers m and n.*

Let's look at a MathCounts problem.

Example 12.4. John has an ample supply of 10-cent and 15-cent stamps. He will buy an ample supply of stamps of one more denomination, which is a whole number. He needs to be able to combine the stamps to make any value of 30 cents or more. In cents, what is the greatest denomination of stamps he can buy which will enable him to do this?

Answer: 6-cent

Solution: Let the new stamp be an x-cent stamp. Clearly $\gcd(x, 5) = 1$, because otherwise we will have infinitely many values that cannot be represented. By the Chicken McNugget Theorem, the largest value that cannot be represented with

x-cent stamps and 5-cent stamps is $5x - x - 5 = 4x - 5$. Note that if a value cannot be represented with x and 5, then this value cannot be represented with x, 10, and 15. So the largest value, call it y, that cannot be represented with x-cent, 10-cent, and 15-cent stamps must be greater than or equal to $4x - 5$. Thus, $4x - 5 \le y \le 29$, $x \le 8.5$. When $x = 8$, we see that 37 cannot be represented with 8, 10, and 15. When $x = 7$, we see that 33 cannot be represented with 7, 10, and 15. So, 7 and 8 do not work. When $x = 6$, with 6, 10 and 15, we can represent **30** $= 3 \cdot 10$, **31** $= 10 + 15 + 6$, **32** $= 20 + 12$, **33** $= 3 \cdot 6 + 15$, **34** $= 10 + 24$, and **35** $= 20 + 15$. Any number larger than 35 can be represented with a multiple of 6 plus one of the numbers from 30 to 35. Thus, $\boxed{6\text{-cent}}$ is the greatest denomination of stamps he can buy.

The second part of Theorem 12.3 tells us that if $\gcd(a, b) = 1$, then there are exactly $\frac{1}{2}(a-1)(b-1)$ positive integers that cannot be expressed in the form $ma + nb$ for nonnegative integers m and n. We will use this fact in our next example, which is adapted from a USAMTS problem.

Example 12.5. Let a and b be positive integers such that all but 65 positive integers are expressible in the form $ma + nb$, where m and n are nonnegative integers. If 60 is one of the numbers that is not expressible, find $a + b$.

Answer: 25

Solution: Clearly, a and b are relatively prime because if $\gcd(a, b) > 1$, then only multiples of $\gcd(a, b)$ could be expressed in the form $ma + nb$. We would have infinitely many positive integers that are not expressible, a contradiction. Without loss of generality, let's assume that $a \le b$. By the Chicken McNugget Theorem, we have
$$\frac{1}{2}(a-1)(b-1) = 65, \qquad (a-1)(b-1) = 130.$$
The possible pairs of (a, b) are $(2, 131)$, $(3, 66)$, $(6, 27)$, and $(11, 14)$. Since $\gcd(a, b) = 1$, we rule out $(3, 66)$ and $(6, 27)$. The only pairs left are $(2, 131)$ and $(11, 14)$. Since 60 is expressible with $a = 2$ and $b = 131$, the pair $(2, 131)$ does not work. If $a = 11$ and $b = 14$, then the largest number that is not expressible is $11 \cdot 14 - 11 - 14 = 129$. Since $129 - 60 = 69 = 11 \cdot 5 + 14$ is expressible, 60 is not expressible in the form $11m + 14n$ by the Chicken McNugget Theorem. So $(11, 14)$ is the desired pair. Therefore, $a + b = \boxed{25}$.

12.4 Euler's Theorem

In MathCounts, we are often asked to find the units digit or the last two digits of a large number. One powerful tool to solve a problem of this type is Euler's Theorem. Let's first give some definitions.

Let $m \neq 0$ be an integer. We say that a is *congruent* to b modulo m, denoted as $a \equiv b \pmod{m}$, if $m|(a-b)$. For any natural number n, Euler's totient function $\phi(n)$ is the number of positive integers less than or equal to n that are relatively prime to n. Euler's totient function is an important function in number theory. It is also easy to compute because of its nice properties.

Theorem 12.4. *Let p be a prime number. Let a, b, and n be natural numbers and $\gcd(a,b) = 1$. Then*

$$\phi(ab) = \phi(a)\phi(b), \qquad \phi(p^n) = p^n - p^{n-1}.$$

For example, $\phi(100) = \phi(2^2 \cdot 5^2) = \phi(2^2) \cdot \phi(5^2) = (2^2 - 2^1) \cdot (5^2 - 5^1) = 40$.

Theorem 12.5. (Euler's Theorem) *Let a and n be relatively prime natural numbers. Then $a^{\phi(n)} \equiv 1 \pmod{n}$.*

One special case of Euler's Theorem is Fermat's Little Theorem. We see that for any prime number p, $\phi(p) = p - 1$. So we have:

Theorem 12.6. (Fermat's Little Theorem) *Let a and p be natural numbers with p a prime and $\gcd(a,p) = 1$. Then $a^{p-1} \equiv 1 \pmod{p}$.*

Our next problem comes from the Princeton University Math Competition.

Example 12.6. Let $f(x) = x^{x^{x^x}}$. What are the last two digits of $f(17)$?

Answer: 77

Solution: We want $f(17) = 17^{17^{17^{17}}} \pmod{100}$. Since $\phi(100) = 40$ and $\gcd(17, 100) = 1$, Euler's theorem tells us that $17^{40} \equiv 1 \pmod{100}$. Thus, we want to find $17^{17^{17}} \pmod{40}$, because if $17^{17^{17}} \equiv y \pmod{40}$, then $f(x) \equiv 17^y \pmod{100}$. Since 17 is relatively prime to 40 and $\phi(40) = (2^3 - 2^2) \cdot (5 - 1) = 16$, $17^{16} \equiv 1 \pmod{40}$. As before, we now want $17^{17} \pmod{16}$, because if $17^{17} \equiv z \pmod{16}$, then $17^{17^{17}} \equiv 17^z \pmod{40}$. Since $17^{17} = (16+1)^{17} \equiv 1 \pmod{16}$, $17^{17^{17}} \equiv 17^1 \pmod{40}$. This result and the Binomial Theorem give us that:

$$f(17) \equiv 17^{17} \equiv (10+7)^{17} \equiv 17 \cdot 10 \cdot 7^{16} + 7^{17} \equiv (170+7) \cdot 7^{16} \equiv 11 \cdot 7^{17} \pmod{100}.$$

Since
$$7^{17} = 7 \cdot 7^{16} = 7 \cdot 49^8 = 7(50-1)^8 \equiv 7 \cdot (-1)^8 \equiv 7 \pmod{100},$$

we have $f(17) \equiv 77 \pmod{100}$. Therefore, the last two digits of $f(17)$ are $\boxed{77}$.

Problems for Chapter 12

Problem 12.1. Chicken McNuggets can be purchased in quantities of 6, 9, and 20 pieces. You can buy exactly 15 pieces by purchasing a 6 and a 9, but you can't buy exactly 10 McNuggets. What is the largest number of McNuggets that can NOT be purchased?

Problem 12.2. How many base-10 three-digit numbers are also three-digit numbers in both base-9 and base-11? (AMC 10)

Problem 12.3. Determine the base (-2) representation of 34.

Problem 12.4. (MAΘ) Find the largest integer d for which there are no nonnegative integer solutions (a, b, c) which satisfy the equation

$$5a + 7b + 11c = d.$$

Problem 12.5. On a true-false test of 100 items, every question that is a multiple of 4 is true, and all others are false. If a student marks every item that is a multiple of 3 false and all others true, how many of the 100 items will be correctly answered? (MathCounts)

Problem 12.6. How many whole numbers n, such that $100 \leq n \leq 1000$, have the same number of odd factors as even factors? (MathCounts)

Problem 12.7. Find the base (-4) representation of $33\frac{1}{3}$.

Problem 12.8. (ARML) For a positive integer n, let $C(n)$ be the number of pairs of consecutive 1's in the binary representation of n. For example,

$$C(183) = C(10110111_2) = 3.$$

Compute
$$C(1) + C(2) + C(3) + \cdots + C(256).$$

Problem 12.9. The integers 1 through 2010 are written on a white board. The integer 1 is erased. Every integer that is either 7 or 11 greater than an erased integer will be erased. At the end of the process what is the largest integer remaining on the board? (MathCounts)

Problem 12.10. Determine the last two digits of $7^{7^{7^{7}}}$.

Problem 12.11. (IMO) Find the smallest natural number n which has the following properties:

(a) Its decimal representation has 6 as the last digit.

(b) If the last digit 6 is erased and placed in front of the remaining digits, the resulting number is four times as large as the original number n.

Problem 12.12. To weigh an object by using a balance scale, Brady places the object on one side of the scale and places enough weights on each side to make the two sides of the scale balanced. Brady's set of weights contains the minimum number necessary to measure the whole-number weight of any object from 1 to 40 pounds, inclusive. What is the greatest weight, in pounds, of a weight in Brady's set? (MathCounts)

Problem 12.13. A game of solitaire is played as follows. After each play, according to the outcome, the player receives either a or b points, where a and b are positive integers such that $a > b$. The player's score accumulates from play to play. She notices that there are 35 unattainable scores and that one of these is 58. Find a and b as an ordered pair (a, b). (Putnam)

Problem 12.14. Let S be a subset of $\{1, 2, 3, ..., 50\}$ such that no pair of distinct elements in S has a sum divisible by 7. What is the maximum number of elements in S? (AHSME)

Problem 12.15. Find the least positive integer n for which $\dfrac{n-13}{5n+6}$ is a non-zero reducible fraction. (AHSME)

Problem 12.16. Let n be the smallest positive integer that is a multiple of 75 and has exactly 75 positive integer divisors, including 1 and itself. Find $\dfrac{n}{75}$. (AIME)

Problem 12.17. A faulty car odometer proceeds from digit 3 to digit 5, always skipping the digit 4, regardless of position. For example, after traveling one mile the odometer changed from 000039 to 000050. If the odometer now reads 002005, how many miles has the car actually traveled? (AMC 12)

Problem 12.18. Begin with the 200-digit number 9876543210987...43210, which repeats the digits 0-9 in reverse order. From the left, choose every third digit to form a new number. Repeat the same process with the new number. Continue the process repeatedly until the result is a two-digit number. What is the resulting two-digit number? (MathCounts)

Problem 12.19. How many integers from 1 to 1992 inclusive have a base three representation that does not contain the digit 2? (Mandelbrot)

Problem 12.20. Find the remainder when $3^3 \cdot 33^{33} \cdot 333^{333} \cdot 3333^{3333}$ is divided by 100. (Purple Comet)

Chapter 13

Modular Arithmetic

Given natural numbers a, b, and m, a is congruent to b modulo m if and only if m divides $a - b$ evenly. That is, if and only if a and b have the same remainder when divided by m. Bézout's Identity tells us that for any natural numbers a and b, there are integers x and y such that $\gcd(a, b) = ax + by$. This identity plays an important role in our study of modular arithmetic.

13.1 Chinese Remainder Theorem

One ancient Chinese puzzle goes like this:

> There are certain things whose number is unknown. Repeatedly divided by 3, the remainder is 2; by 5 the remainder is 3; and by 7 the remainder is 2. What will be the least number?

We can solve this puzzle (Problem 13.1) using the Chinese Remainder Theorem. But, before we learn this theorem, let's first introduce the concept of multiplicative inverse.

Given natural numbers a and m, an integer x is said to be a *modular multiplicative inverse*, or *multiplicative inverse*, of a modulo m if $a \cdot x \equiv 1 \pmod{m}$. Note that a has a multiplicative inverse (mod m) if and only if $\gcd(a, m) = 1$. For example, for any integer x, $2x \not\equiv 1 \pmod{6}$. So, 2 has no multiplicative inverse modulo 6. Note also that if x is a multiplicative inverse of a modulo m, then so is $x + km$ for any integer k.

To find a multiplicative inverse of a modulo m when $\gcd(a, m) = 1$, we first use the Euclidean Algorithm to get $\gcd(a, m)$. Next, we reverse the process to get integers x and y such that $a \cdot x + m \cdot y = \gcd(a, m) = 1$. We see that this x is a multiplicative inverse of a modulo m. As an example, let's find a multiplicative inverse of 11 modulo 13. We have:

$$13 = 11 + 2, \quad 11 = 5 \cdot 2 + 1, \quad 1 = 11 - 5 \cdot 2 = 11 - 5(13 - 11) = 6 \cdot 11 - 5 \cdot 13.$$

Therefore, one multiplicative inverse of 11 modulo 13 is 6.

Example 13.1. Compute 2^{972} (mod 977). (AwesomeMath)

Answer: 916

Solution: First, we note that 977 is a prime because no prime number less than or equal to $\sqrt{977} \approx 31.257$ divides it evenly. By Fermat's Little Theorem, $2^{976} \equiv 1$ (mod 977). That is, $16 \cdot 2^{972} \equiv 1$ (mod 977).

Thus, if we know a multiplicative inverse of 16 modulo 977, then we can multiply both sides of the equation by it and cancel out the 16. Since $977 - 61 \cdot 16 = 1$, -61 is a multiplicative inverse of 16 modulo 977. Thus

$$2^{972} \equiv 1 \cdot 2^{972} \equiv -61 \cdot 16 \cdot 2^{972} \equiv -61 \cdot 2^{976} \equiv -61 \cdot 1 \equiv \boxed{916} \pmod{977}.$$

Now we are ready to introduce the Chinese Remainder Theorem.

Theorem 13.1. (Chinese Remainder Theorem) *Let $m_1, m_2, ..., m_n$ be pairwise relatively prime positive integers. Let $M = m_1 m_2 \cdots m_n$. For any integers $y_1, y_2, ..., y_n$, there is an integer x such that*

$$x \equiv y_1 \pmod{m_1},$$
$$x \equiv y_2 \pmod{m_2},$$
$$\vdots$$
$$x \equiv y_n \pmod{m_n},$$

and x is unique modulo M.

To find x, we let $a_i = \frac{M}{m_i}$. Next, for each $1 \le i \le n$, we find a multiplicative inverse b_i of a_i modulo m_i. Then a solution for x is:

$$x \equiv a_1 b_1 y_1 + a_2 b_2 y_2 + \cdots + a_n b_n y_n \pmod{M}.$$

Let's look at a MathCounts problem.

Example 13.2. The marching band has more than 100 members but fewer than 200 members. When they line up in rows of 4 there is one extra person; when they line up in rows of 5 there are two extra people; and when they line up in rows of 7 there are three extra people. How many members are in the marching band?

Answer: 157

13.2 Solving Linear Diophantine Equations

Solution: Let x be the number of people in the marching band. We have $x \equiv 1 \pmod 4$, $x \equiv 2 \pmod 5$, and $x \equiv 3 \pmod 7$. Let $M = 4 \cdot 5 \cdot 7 = 140$. Let $a_1 = 5 \cdot 7 = 35$, $a_2 = 4 \cdot 7 = 28$, and $a_3 = 4 \cdot 5 = 20$.

To find a multiplicative inverse b_1 of 35 modulo 4, we have

$$35 = 8 \cdot 4 + 3, \quad 4 = 3 + 1, \quad 1 = 4 - 3 = 4 - (35 - 8 \cdot 4) = (-1) \cdot 35 + 9 \cdot 4.$$

So $b_1 = -1$. To find a multiplicative inverse b_2 of 28 modulo 5, we have

$$28 = 5 \cdot 5 + 3, \quad 5 = 3 + 2, \quad 3 = 2 + 1.$$

So $1 = 3 - 2 = 3 - (5 - 3) = 2 \cdot 3 - 5 = 2 \cdot (28 - 5 \cdot 5) - 5 = 2 \cdot 28 + (-11) \cdot 5$. Thus $b_2 = 2$.

To find a multiplicative inverse b_3 of 20 modulo 7, we have

$$20 = 2 \cdot 7 + 6, \quad 7 = 6 + 1, \quad 1 = 7 - 6 = 7 - (20 - 2 \cdot 7) = (-1) \cdot 20 + 3 \cdot 7.$$

Thus $b_3 = -1$. Therefore,

$$x \equiv 35 \cdot (-1) \cdot 1 + 28 \cdot 2 \cdot 2 + 20 \cdot (-1) \cdot 3 \equiv 17 \pmod{140}.$$

Since the band has between 100 and 200 members, the number of people in the band is $17 + 140 = \boxed{157}$.

13.2 Solving Linear Diophantine Equations

A *Diophantine equation* is a polynomial equation with integral coefficients where only integer solutions are allowed. A linear Diophantine equation in two variables x and y is a Diophantine equation of the form $ax + by = c$, where a, b, and c are integers and we seek integer solutions for x and y. Many linear Diophantine equations can be solved using modular arithmetic.

Example 13.3. Exactly one ordered pair of positive integers (x, y) satisfies the equation $37x + 73y = 2016$. What is the sum $x + y$? (MathCounts)

Answer: 36

Solution: We can rewrite the equation as $37(x + 2y) - y = 2016$. Let $z = x + 2y$. We solve $37z - y = 2016$ first. Taking both sides of the equation modulo 37, we get $-y \equiv 18 \pmod{37}$. Thus $y \equiv 19 \pmod{37}$. Since $37x + 73y = 2016$, $y \leq \frac{2016}{73} < 28$. So the only positive solution for y is $y = 19$. Plugging it in the equation $37z - y = 2016$, we get $z = 55$. Therefore, $x = z - 2y = 17$ and the sum $x + y = 17 + 19 = \boxed{36}$.

To solve $ax + by = c$ in general, we notice that c must be divisible by $\gcd(a, b)$. Otherwise $ax + by = c$ has no integer solutions. So without loss of generality, we can assume that $\gcd(a, b) = 1$. To solve $ax + by = c$ with $\gcd(a, b) = 1$, we first use the Euclidean Algorithm to get integers m and n such that $a \cdot m + b \cdot n = 1$. Next, we multiply both sides by c and get $a \cdot (mc) + b \cdot (nc) = c$. Then for any integer k,

$$a(mc + kb) + b(nc - ka) = a(mc) + b(nc) + akb - bka = c.$$

That is, for any integer k, the integer pair $(mc + kb, nc - ka)$ is a solution to $ax + by = c$ when $\gcd(a, b) = 1$.

Theorem 13.2. *If $\gcd(a, b) = 1$, then all integer solutions to the equation $ax + by = c$ may be written as:*
$$(x, y) = (mc + kb, nc - ka)$$
where k can be any integer and m and n are integers such that $ma + nb = 1$.

Example 13.4. How many positive integer pairs (x, y) satisfy $10x + 14y = 1742$?

Answer: 25

Solution: The equation is equivalent to $5x + 7y = 871$. From the Euclidean Algorithm, we have

$$7 = 5 + 2, \qquad 5 = 2 \cdot 2 + 1, \qquad 1 = 5 - 2 \cdot 2 = 5 - 2 \cdot (7 - 5) = 3 \cdot 5 - 2 \cdot 7.$$

Therefore, for any integer k, the integer pair $(3 \cdot 871 + 7k, -2 \cdot 871 - 5k)$ is a solution to $10x + 14y = 1742$. To make the solutions positive, we must have

$$3 \cdot 871 + 7k > 0, \qquad \text{and} \qquad -2 \cdot 871 - 5k > 0.$$

Therefore,
$$\frac{-2613}{7} < k < \frac{-1742}{5}.$$

The only integers k that satisfy the requirements are: $k = -373, -371, ..., -349$. So there are in total $-349 - (-373) + 1 = \boxed{25}$ positive solutions.

13.3 Solving Diophantine Equations Using Inequalities

Sometimes, one side of a Diophantine equation grows faster than the other side when the variables change. This observation motivates us to establish bounds for the variables using inequalities. Usually such an approach helps us narrow down the possible ranges of the variables. Let's look at a MathCounts problem.

13.3 Solving Diophantine Equations Using Inequalities

Example 13.5. The consecutive integers from 1 to n were written on a chalkboard. One of the integers was erased, and the mean of the remaining integers was $35\frac{7}{17}$. What integer was erased?

Answer: 7

Solution: Suppose the erased number is k. Then we have

$$\frac{1+2+\cdots+n-k}{n-1} = 35\frac{7}{17},$$

$$\frac{n(n+1)-2k}{2} = \frac{602}{17}(n-1).$$

Note that the left-hand side of the equation is quadratic and the right-hand side is linear. Since a quadratic function grows faster than a linear function, we can set up bounds to ensure that the quadratic will not become too large. These bounds are obtained from the extreme cases. In the case that the number 1 is erased, the sum of the remaining $n-1$ numbers will be

$$2+3+\cdots+n = \frac{(n+2)(n-1)}{2}.$$

Then the mean of the remaining numbers is $\frac{n+2}{2}$.

$$35\frac{7}{17} \leq \frac{n+2}{2}, \qquad \frac{602}{17} \leq \frac{n+2}{2}, \qquad n \geq \frac{1170}{17}.$$

Since n is an integer, $n \geq 69$. In the case that the number n is erased, the sum of the remaining $n-1$ numbers will be

$$1+2+\cdots+(n-1) = \frac{n(n-1)}{2}.$$

Then the mean of the remaining numbers is $\frac{n}{2}$.

$$\frac{n}{2} \leq 35\frac{7}{17}, \qquad n \leq \frac{1204}{17}.$$

Since n is an integer, $n \leq 70$. Therefore, $n = 69$ or $n = 70$. If $n = 69$, we have

$$\frac{1+2+\cdots+69-k}{69-1} = 35\frac{7}{17}, \qquad k = \frac{69 \cdot 70}{2} - \frac{68 \cdot 602}{17} = 7.$$

If $n = 70$, we have

$$\frac{1+2+\cdots+70-k}{70-1} = 35\frac{7}{17}, \qquad k = \frac{70 \cdot 71}{2} - \frac{69 \cdot 602}{17} = \frac{707}{17}.$$

Since $\frac{707}{17}$ is not an integer, $n = 70$ does not work. Therefore, $n = 69$ and the erased integer is $\boxed{7}$.

13.4 The Floor Function

We briefly introduced the floor function in Chapter 2. Because of its importance, we devote one section to it here. For any real number x, we use $\lfloor x \rfloor$ to denote the greatest integer less than or equal to x. We call $\lfloor x \rfloor$ the *floor* of x. Letting $m = \lfloor x \rfloor$, we see that $m \leq x < m+1$. We call the difference $x - \lfloor x \rfloor$ the *fractional part* of x and use $\{x\}$ to denote it. That is, $\{x\} = x - \lfloor x \rfloor$. We use $\lceil x \rceil$ to denote the least integer greater than or equal to x. We call $\lceil x \rceil$ the *ceiling* of x. Letting $n = \lceil x \rceil$, we see that $n - 1 < x \leq n$. The floor and ceiling functions are closely related. For any real number x, $\lceil x \rceil = -\lfloor -x \rfloor$.

Note that both the floor and ceiling functions are monotonic non-decreasing functions. This property is a useful tool when we solve problems involving these functions. Our next example comes from the Canadian Mathematical Olympiad.

Example 13.6. Let n be any positive integer. Evaluate

$$\lfloor \sqrt{4n+1} \rfloor - \lfloor \sqrt{n} + \sqrt{n+1} \rfloor.$$

Answer: 0

Solution: When we need to compare two entities involving square roots, a common method is to get rid of the square roots by squaring. Let's square $\sqrt{n} + \sqrt{n+1}$. We get

$$(\sqrt{n} + \sqrt{n+1})^2 = 2n + 1 + 2\sqrt{n^2 + n}.$$

Since $4n + 1 = 2n + 1 + 2n < 2n + 1 + 2\sqrt{n^2 + n} = (\sqrt{n} + \sqrt{n+1})^2$, we have

$$4n + 1 < (\sqrt{n} + \sqrt{n+1})^2 = 2n + 1 + 2\sqrt{n^2 + n}$$

$$< 2n + 1 + 2\sqrt{n^2 + n + \frac{1}{4}}$$

$$= 2n + 1 + 2\left(n + \frac{1}{2}\right) = 4n + 2. \qquad (*)$$

Note that $\lfloor \sqrt{m} \rfloor$ increases if and only if m is a square. Since the square of an even number is 0 modulo 4 and the square of an odd number is 1 modulo 4, $4n + 2$ is never a square. Thus,

$$\lfloor \sqrt{4n+1} \rfloor = \lfloor \sqrt{4n+2} \rfloor,$$

for all positive integers n. So from $(*)$, we see that for all positive integers n,

$$\lfloor \sqrt{4n+1} \rfloor = \lfloor \sqrt{n} + \sqrt{n+1} \rfloor.$$

Therefore the difference $\lfloor \sqrt{4n+1} \rfloor - \lfloor \sqrt{n} + \sqrt{n+1} \rfloor$ is always $\boxed{0}$.

Problems for Chapter 13

Problem 13.1. There are certain things whose number is unknown. Repeatedly divided by 3, the remainder is 2; by 5 the remainder is 3; and by 7 the remainder is 2. What will be the least number?

Problem 13.2. In the non-decreasing sequence of odd integers $\{a_1, a_2, a_3, ...\} = \{1, 3, 3, 3, 5, 5, 5, 5, ...\}$, each odd positive integer k appears k times. The nth term can be written as $a_n = b\lfloor \sqrt{n+c} \rfloor + d$ for some integers b, c, and d. What is $b+c+d$? (AHSME)

Problem 13.3. Zan has created this iterative rule for generating sequences of whole numbers:

1) If a number is 25 or less, double the number.

2) If a number is greater than 25, subtract 12 from it.

Let F be the first number in a sequence generated by the rule above. F is a "sweet number" if 16 is not a term in the sequence that starts with F. How many of the whole numbers 1 through 50 are "sweet numbers"? (MathCounts)

Problem 13.4. What is the largest positive integer n for which there is a unique integer k such that $\dfrac{8}{15} < \dfrac{n}{n+k} < \dfrac{7}{13}$? (AIME)

Problem 13.5. Three planets orbit a star circularly in the same plane. Each moves in the same direction and moves at constant speed. Their periods are 60, 84, and 140 years. The three planets and the star are currently collinear. What is the fewest number of years from now that they will all be collinear again? (AIME)

Problem 13.6. Benji pays $2.78 for some apples and oranges. If each apple costs $0.35 and each orange costs $0.69, how many apples did he buy?

Problem 13.7. How many pairs of integers (x, y) satisfy the equation $x^2 - 3y^2 = 2$?

Problem 13.8. When Mr. Smith cashed a check at his bank, the teller mistook the number of cents for the number of dollars and vice versa. Unaware of this, Mr. Smith spent 68 cents and then noticed to his surprise that he had twice the amount of the original check. Determine the smallest value for which the check could have been written. (Burton)

Problem 13.9. In the United States, coins have the following thicknesses: penny, 1.55 mm; nickel, 1.95mm; dime, 1.35 mm; quarter, 1.75 mm. If a stack of these coins is exactly 14 mm high, how many coins are in the stack? (AMC 10)

Problem 13.10. A band of 17 pirates stole a sack of gold coins. When they tried to divide the fortune into equal portions, 3 coins remained. In the ensuing brawl over who should get the extra coins, one pirate was expelled. The wealth was redistributed, but this time an equal division left 10 coins. Again an argument developed in which another pirate was expelled. But now the total fortune was evenly distributed among the survivors. What was the least number of coins that could have been stolen? (Burton)

Problem 13.11. Let a, b, and c be positive integers such that $29a+30b+31c = 366$. Find $19a+20b+21c$. (Purple Comet)

Problem 13.12. Let $a_n = 6^n + 8^n$. Determine the remainder when a_{83} is divided by 49. (AIME)

Problem 13.13. Find the smallest positive integer x such that $x \equiv 1 \pmod 3$, $x \equiv 3 \pmod 5$, $x \equiv 5 \pmod 7$, $x \equiv 9 \pmod{11}$, and $x \equiv 2 \pmod{13}$. (PUMaC)

Problem 13.14. Determine the number of positive integer solutions to $43x + 17y = 1500$.

Problem 13.15. Real numbers x, y, and z satisfy the following system of equations:

$$x + \lfloor y \rfloor + \{z\} = 200.0,$$
$$\{x\} + y + \lfloor z \rfloor = 190.1,$$
$$\lfloor x \rfloor + \{y\} + z = 178.8.$$

What is the value of x? (Australia)

Problem 13.16. Find the smallest n such that $n!$ ends in 290 zeroes. (HMMT)

Problem 13.17. Suppose that r is a real number for which

$$\left\lfloor r + \frac{19}{100} \right\rfloor + \left\lfloor r + \frac{20}{100} \right\rfloor + \cdots + \left\lfloor r + \frac{91}{100} \right\rfloor = 546.$$

Find $\lfloor 100r \rfloor$. (AIME)

Problem 13.18. What is the remainder when 4444^{4444} is divided by 18? (Cornell)

Problem 13.19. Given that 2^{2004} is a 604-digit number whose first digit is 1, how many elements of the set $S = \{2^0, 2^1, 2^2, \ldots, 2^{2003}\}$ have a first digit of 4? (AMC 12)

Problem 13.20. (WOOT) Determine the number of real solutions x to the equation

$$\left\lfloor \frac{x}{2} \right\rfloor + \left\lfloor \frac{x}{3} \right\rfloor + \left\lfloor \frac{x}{5} \right\rfloor = x.$$

Chapter 14

Counting

Counting is a kindergarten subject, but it is also one of the hardest MathCounts topics. That's because many MathCounts counting problems need both grit and strategies. Some strategies, such as complementary counting, are easy to learn, while others require a lot of practice.

14.1 Stars and Bars

The stars and bars method is a powerful counting strategy popularized by Princeton professor William Feller in his book *An Introduction to Probability Theory and Its Applications*. For example, if we are asked to find the number of nonnegative integer solutions $(x_1, x_2, x_3, x_4, x_5)$ to the Diophantine equation $x_1 + x_2 + x_3 + x_4 + x_5 = 17$, we can use 17 stars to represent the number 17, and $5-1$ bars separating the stars to represent the partitions. One possible arrangement is this:

$$* * * | * * | * * * * * * * | * * * * * |$$

This arrangement corresponds to the solution $(3, 2, 7, 5, 0)$. Since we can choose $5-1$ slots from the total $17+5-1$ slots to place $5-1$ bars, the number of nonnegative integer solutions to the given equation is $\binom{17+5-1}{5-1}$.

Theorem 14.1. (Stars and Bars) *The number of ways to distribute n indistinguishable objects into k distinct bins is*

$$\binom{n+k-1}{k-1}.$$

If we are asked to find the number of *positive* integer solutions $(x_1, x_2, x_3, x_4, x_5)$ to the Diophantine equation $x_1 + x_2 + x_3 + x_4 + x_5 = 17$, then no two bars can be adjacent. Therefore, we can place the $5-1$ bars among the $17-1$ spaces between the 17 stars. So the number of positive integer solutions to the Diophantine equation $x_1 + x_2 + x_3 + x_4 + x_5 = 17$ is $\binom{17-1}{5-1}$.

Theorem 14.2. *The number of ways to distribute n indistinguishable objects into k distinct bins such that no bin remains empty is*

$$\binom{n-1}{k-1}.$$

Recasting the original problem you want to solve as a "stars and bars" problem is often the most important step when you try to use this method.

Example 14.1. How many 7-digit positive integers are there such that their digits are in non-decreasing order? (AoPS)

Answer: 6435

Solution: Note that the number is fixed when we get all 7 digits. Note also that the digits can be repeated and they cannot be zero. Let's use stars to represent the digits. Let's place the digits into 9 bins so that if it is in bin 1, then it is 1; if it is in bin 2, then it is 2; and so on. So, we have 7 stars and $9-1 = 8$ bars to separate the stars. For example,

$$\| * \|\| * * * | * \| * *$$

represents the number 3666799. Thus the total number of such 7-digit positive integers is $\binom{7+9-1}{9-1} = \boxed{6435}$.

Example 14.2. How many integers from 1 to 10000 are there whose digits sum to 19?

Answer: 660

Solution: Since the sum of the digits of 10000 is not equal to 19, we only need to consider integers $x_1 x_2 x_3 x_4$ such that $0 \leq x_1, x_2, x_3, x_4 \leq 9$ and $x_1 + x_2 + x_3 + x_4 = 19$. Here $x_1 x_2 x_3 x_4$ represents an integer with x_1 as its leading digit. Note that 0 is allowed as a leading digit here because the numbers range from 1 to 9999, or 0001 to 9999. If x_1, x_2, x_3, x_4 could be any nonnegative integers, then we would have $\binom{19+4-1}{4-1} = 1540$ integers by using stars and bars. Now let's consider the "bad" case when $x_1 \geq 10$. In this case, let $x_1' = x_1 - 10$. Then we only need to consider integers $x_1' x_2 x_3 x_4$ such that $0 \leq x_1', x_2, x_3, x_4 \leq 9$ and $x_1' + x_2 + x_3 + x_4 =$

$19 - 10 = 9$. Again, using stars and bars, we have $\binom{9+4-1}{4-1} = 220$ "bad" integers. By symmetry, each of $x_2 \geq 10$, $x_3 \geq 10$, and $x_4 \geq 10$ gives us 220 "bad" integers. We see that it is not possible to have more than one $x_i \geq 10$ because then the sum of the digits would be ≥ 20. So the number of integers from 1 to 10000 whose digits sum to 19 is $1540 - 4 \cdot 220 = \boxed{660}$.

14.2 Principle of Inclusion-Exclusion

In terms of mathematics, strategic overcounting is a counting technique in which we deliberately overcount and then subtract the overcounted parts systematically. The principle of inclusion-exclusion results from strategic overcounting.

Theorem 14.3. (Principle of Inclusion-Exclusion) *Given finite sets A, B, and C,*

$$|A \cup B \cup C| = |A| + |B| + |C| - |A \cap B| - |A \cap C| - |B \cap C| + |A \cap B \cap C|.$$

Our next example builds upon Example 14.2.

Example 14.3. How many four-digit positive integers are there whose digits sum to 23?

Answer: 465

Solution: As in Example 14.2, let the first digit be x_1 and the second, third, and fourth digits be x_2, x_3, and x_4, respectively. We have $x_1 + x_2 + x_3 + x_4 = 23$. Since $x_1 x_2 x_3 x_4$ is a four-digit positive integer, $x_1 \geq 1$. So we let $x_1' = x_1 - 1$. Then we have $0 \leq x_1', x_2, x_3, x_4 \leq 9$, and $x_1' + x_2 + x_3 + x_4 = 22$. If each digit, x_1', x_2, x_3, and x_4, could be any nonnegative integer, then we would have $\binom{22+4-1}{4-1} = 2300$ integers by stars and bars. Next, we need to systematically subtract the overcounted integers. Let A be the set of solutions where $x_1' \geq 9$. Let B, C, and D be the sets of solutions where $x_2 \geq 10$, $x_3 \geq 10$, and $x_4 \geq 10$, respectively. Letting $x_1'' = x_1' - 9$, we have $x_1'' + x_2 + x_3 + x_4 = 22 - 9 = 13$. By stars and bars, $|A| = \binom{13+4-1}{4-1} = 560$. Letting $x_2' = x_2 - 10$, we have $x_1' + x_2' + x_3 + x_4 = 22 - 10 = 12$. So $|B| = \binom{12+4-1}{4-1} = 455$. Similarly, $|C| = |D| = |B| = 455$.

Finally, we need to systematically add the under-counted integers. $A \cap B$ is the set of solutions where $x_1' \geq 9$ and $x_2 \geq 10$. When we let $x_1'' = x_1' - 9$ and $x_2' = x_2 - 10$, we have $x_1'' + x_2' + x_3 + x_4 = 22 - 9 - 10 = 3$. Again by stars and bars, $|A \cap B| = \binom{3+4-1}{4-1} = 20$ integers. Similarly, $|A \cap C| = |A \cap D| = 20$. Note that $B \cap C$ is the set where $x_2 \geq 10$ and $x_3 \geq 10$. Letting $x_2' = x_2 - 10$ and $x_3' = x_3 - 10$, we have $x_1' + x_2' + x_3' + x_4 = 22 - 10 - 10 = 2$. Using stars and bars again, we have $|B \cap C| = \binom{2+4-1}{4-1} = 10$ integers. Similarly, $|B \cap D| = |C \cap D| = 10$.

Therefore, by the principle of inclusion-exclusion, the number of four-digit positive integers whose digits sum to 23 is

$$2300 - (|A| + |B| + |C| + |D|)$$
$$+ |A \cap B| + |A \cap C| + |A \cap D| + |B \cap C| + |B \cap D| + |C \cap D|$$
$$= 2300 - 560 - 3 \cdot 455 + 3 \cdot 20 + 3 \cdot 10 = \boxed{465}.$$

If we shuffle a deck of 52 cards well, so that not a single card is in the same position as when we started, then we say that the deck is *deranged*. Formally, let $S = \{1, 2, 3, ..., n\}$ be an ordered set. A *permutation* of S is a rearrangement of the elements of S. We know that when a set has n elements, it has $n!$ permutations. If a permutation of an ordered set S leaves no element in its original position, then it is a *derangement*. We use $D(n)$ to denote the number of derangements of a set with n elements. $D(n)$ can be calculated using the principle of inclusion-exclusion.

Theorem 14.4. *For any ordered set S with n distinct elements, the number of derangements of S is:*

$$D(n) = n!\left(1 - \frac{1}{1!} + \frac{1}{2!} - \frac{1}{3!} + \cdots + (-1)^n \frac{1}{n!}\right).$$

For example,

$$D(6) = 6!(1 - 1 + \frac{1}{2} - \frac{1}{6} + \frac{1}{24} - \frac{1}{120} + \frac{1}{720}) = 265.$$

Example 14.4. Julia is learning how to write the letter C. She has 6 differently-colored crayons, and want to write Cc Cc Cc Cc Cc. In how many ways can she write the ten Cs, in such a way that each upper case C is a different color, each lower case C is a different color, and in each pair the upper case C and lower case C are different colors? (HMMT)

Answer: 222,480

Solution: Julia has 6! ways to pick the 5 different colors for the five upper case Cs. After that, there is one more color left. Let her use this leftover color for an imaginary 6th upper case C. Similarly, we may assume that, after picking 5 different colors for the five lower case Cs, she uses the leftover color for an imaginary 6th lower case C. Since these two (possibly the same) colors for the 6th pair of Cc are uniquely determined by the colors of the first five pairs, adding the 6th pair of Cc does not affect our counting. If these two colors for the 6th pair of Cc are different, then the six lower case Cs are a derangement of the six upper case Cs. In this case, there are $6! \cdot D(6)$ ways. If these two colors are the same, then the first five lower case Cs are a derangement of the first five upper case Cs. In this case, there are $6! \cdot D(5)$ ways. Thus, the number of ways Julia can write the ten Cs is

$$6!\big(D(6) + D(5)\big)$$
$$= 6!\bigg(6!\Big(1 - \frac{1}{1!} + \frac{1}{2!} - \frac{1}{3!} + \frac{1}{4!} - \frac{1}{5!} + \frac{1}{6!}\Big) + 5!\Big(1 - \frac{1}{1!} + \frac{1}{2!} - \frac{1}{3!} + \frac{1}{4!} - \frac{1}{5!}\Big)\bigg)$$
$$= 6!(265 + 44) = \boxed{222,480}.$$

14.3 Counting Using Recurrence Relations

We learned recurrence relations in Chapter 5. Recurrence relations are very useful in solving counting problems because often we can find a recurrence relation that can make the problem simpler. When we are asked to count the number of elements of a particular set, a general strategy is to start from a smaller set and build upon it inductively using recurrence relations. Let's use a MathCounts problem to illustrate this technique.

Example 14.5. The numbers 1, 2, 3, ..., 15 must be arranged in the circles of the figure shown, with one number per circle and each number used exactly once, in such a way that each arrow points from a smaller number to a larger number. How many such arrangements are possible?

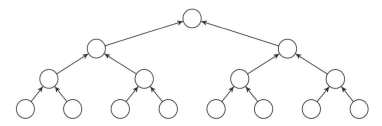

Answer: 21,964,800

Solution: Let a_n be the number of ways to arrange $2^n - 1$ numbers in the fashion described in the problem. When $n = 1$, there is only one number, so $a_1 = 1$. When $n = 2$, there are $2^2 - 1 = 3$ distinct numbers. The largest number must be placed on the top. We have $2^2 - 2$ numbers left. There are $\binom{2^2-2}{2^1-1}$ ways to determine which number should be placed on the left side. After that, each side can be determined in a_1 ways. So we have

$$a_2 = \binom{2^2-2}{2^1-1} \cdot a_1 \cdot a_1 = \binom{2^2-2}{2^1-1} \cdot (a_1)^2 = 2.$$

Similarly, when $n = 3$, there are $2^3 - 1 = 7$ distinct numbers. The largest number is placed on the top. We have $2^3 - 2$ numbers left. There are $\binom{2^3-2}{2^2-1}$ ways to determine which numbers should be placed on the left side. After that, each side can be determined in a_2 ways. So we have

$$a_3 = \binom{2^3-2}{2^2-1} \cdot (a_2)^2 = \binom{6}{3} \cdot 2^2 = 80.$$

Our problem asks us to calculate a_4. With the same arguments, we see that

$$a_4 = \binom{2^4-2}{2^3-1} \cdot (a_3)^2 = \binom{14}{7} \cdot 80^2 = \boxed{21,964,800}.$$

14.4 Counting Geometric Objects

Recasting a given problem in a different setting or a different branch of mathematics is always a good problem solving strategy. This is especially true when we need to count geometric objects. We are often told to "think outside the box." Sometimes we think outside the box when we think inside a box, as we will see in our next example.

Example 14.6. Among the $6 \times 6 \times 6$ grid points (i, j, k) where $1 \le i, j, k \le 6$, how many different sets of six grid points forming a straight line can be found? (Leo Moser)

Answer: 148

Solution: Let each of these $6 \times 6 \times 6$ grid points be the center of a unit cube. Combining all these unit cubes, we get a cube, call it cube A, made of $6 \times 6 \times 6$ unit cubes. Now let's embed cube A in an $8 \times 8 \times 8$ cube. That is, we wrap this $6 \times 6 \times 6$ cube snugly with one layer of unit cubes. Let's call this outer layer box B.

We see that, if a set of six grid points inside cube A forms a straight line, then this line passes through exactly two unit cubes of box B. That is, there is a one-to-

14.4 Counting Geometric Objects

one correspondence between each set of six grid points in A forming a straight line and a set of two unit cubes in B. Since there are $8^3 - 6^3$ unit cubes in box B, the number of different sets of six grid points forming a straight line is $\dfrac{8^3 - 6^3}{2} = \boxed{148}$.

One next example comes from MathCounts.

Example 14.7. The faces of a cube are to be numbered with integers 1 through 6 in such a way that consecutive numbers are always on adjacent faces (not opposite ones). The faces numbered 1 is on top and the face numbered 2 is toward the front. In how many different ways can the remaining faces be numbered?

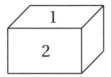

Answer: 10

Solution: Let's represent each face of the cube with a vertex of an octahedron, as shown. Let's label the vertices A, B, C, D, E, and F. We connect two vertices if and only if the two corresponding faces are adjacent.

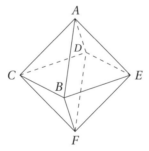

Now the problem is equivalent to finding a path that starts with $A \to B$ and goes through each vertex exactly once. If the path goes from B to vertex C, there are four ways:

$$C \to D \to E \to F,$$
$$C \to D \to F \to E,$$
$$C \to F \to E \to D,$$
$$C \to F \to D \to E.$$

Similarly, there are four ways if the path goes from B to vertex E. If the path goes from B to vertex F, there are two ways:

$$F \to C \to D \to E,$$
$$F \to E \to D \to C.$$

Therefore, in total there are $4 + 4 + 2 = \boxed{10}$ ways.

As we learned in Chapter 7, Pick's Theorem is a useful tool to calculate the area of a lattice polygon. Interestingly, Pick's Theorem can also be used to help us count lattice points as we will see in the next example.

Example 14.8. A bug travels in the coordinate plane, moving only along the lines that are parallel to the x-axis or y-axis. Let $A = (-3, 2)$ and $B = (3, -2)$. Consider all possible paths of the bug from A to B of length at most 20. How many points with integer coordinates lie on at least one of these paths? (AMC 12)

Answer: 195 points

Solution: Let's look at the center rectangle bounded by $x = \pm 3$ and $y = \pm 2$. The bug can travel from A to any point p on the boundary of the center rectangle. From p, the bug can travel a distance of 5 horizontally or vertically and back to p, before it continues to travel to B. Such a path has a length 20. So in fact, all the lattice points inside the polygon shown and on its boundary satisfy the requirements.

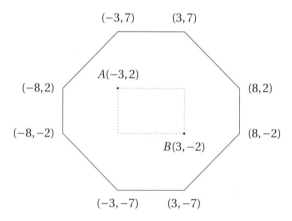

The area of the polygon is the sum of the areas of the top and bottom trapezoids plus the area of a 16 by 4 rectangle in the middle. So it is $(16 + 6) \cdot 5 + 16 \cdot 4 = 174$. The number of boundary points $B = 7 \cdot 2 + 5 \cdot 2 + 4 \cdot 4 = 40$. By Pick's Theorem,

$$\text{Area} = \frac{1}{2} B + I - 1, \qquad 174 = \frac{1}{2} \cdot 40 + I - 1, \qquad I = 155.$$

Therefore, the total number of lattice points satisfying the requirements is

$$I + B = 155 + 40 = \boxed{195 \text{ points}}.$$

Problems for Chapter 14

Problem 14.1. In a school of 100 students, 90 study English, 75 study Spanish, and 42 study French. Every student must study at least one of the three languages. What is the least possible number of students who could be studying all three languages? (MathCounts)

Problem 14.2. How many ways are there to arrange five red, five blue, and five green balls in a row so that no two green balls lie next to each other? (Russia)

Problem 14.3. Given five pairs of gloves of different sizes, how many ways are there for five people each to choose two gloves (one left and one right) with no one getting a matching pair? (Alan Tucker)

Problem 14.4. There are 12 books on a shelf. How many ways are there to choose five of them so that no two of the chosen books stand next to each other? (Russia)

Problem 14.5. Encode the letter A as 0, B as 1, ..., Z as 25. How many 5-letter words have the sum of the codes of its letters equal to 14?

Problem 14.6. Find the number of ordered quadruples (x_1, x_2, x_3, x_4) of odd positive integers such that $x_1 + x_2 + x_3 + x_4 = 98$. (AIME)

Problem 14.7. Assume 12 points are arranged around a circle and all chords are drawn. What is the maximum possible number of intersection points between these chords?

Problem 14.8. One hundred red balls are lined up in a row. Starting from the left end, every fourth ball is replaced with a green ball. Then, starting from the right end, every fifth ball is replaced with a white ball. Finally, starting from the left end, every sixth ball is replaced with a yellow ball. How many red balls remain in the row? (MathCounts)

Problem 14.9. Two red, two yellow, and two green faces, all unit squares, are available for building a cube. How many distinct cubes can be built? (MathCounts)

Problem 14.10. From the first twenty positive integers, how many ways can we select 6 integers so that there are no consecutive integers among the six chosen integers?

Problem 14.11. A game show offers a contestant three prizes A, B, and C, each of which is worth a whole number of dollars from $1 to $9999 inclusive. The contestant wins the prizes by correctly guessing the price of each prize in the order

A, B, C. As a hint, the digits of the three prices are given. On a particular day, the digits given were 1, 1, 1, 1, 3, 3, 3. Find the total number of possible guesses for all three prizes consistent with the hint. (AIME)

Problem 14.12. Eight congruent equilateral triangles, each of a different color, are used to construct a regular octahedron. How many distinguishable ways are there to construct the octahedron? Two colored octahedrons are distinguishable if neither can be rotated to look just like the other. (AMC 12)

Problem 14.13. Each of the faces of a cube is colored by a different color. How many of the colorings are distinct? (Engel)

Problem 14.14. In how many ways can the integers 1, 2, ..., 8 be arranged in a row so that no odd integer is in its natural position?

Problem 14.15. How many ordered pairs of subsets (A, B) of $\{1, 2, ..., 10\}$ are there such that A and B are disjoint? Disjoint sets are defined as sets that have no common elements. (UIUC)

Problem 14.16. Given eight distinguishable rings, let n be the number of possible five-ring arrangements on the four fingers (not the thumb) of one hand. The order of rings on each finger is significant, but it is not required that each finger have a ring. Find the leftmost three nonzero digits of n. (AIME)

Problem 14.17. A positive integer is called snakelike if its decimal representation $a_1 a_2 \cdots a_k$ satisfies $a_i < a_{i+1}$ if i is odd and $a_i > a_{i+1}$ if i is even. How many snakelike integers between 1000 and 9999 have four distinct digits? (AIME)

Problem 14.18. Find the number of ordered triples of divisors (d_1, d_2, d_3) of 360 such that the product $d_1 \cdot d_2 \cdot d_3$ is also a divisor of 360. (HMMT)

Problem 14.19. Let S be the set $\{1, 2, 3, ..., 10\}$. Let n be the number of sets of two non-empty disjoint subsets of S. Find the remainder obtained when n is divided by 1000. (AIME)

Problem 14.20. There is an unlimited supply of congruent equilateral triangles made of colored paper. Each triangle is a solid color with the same color on both sides of the paper. A large equilateral triangle is constructed from four of these paper triangles as shown. Two large triangles are considered distinguishable if it is not possible to place one on the other, using translations, rotations, and/or reflections, so that their corresponding small triangles are of the same color. Given that there are six different colors of triangles from which to choose, how many distinguishable large equilateral triangles can be constructed? (AIME)

Chapter 15

Probability and Statistics

In mathematical terms, when we toss a coin or roll a die, we are conducting an *experiment*: an activity with observable outcomes. The set of all possible outcomes of an experiment is called the *sample space*. An *event* is a subset of the sample space. Probability measures the likelihood that an event will occur, while statistics analyzes the actual outcomes of experiments. Given a finite sample space S and an event $E \subseteq S$, the probability that E occurs is $P(E) = \frac{|E|}{|S|}$.

15.1 Conditional Probability

Sometimes we need to know the probability that event B occurs given that event A has already occurred. This is called *conditional probability*. We use $P(B|A)$ to denote the probability of B given A.

$$P(B|A) = \frac{P(A \cap B)}{P(A)}.$$

Conditional probability can be quite counter-intuitive, as we will see when we compare the following two examples. Both of them are from *The Drunkard's Walk* by Leonard Mlodinow.

Example 15.1. In a family with two children, what are the chances, if one of the children is a girl, that both children are girls?

Answer: $\frac{1}{3}$

Solution: When a family has two children, the possible outcomes are: (boy, boy), (boy, girl), (girl, boy), and (girl, girl), when we take birth order into consideration.

Among the four outcomes, three of them have a girl. So the probability that one of the children is a girl is $\frac{3}{4}$. Since there is $\frac{1}{4}$ chance that both are girls, the probability that both are girls given that one is a girl is

$$\frac{\frac{1}{4}}{\frac{3}{4}} = \boxed{\frac{1}{3}}.$$

Surprisingly, the answer will be different if we twist the problem a little.

Example 15.2. In a family with two children, what are the chances, if one of the children is a girl named Florida, that both children are girls?

At first glance, the conditions "one of the children is a girl" and "one of the children is a girl named Florida" do not seem to be that different. After all, everyone has a name. But Florida is a rare name. According to Mlodinow, about one out of every one million girls is named Florida. This twist changes the probability.

Answer: $\approx \frac{1}{2}$

Solution: We use B to represent that a child is a boy. We use G_F and G_{NF} to represent that a child is a girl named Florida and that a child is a girl not named Florida, respectively. Let $P(G_F) = \alpha$. We see that $P(B) = \frac{1}{2}$ and $P(G_{NF}) = \frac{1}{2} - \alpha$. In a two-child family with one child a girl named Florida, the possible outcomes are: (B, G_F), (G_F, B), (G_F, G_{NF}), (G_{NF}, G_F), and (G_F, G_F). We have

$$P(B, G_F) = \frac{1}{2}\alpha = P(G_F, B), \quad P(G_F, G_{NF}) = (\frac{1}{2} - \alpha)\alpha = P(G_{NF}, G_F), \quad P(G_F, G_F) = \alpha^2.$$

So the probability that both are girls is: $2 \cdot (\frac{1}{2} - \alpha)\alpha + \alpha^2 = \alpha - \alpha^2$. The probability that one child is a girl named Florida is:

$$2 \cdot \frac{1}{2}\alpha + 2 \cdot (\frac{1}{2} - \alpha)\alpha + \alpha^2 = 2\alpha - \alpha^2.$$

Thus the probability that both are girls given that one is a girl named Florida is

$$\frac{\alpha - \alpha^2}{2\alpha - \alpha^2} = \frac{1 - \alpha}{2 - \alpha} \approx \boxed{\frac{1}{2}}.$$

Here the answer is close to $\frac{1}{2}$ because Florida is not a common name and thus α is small. If all girls are named Florida, then $\alpha = \frac{1}{2}$ and the answer will be $\frac{1}{3}$ as in the first example.

15.2 Geometric Probability

Sometimes an event occurs in an infinite sample space. For example, given a circle with radius 1 inscribed in a 2 × 2 square, we are asked to find the probability that a randomly chosen point inside the square is also inside the circle. In such circumstances, we compare areas rather than numbers of points. Since the area of the circle is $\pi \cdot 1^2 = \pi$ and the area of the square is $2 \cdot 2 = 4$, the probability is $\frac{\pi}{4}$. In general, geometric probability measures the distributions of length, area, volume, etc. Given a sample space S and an event $E \subseteq S$,

$$P(E) = \frac{\text{Feasible Region of } E}{\text{Total Region of } S}.$$

Example 15.3. Two mathematicians take a morning coffee break each day. They arrive at the cafeteria independently, at random times between 9 am and 10 am, and stay for exactly m minutes. The probability that either one arrives while the other is in the cafeteria is $\frac{2}{5}$. Find m. (AIME)

Answer: $60 - 12\sqrt{15}$

Solution: We use the x-axis to represent the time in minutes after 9 am that the first person arrives at the cafeteria. Similarly, we use the y-axis to represent the time that the second person arrives at the cafeteria. A point (x, y) is in the feasible region if and only if the two mathematicians meet each other. That is, if and only if $0 \le x \le 60$, $0 \le y \le 60$, and $|x - y| \le m$.

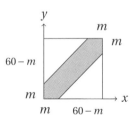

The total area of the sample space is a 60×60 square. The feasible region has area

$$60 \cdot 60 - 2 \cdot \frac{1}{2}(60 - m)^2.$$

Therefore,

$$\frac{60 \cdot 60 - 2 \cdot \frac{1}{2}(60 - m)^2}{60 \cdot 60} = \frac{2}{5}, \qquad (60 - m)^2 = \frac{3}{5} \cdot 60^2.$$

So $m = 60 \pm 12\sqrt{15}$. Since $m < 60$, we have $m = \boxed{60 - 12\sqrt{15}}$ minutes.

15.3 Mean, Median, Mode, and Range

In statistics, there are many ways to describe "average." Given a list of numbers $A = (a_1, a_2, ..., a_n)$, the *mean* of A is equal to $\dfrac{a_1 + a_2 + \cdots + a_n}{n}$. Arranging the numbers of A in non-decreasing order: $a'_1 \le a'_2 \le \cdots \le a'_n$, the median of A is the middle number in this arrangement. In particular,

$$\text{median} = \begin{cases} a'_{\frac{n+1}{2}} & \text{if } n \text{ is odd,} \\ \frac{1}{2}\left(a'_{\frac{n}{2}} + a'_{\frac{n}{2}+1}\right) & \text{if } n \text{ is even.} \end{cases}$$

The *mode* of A is the number(s) that occurs most frequently in A. A list might have more than one mode. The *range* of A is the difference between its largest number and its smallest number. That is, the range of A is $a'_n - a'_1$.

Our next example comes from MathCounts.

Example 15.4. The sum of a list of seven positive integers is 42. The mean, median, and mode are consecutive integers, in some order. What is the largest possible integer in the list?

Answer: 22

Solution: The mean of the list is $\dfrac{42}{7} = 6$. In non-decreasing order, let the list be

$$a, b, c, \text{median}, d, e, f.$$

Since $f = 42 - (a + b + c + \text{median} + d + e)$, we would like the other six numbers to be as small as possible in order to make f large. Since the mean, median, and mode are consecutive integers, the smallest value of the median is 4. Note that mode = 4 and median = 5 would not give us a large f. So, the mode is 5. That is, $d = e = 5$. Since the frequency of the mode is 2, a, b, and c must be distinct. When we let a, b, and c be as small as possible, we get

$$1, 2, 3, 4, 5, 5, f.$$

So the largest possible integer is $42 - (1 + 2 + 3 + 4 + 5 + 5) = \boxed{22}$.

15.4 Expected Value

In statistics, a *random variable* is a variable whose value will vary from trial to trial as the experiment is repeated. If a random variable X takes value $x_1, x_2, ...,$

15.4 Expected Value

x_k with probabilities $p_1, p_2, \ldots, p_k$, respectively, then the *expected value* of X is:

$$E(X) = x_1 \cdot p_1 + x_2 \cdot p_2 + \cdots + x_k \cdot p_k.$$

Expected value is just a more general way to say "average." It is a probability-weighted average. For example, the expected outcome you get when you roll a fair die is $\frac{1+2+3+4+5+6}{6} = 3.5$ because the probability of each value is $\frac{1}{6}$.

Example 15.5. 64 teams play in a single elimination tournament. In total, there are 6 rounds. You need to predict all the winners in all 63 games. Your score is computed as follows: 32 points for correctly predicting the final winner, 16 points for each correct finalist, and so on, down to 1 point for every correctly predicted winner for the first round. You flip fair coins to decide every one of your 63 bets. What is your expected number of points? (Barsky)

Answer: 31.5 points

Solution: The expected number of points you get for the first round is $\frac{1}{2} \cdot 1 \cdot 2^5$. In order to get points for round 2, you need to guess correctly for both round 1 and round 2. So the expected number of points you get for the second round is $\frac{1}{2^2} \cdot 2 \cdot 2^4$. We calculate the expected number of points for the other rounds similarly. The expected number of points you get after all 6 rounds is

$$\frac{1}{2} \cdot 1 \cdot 2^5 + \frac{1}{2^2} \cdot 2 \cdot 2^4 + \cdots + \frac{1}{2^6} \cdot 2^5 \cdot 2^0$$
$$= 2^4 + 2^3 + 2^2 + 2^1 + 2^0 + 2^{-1} = \boxed{31.5 \text{ points}}.$$

Example 15.6. Given n strings, you randomly pair the $2n$ ends and tie together each pair. What is the expected number of resulting loops? (Snell)

Answer: $1 + \frac{1}{3} + \frac{1}{5} + \cdots + \frac{1}{2n-1}$ loops

Solution: Let $E(n)$ be the expected number of loops when you have n strings. We see that $E(1) = 1$. Given n strings, you randomly pick one end. You can tie it with any of the remaining $2n-1$ ends each with equal probability. If you tie it with the other end of the same string, you end up with $1 + E(n-1)$ loops. Otherwise, you get $n-1$ strings. Therefore,

$$E(n) = \frac{1}{2n-1}\bigl(1 + E(n-1)\bigr) + \frac{2n-2}{2n-1} \cdot E(n-1) = \frac{1}{2n-1} + E(n-1).$$

By induction, we get

$$E(n) = \boxed{1 + \frac{1}{3} + \frac{1}{5} + \cdots + \frac{1}{2n-1} \text{ loops}}.$$

Problems for Chapter 15

Problem 15.1. In the city of Trichotomy, every day the weather is exactly one of the following: sunny, cloudy, or rainy. Each day has a 50% chance of having the same weather as the day before and a 25% chance of having each of the other two types of weather. If it does not rain on Friday, what is the probability that there will be no rain during the weekend (Saturday and Sunday)? Express your answer as a common fraction. (MathCounts)

Problem 15.2. Each face of a cube is given a single narrow stripe painted from the center of one edge to the center of its opposite edge. The choice of the edge pairing is made at random and independently for each face. What is the probability that there is a continuous stripe encircling the cube? Express your answer as a common fraction. (AMC 10)

Problem 15.3. Given that more boys are named David than are named Delta, which of the following two probabilities is higher?

(A) In a family with two children, if one of the children is a boy named David, the probability that both children are boys.

(B) In a family with two children, if one of the children is a boy named Delta, the probability that both children are boys.

Problem 15.4. Before you are three doors. Behind exactly one of them is a prize, which you will win if you choose its door correctly. First you pick a door. Monty, who knows where the prize is and will not reveal it, deliberately opens *another* door, revealing it to be empty. He then gives you the opportunity to switch to the remaining door. Are you more likely to win by switching than by sticking with your original door? (Monty Hall)

Problem 15.5. One half percent of the population has a particular disease. A test is developed for the disease. The test gives a false positive 3% of the time and a false negative 2% of the time. What is the probability that a person tests positive actually has the disease? Express your answer as a decimal to the nearest hundredth. (SUNY)

Problem 15.6. Mr. Canada chooses a positive real a uniformly at random from $(0,1]$, chooses a positive real b uniformly at random from $(0,1]$, and then sets $c = \frac{a}{a+b}$. What is the probability that c lies between $\frac{1}{4}$ and $\frac{3}{4}$? Express your answer as a common fraction. (HMMT)

Problem 15.7. In any 15-minute interval, there is a 20% probability that you will see at least one shooting star. What is the probability that you see at least one shooting star in the period of an hour? Express your answer as a decimal to the nearest hundredth.

Problems for Chapter 15

Problem 15.8. In any one hour interval, there is a 40% probability that you will see at least one shooting star. What is the probability that you see at least one shooting star in the period of half an hour? Express your answer as a decimal to the nearest thousandth.

Problem 15.9. The mean, median, unique mode, and range of a collection of eight integers are all equal to 8. What is the largest integer that can be an element of this collection? (AMC 12)

Problem 15.10. A spaghetti stick is dropped on the floor and breaks at random into three pieces. What is the probability that the three parts obtained are the sides of a triangle? Express your answer as a common fraction.

Problem 15.11. A spaghetti stick is dropped on the floor and breaks at random into four pieces. What is the probability that the four parts obtained are the sides of a quadrilateral? Express your answer as a common fraction.

Problem 15.12. Urn A contains 4 white balls and 2 red balls. Urn B contains 3 red balls and 3 black balls. An urn is randomly selected, and then a ball inside of that urn is removed. We then repeat the process of selecting an urn and drawing out a ball, without returning the first ball. What is the probability that the first ball drawn is red, given that the second ball drawn is black? Express your answer as a common fraction. (HMMT)

Problem 15.13. A fair die is rolled four times. What is the probability that each of the final three rolls is at least as large as the roll preceding it? Express your answer as a common fraction. (AIME)

Problem 15.14. Jenny places 100 pennies on a table, 30 showing heads and 70 showing tails. She chooses 40 of the pennies at random (all different) and turns them over. That is, if a chosen penny was showing heads, she turns it to show tails; if a chosen penny was showing tails, she turns it to show heads. At the end, what is the expected number of pennies showing heads? (MPfG)

Problem 15.15. All the students in an algebra class took a 100-point test. Five students scored 100, each student scored at least 60, and the mean score was 76. What is the smallest possible number of students in the class? (AMC 12)

Problem 15.16. A list of integers has mode 32 and mean 22. The smallest number on the list is 10. The median m of the list is a member of the list. If the list member m were replaced by $m+10$, the mean and median of the new list would be 24 and $m+10$, respectively. If m were instead replaced by $m-8$, the median of the new list would be $m-4$. What is m? (AHSME)

Problem 15.17. One hundred people line up to board an airplane. Each has a boarding pass with assigned seat. However, the first person to board has lost his boarding pass and takes a random seat. After that, each person takes the assigned seat if its unoccupied, and one of unoccupied seats at random otherwise. What is the probability that the last person to board gets to sit in his assigned seat? Express your answer as a common fraction. (Winkler)

Problem 15.18. You have coins $C_1, C_2, ..., C_n$. For each k, C_k is biased so that it has probability $\dfrac{1}{2k+1}$ of landing heads when tossed. If the n coins are tossed, what is the probability that the number of heads is odd? (Putnam)

Problem 15.19. An ant is on one face of a cube. At every step, the ant walks to one of its four neighboring faces with equal probability. What is the expected number of steps for it to reach the face opposite its starting face? (MPfG)

Problem 15.20. The army needs to identify soldiers with a disease called *klep*. So we group the n soldiers into groups of k. Blend the blood samples of each group and apply the test once to each blended sample. If the group-blend does not have klep, we are done with that group after one test. If the group-blend fails the test, then someone in the group has klep, and we individually test all the soldiers in the group. If each soldier has klep with probability p, what is the expected number of tests as a function of n, p, and k? (Assume that n is divisible by k.) (MIT)

Problem 15.21. In his spare time, Richard Rusczyk shuffles a standard deck of 52 cards. He then turns the cards up one by one from the top of the deck until the third ace appears. What is the expected number of cards Richard will turn up? (AoPS)

Problem 15.22. Sherry starts at the number 1. Whenever she is at 1, she moves one step to 2. Whenever she is at a number strictly between 1 and 10, she moves one step up or one step down, each with probability $\dfrac{1}{2}$. When she reaches 10, she stops. What is the expected number of steps that Sherry will take? (MPfG)

Problem 15.23. The probability that a set of three distinct vertices chosen at random from among the vertices of a regular n-gon determines an obtuse triangle is $\dfrac{93}{125}$. Find the sum of all possible values of n. (AIME)

Answers

Answers for Chapter 1

1.1	21		**1.2**	1
1.3	true		**1.4**	no
1.5	there are		**1.6**	no
1.7	possible		**1.8**	7
1.9	he can		**1.10**	impossible
1.11	true		**1.12**	impossible
1.13	you can		**1.14**	impossible
1.15	5		**1.16**	there is
1.17	no		**1.18**	true
1.19	there is		**1.20**	they can

Answers for Chapter 2

2.1	2		**2.2**	7
2.3	(3,6)		**2.4**	500
2.5	$\frac{43}{19}$		**2.6**	53
2.7	$\pm\frac{1}{2}$, ± 1		**2.8**	19,683
2.9	$\frac{121}{12}$		**2.10**	3 and 8
2.11	66		**2.12**	166
2.13	14		**2.14**	10
2.15	44 days		**2.16**	-2240
2.17	152		**2.18**	373
2.19	816		**2.20**	$\frac{3}{4}$
2.21	-2		**2.22**	$48\sqrt{6}$
2.23	600			

Answers for Chapter 3

3.1	37.5%		**3.2**	33
3.3	45 mph		**3.4**	54 months
3.5	190		**3.6**	40 kg
3.7	334 minutes		**3.8**	90 cents
3.9	1800 yards		**3.10**	8
3.11	bronze		**3.12**	$\frac{22}{27}$ miles
3.13	54		**3.14**	A, A, D, C
3.15	17 minutes		**3.16**	55 floors
3.17	78 days		**3.18**	"One"
3.19	6:23		**3.20**	6 minutes
3.21	30 students		**3.22**	13 judges
3.23	120 steps			

Answers for Chapter 4

4.1	18	**4.2**	50
4.3	$-x+118$	**4.4**	-11
4.5	$-\frac{1}{9}$	**4.6**	-3
4.7	$-\frac{59}{49}$	**4.8**	-2
4.9	$5x$	**4.10**	$(b+c)^2 - c(a+1)^2$
4.11	86	**4.12**	6
4.13	$\frac{83}{74}$	**4.14**	$\frac{-1+\sqrt{57}}{2}$
4.15	5	**4.16**	$2^{20}-1$
4.17	55	**4.18**	0
4.19	$\frac{(-1)^{n+1}+n+1}{n+2}$	**4.20**	20

Answers for Chapter 5

5.1	8775	**5.2**	55
5.3	179	**5.4**	9902
5.5	194	**5.6**	3722
5.7	-6561	**5.8**	65
5.9	819	**5.10**	348
5.11	12	**5.12**	$\frac{2}{3}$
5.13	981	**5.14**	1999
5.15	2	**5.16**	9
5.17	$\frac{3{,}999{,}999}{2000}$	**5.18**	3
5.19	$\frac{13}{36}$	**5.20**	225

Answers for Chapter 6

6.1	$\sqrt[3]{2}$	6.2	$f(x) = \dfrac{-x^3 + 2x^2 + x - 1}{x^2 - x}$
6.3	96	6.4	19
6.5	No such f exists	6.6	$1988x$
6.7	1	6.8	$P(x) = x^3 +$ a constant
6.9	561	6.10	1
6.11	$f(x) = \dfrac{-x^3 + 3x^2 - 2x + 1}{2x^2 - 2x}$	6.12	$f(x) = 0$
6.13	$f(n) = n$	6.14	763
6.15	364	6.16	$f(x) = 0$
6.17	sum of digits of n in base 2	6.18	$f(n) = n$
6.19	$f(n) = n$	6.20	No such f exists

Answers for Chapter 7

7.1	$2 - \sqrt{3}$	7.2	$\dfrac{60}{37}$
7.3	180	7.4	36
7.5	122	7.6	58
7.7	$-\dfrac{4}{7}$	7.8	20
7.9	25	7.10	20
7.11	110	7.12	17
7.13	408	7.14	6 km
7.15	$\sqrt{3}$	7.16	32
7.17	$\dfrac{50}{3}$	7.18	$90°$
7.19	$\dfrac{\sqrt{3}}{8}$	7.20	6
7.21	$3\sqrt{5}$		

Answers for Chapter 8

8.1	$\frac{26}{9}\pi$	8.2	46 in^2
8.3	$\frac{8}{9}$	8.4	$\frac{5}{3}$
8.5	$2+\sqrt{3}$ cm	8.6	$\frac{7}{10}$ in
8.7	$\frac{108}{\pi}$	8.8	$\frac{5}{16}$
8.9	$\sqrt{130}$	8.10	$6\sqrt{5}$
8.11	$\frac{\pi}{6}$	8.12	2
8.13	3	8.14	12
8.15	5	8.16	$y-z$
8.17	$\frac{45\sqrt{17}}{17}$	8.18	13
8.19	$\frac{15}{8}$	8.20	$90°$

Answers for Chapter 9

9.1	11	9.2	18
9.3	6	9.4	5
9.5	$\frac{\sqrt{6}+\sqrt{2}}{2}$	9.6	8
9.7	408	9.8	450 cubic units
9.9	7 faces	9.10	$24\sqrt{3} \text{ in}^3$
9.11	$1+2\sqrt{3}$	9.12	$\frac{29}{2}$ feet
9.13	288	9.14	$\frac{5}{6}$
9.15	$\frac{6\sqrt{34}}{17}$	9.16	137
9.17	13	9.18	$12-3\sqrt[3]{37}$ inches
9.19	840	9.20	$\sqrt{7}$
9.21	$\frac{2}{27}$		

Answers for Chapter 10

10.1	15°	**10.2**	80°
10.3	50°	**10.4**	360°
10.5	291	**10.6**	30°
10.7	66°	**10.8**	19°
10.9	90°	**10.10**	27°
10.11	60°	**10.12**	40°
10.13	60°	**10.14**	30°
10.15	15°	**10.16**	55°
10.17	45°	**10.18**	16°
10.19	81°	**10.20**	90°

Answers for Chapter 11

11.1	$2:9$	**11.2**	$\dfrac{56}{11}$
11.3	30 in^2	**11.4**	65
11.5	21	**11.6**	$87:25$
11.7	$\dfrac{ab(c+d)}{cd(a+b)}$	**11.8**	$12:5$
11.9	$2:1$	**11.10**	315
11.11	$1:5$	**11.12**	177
11.13	$1:2$	**11.14**	94
11.15	441	**11.16**	923
11.17	108	**11.18**	$36:29$
11.19	$1:2$	**11.20**	$\dfrac{4}{13}S$

Answers for Chapter 12

12.1	43	**12.2**	608
12.3	$1,100,110_{(-2)}$	**12.4**	13
12.5	42	**12.6**	225
12.7	$202.\overline{32}_{(-4)}$	**12.8**	448
12.9	60	**12.10**	43
12.11	153,846	**12.12**	27
12.13	(11, 8)	**12.14**	23
12.15	84	**12.16**	432
12.17	1462 miles	**12.18**	98
12.19	127	**12.20**	19

Answers for Chapter 13

13.1	23	**13.2**	2
13.3	16	**13.4**	112
13.5	105 years	**13.6**	4 apples
13.7	0 pairs	**13.8**	$10.21
13.9	8 coins	**13.10**	3930 coins
13.11	246	**13.12**	35
13.13	12,703	**13.14**	2
13.15	94.65	**13.16**	1170
13.17	743	**13.18**	16
13.19	195	**13.20**	30

Answers for Chapter 14

14.1	7 students	**14.2**	116,424
14.3	5280	**14.4**	56
14.5	3060 words	**14.6**	19,600
14.7	495 points	**14.8**	54 red balls
14.9	6 cubes	**14.10**	5005
14.11	420	**14.12**	1680
14.13	30	**14.14**	24,024
14.15	59,049	**14.16**	376
14.17	882	**14.18**	800
14.19	501	**14.20**	336

Answers for Chapter 15

15.1	$\frac{9}{16}$	**15.2**	$\frac{3}{16}$
15.3	(B)	**15.4**	yes
15.5	0.14	**15.6**	$\frac{2}{3}$
15.7	0.59	**15.8**	0.225
15.9	14	**15.10**	$\frac{1}{4}$
15.11	$\frac{1}{2}$	**15.12**	$\frac{7}{15}$
15.13	$\frac{7}{72}$	**15.14**	46
15.15	13 students	**15.16**	20
15.17	$\frac{1}{2}$	**15.18**	$\frac{n}{2n+1}$
15.19	6 steps	**15.20**	$n\left(1-(1-p)^k+\frac{1}{k}\right)$
15.21	$\frac{159}{5}$	**15.22**	81 steps
15.23	503		

Solutions

Solutions for Chapter 1

Solution to 1.1 If there are 7 apples, 5 bananas, and 8 oranges in the basket, then one more apple, or banana, or orange will satisfy the requirement. Thus the smallest number of fruit that should be put in the basket is $7+5+8+1= \boxed{21}$.

Solution to 1.2 Say these six positive integers are $a_1, a_2, ..., a_6$. For each $1 \leq i \leq 6$, let's consider $a_i \pmod 5$. It can only be one of the five values 0, 1, 2, 3, or 4. So two of them must have the same value (mod 5). That is, this pair has a difference that is a multiple of 5. Thus the probability is $\boxed{1}$.

Solution to 1.3 A person can have 0, 1, 2, ..., or 7 friends in the group. If everyone had a different number of friends, then one person would have no friends, and another one would have 7 friends. But, one person having 7 friends implies that no one can have zero friends, a contradiction. So it is $\boxed{\text{true}}$ that there are two people who have the same number of friends among the people in the group.

Solution to 1.4 Let's pick a soldier A. Whenever A is on duty, two others are with him. If A had shared duty with everyone else exactly once, then we could have paired the others one pair per day. But 99 is not even. So the answer is $\boxed{\text{no}}$.

Solution to 1.5 Let's arrange the ages of the students into a non-decreasing sequence: $a_1 \leq a_2 \leq \cdots \leq a_{33}$. If the sum of the ages of the oldest 20 students were at most 260, then the average age of these 33 students would be at most 13. But $430 > 33 \cdot 13$, a contradiction. Therefore, $\boxed{\text{there are}}$ 20 students in the class such that the sum of their ages is greater than 260.

Solution to 1.6 The sum of any two consecutive numbers is odd. The sum of 25 odd numbers is odd. So the answer is $\boxed{\text{no}}$.

Solution to 1.7 We randomly separate the house into two houses. For any member A of the parliament, if A has two or more enemies in the same house, we move A into the other house. Since there are only finitely many members in the parliament, after finitely many such switches, we get two houses such that each member has at most one enemy in his or her own house. So it is $\boxed{\text{possible}}$.

Solution to 1.8 Let's consider the scenario of 7 senators S_0, S_1, S_2, S_3, S_4, S_5, and S_6, where for each $0 \le i \le 6$, S_i hates S_{i+1}, S_{i+2}, and S_{i+3}. Here the indices are modulo 7. We see that none of the 7 senators could share a committee with anyone else among the seven. So, we need at least 7 committees. Next, we prove that 7 is enough by induction. Clearly 7 is enough if we have one senator. Suppose 7 committees are enough for k senators each of whom hates at most 3 other senators. Here we relax the condition of strictly three to at most three to make the induction work. Let us define a senator's hate number to be the number of senators who hate him. With $k+1$ senators, since the total hate number is at most $3(k+1)$, at least one senator, say S, is hated by at most 3 others. We first place the other k senators in 7 committees. Then we place senator S into a committee where senator S does not hate anyone and no one in the committee hates him. With 7 committees, such an arrangement is feasible. So 7 is enough for $k+1$ senators, and so is enough for any natural number. Thus the smallest number is $\boxed{7}$.

Solution to 1.9 Dmitri can put the chosen coin aside and place 50 coins in one pan and another 50 coins in the other pan. Note that if we place 50 genuine coins in one pan and 50 counterfeit coins in the other pan, then the difference of the weights is even. With this initial configuration, if we subsequently switch coins from one pan to another, the difference of the weights will remain even. On the other hand, if we place 50 genuine coins in one pan and 1 genuine plus 49 counterfeit coins in the other pan, then the difference of the weights is odd. With this initial configuration, if we subsequently switch coins from one pan to another, the difference of the weights will remain odd. Therefore, if the difference between the weights of the two pans is even, then Dmitri's coin is a genuine one, otherwise his coin is counterfeit. So $\boxed{\text{he can}}$ find it out in one weighing.

Solution to 1.10 We consider the number of stones (mod 3). Then, the three piles have 1, 2, and 0 stones, respectively. Transferring one stone from each of two piles to the third pile is equivalent to subtracting one stone (mod 3) from each pile since $2 \equiv -1 \pmod{3}$. So the three piles still have 0, 1, and 2 stones (mod 3). That is, such a transformation will not change $(1,2,0)$ into $(0,0,0)$. So it is $\boxed{\text{impossible}}$.

Solution to 1.11 Given a polyhedron, suppose n is the maximum number of edges any face of the polyhedron could have. Pick a face of the polyhedron that has n edges. Each of the n neighboring faces of this chosen face has between 3 to n edges. With n faces and $n-2$ possible numbers of edges, at least two of these n faces must have the same number of edges. So it is $\boxed{\text{true}}$.

Solutions for Chapter 1   149

Solution to 1.12 When we consider the number of chameleons modulo 3 for each color, we get a $(0, 1, 2)$ (mod 3) configuration. Since $2 \equiv -1$ (mod 3), each swap is equivalent to subtracting one chameleon from each color. So we still have a $(0, 1, 2)$ (mod 3) configuration after each swap. Therefore, it is $\boxed{\text{impossible}}$ for all chameleons to become one color.

Solution to 1.13 Let's look at the first column first. If every integer in the first column is greater than one, we subtract 1 from each number of the first column. We keep doing this until we see ones in the first column. If not all the numbers in the first column are ones, then for each "1" in the first column, we double the row where this "1" belongs. After this is done, we subtract 1 from each number of the first column again. Repeating the process, we will eventually get all ones in the first column. Then, we subtract 1 from each number of the first column and the first column will be all zeros. Next we work on the next column ... Eventually we get a table of zeros. So $\boxed{\text{you can}}$.

Solution to 1.14 Let's look at the perimeter, calling it x, of the infected squares. Initially, $x \leq 36$. When a square with 2 infected neighbors is infected, x does not change. When a square with 3 infected neighbors is infected, x decreases by 2. When a square with 4 infected neighbors is infected, x decreases by 4. Thus x never increases. Since the perimeter of a 10×10 grid is $40 > 36 \geq x$, it is $\boxed{\text{impossible}}$ for all 100 squares to get infected.

Solution to 1.15 Let's begin from the smallest losing number and work backwards. Clearly, 1 is the smallest losing number. If there are between 2 to 6 toothpicks, you can always leave 1 toothpick for your opponent. But, if there are $1 + 6$ toothpicks and it's your turn, then you will lose. No matter how many, say k, toothpicks you remove, there are at least 2 and at most 6 toothpicks left. So, your opponent could take $6 - k$ toothpicks the next turn, forcing you to take the last one. So 7 is the second smallest losing number. Similarly, we see that $1 + 2 \cdot 6$ is the third losing number. Using induction, we see that the largest losing number less than or equal to 300 is $1 + 49 \cdot 6 = 295$. So the first player should remove $\boxed{5}$ toothpicks in the first turn. Thereafter, no matter how many, say k, the second player removes, the first player can always remove $6 - k$ toothpicks. Eventually, the second player has to take the last toothpick.

Solution to 1.16 Let's consider a player, say A, who lost the most games. Note that A does not have to be unique. If A were not an unfortunate player such that every other player either beat him or beat someone who beat him, then there would be a player B such that B neither beat A nor beat anyone who beat A. So A beat B and everyone who beat A beat B. Then B would have lost more games than A did. But A lost the most games, a contradiction. Therefore, $\boxed{\text{there is}}$ such an unfortunate player, namely, a player who lost the most games.

Solution to 1.17 For any a and b, $(0.6a - 0.8b)^2 + (0.8a + 0.6b)^2 = a^2 + b^2$. Thus If the set $\{3, 4, 12\}$ is transformed to the set $\{a, b, c\}$, then $a^2 + b^2 + c^2 = 3^2 + 4^2 + 12^2$. Since $4^2 + 6^2 + 12^2 \neq 3^2 + 4^2 + 12^2$, the answer is $\boxed{\text{no}}$.

Solution to 1.18 Let g_i be the total number of games the chess player has played up to the end of the ith day. We have $1 \leq g_1 < g_2 < \cdots < g_{56} \leq 88$. Let's consider the following 112 numbers:

$$g_1, g_2, \ldots, g_{56}, g_1 + 23, g_2 + 23, \ldots, g_{56} + 23.$$

We have 112 numbers, but the largest one is less than or equal to $88 + 23 = 111$. By the pigeonhole principle, at least two of the numbers must be equal. Since the player plays at least one game per day, $\{g_1, g_2, \ldots\}$ is a strictly increasing sequence. So there must be some positive integers m and n such that $m > n$ and

$$g_m = g_n + 23, \qquad g_m - g_n = 23.$$

Therefore, it is $\boxed{\text{true}}$ that from the $(n+1)$th day to the mth day, she plays exactly 23 games.

Solution to 1.19 Let's number the n cars $c_1, c_2, \ldots, c_n$ according to their order on the circular track. Let's get another identical car with plenty of gas, call it C, and let it collect gas from the n cars starting with c_1 on its way around. Each time before it collects gas from c_i, we measure the gas level of C and record it as m_i. Among the n measures $m_1, m_2, \ldots, m_n$, there must be a minimal number m_i. We see that the car c_i is a car that can complete a lap by collecting gas from the other cars on its way around because c_i is always able to reach other cars before it runs out of gas. Otherwise m_i would not be minimal. Thus $\boxed{\text{there is}}$ such a car.

Solution to 1.20 The prisoners can count the parity of the hats they see. Let the 100th prisoner speak first. If he sees an even number of white hats and an odd number of black hats, then he will say "black"; otherwise there must be an odd number of white hats and he will say "white". Without loss of generality, suppose the 100th prisoner says "black", then the 99th prisoner will know that the 100th prisoner sees an odd number of black hats. If the 99th prisoner also sees an odd number of black hats, then his hat must be white and he will say "white". If he sees an even number of black hats, then he must have a black hat on and so he will say "black". Similarly, if the 100th says "black" and the 99th says "white", then the 98th prisoner will know that, counting the white hat on the head of the 99th prisoner, there are an odd number of black hats and an even number of white hats among the first 99 hats. So among the first 98 hats, there are an odd number of black hats and an odd number of white hats. He can then correctly calculate the color of his hat with this knowledge together with the parity of the first 97 hats he sees. Repeating the process, we see that except for the 100th, all other prisoners can tell the color of his hat correctly. So $\boxed{\text{they can}}$ survive.

Solutions for Chapter 2

Solution to 2.1 For any positive numbers a, b, c, and d, if $\frac{a}{b} = \frac{c}{d}$, then $\frac{a}{b} = \frac{a+c}{b+d}$. This is because

$$\frac{a}{b} = \frac{c}{d}, \quad ad = bc, \quad ab + ad = ab + bc, \quad a(b+d) = b(a+c), \quad \frac{a}{b} = \frac{a+c}{b+d}.$$

So we can sum the three numerators and the three denominators, and get

$$\frac{y}{x-z} = \frac{x+y}{z} = \frac{x}{y} = \frac{y+x+y+x}{x-z+z+y} = \frac{2x+2y}{x+y} = \boxed{2}.$$

Solution to 2.2 Multiplying both sides of the equation by $12xy$, we get $5xy = 12x + 12y$. Dividing both sides by 5, we get

$$xy - \frac{12}{5}x - \frac{12}{5}y = 0, \quad \left(x - \frac{12}{5}\right)\left(y - \frac{12}{5}\right) = \frac{144}{25}.$$

Multiplying both sides by 25, we get

$$(5x - 12)(5y - 12) = 144 = 2^4 \cdot 3^2.$$

We do not need to consider the case when $5x - 12 \leq 0$ and $5y - 12 \leq 0$ because then the positive integers x and y would be too small to satisfy the equation above. We only need to consider the case when each of them is positive. Since $x < y$,

$$0 < 5x - 12 < \sqrt{144} = 12.$$

Therefore

$$12 < 5x < 24, \quad 3 \leq x \leq 4.$$

When $x = 4$, $5x - 12 = 8$ and $5y - 12 = 18$. So $y = 6$. When $x = 3$, $5x - 12 = 3$ and $5y - 12 = 48$. So $y = 12$. Both satisfy the original equation. Thus the sum of all possible x values is $3 + 4 = \boxed{7}$.

Solution to 2.3 By Simon's Favorite Factoring Trick, we have

$$xy + x - 2y - 2 = 9 - 2, \quad (x-2)(y+1) = 7.$$

Since both x and y are positive, we have only two cases: $x - 2 = 7$ and $y + 1 = 1$; or $x - 2 = 1$ and $y + 1 = 7$. The first case does not give us any positive y value. The second case gives us $x = 3$ and $y = 6$. So the only positive integral pair is $\boxed{(3,6)}$.

Solution to 2.4 When we expand $\left(\frac{1}{2} - x\right)^{2001}$, the last term is $-x^{2001}$. It cancels with x^{2001} and thus the equation is a 2000th degree polynomial and has 2000 roots. We note that if x is a root, then so is $\frac{1}{2} - x$. We also note that $x \neq \frac{1}{2} - x$, because $x = \frac{1}{4}$ is not a root. Since the sum of the pair x and $\frac{1}{2} - x$ is $\frac{1}{2}$, the sum of all the roots is $\frac{1}{2} \cdot 2000 \cdot \frac{1}{2} = \boxed{500}$.

Solution to 2.5 Let $f^{-1}(27) = t$, then $f(t) = 27$. When $5x - 2 = 27$, $x = \frac{29}{5}$. Thus

$$f\left(\frac{2x-3}{x-2}\right) = f\left(\frac{2(\frac{29}{5})-3}{\frac{29}{5}-2}\right) = f\left(\frac{43}{19}\right) = 27. \quad \text{So } f^{-1}(27) = t = \boxed{\frac{43}{19}}.$$

Solution to 2.6 From $\frac{1}{a} + \frac{1}{b} + \frac{1}{c} = 5$, we get $ab + ac + bc = 5abc = 5$. So

$$a^2 + b^2 + c^2 = (a+b+c)^2 - 2(ab+ac+bc) = 15.$$

Therefore,

$$a^3 + b^3 + c^3 = 3abc + (a+b+c)(a^2+b^2+c^2-ab-ac-bc) = 3 + 5 \cdot (15-5) = \boxed{53}.$$

Solution to 2.7 Let $f(1) = a$ and $f(-1) = b$. When $x = 1$, we have $a = 2a^2 - 1$. So $a = -\frac{1}{2}$ or $a = 1$. When $f(1) = -\frac{1}{2}$, we have

$$-\frac{1}{2} = f(1) = f((-1)^2) = 2b^2 - 1, \quad b^2 = \frac{1}{4}, \quad b = \pm\frac{1}{2}.$$

When $f(1) = 1$, we have

$$1 = f(1) = f((-1)^2) = 2b^2 - 1, \quad b^2 = 1, \quad b = \pm 1.$$

So all possible values of $f(-1)$ are $\boxed{\pm\frac{1}{2}, \pm 1}$.

Solution to 2.8 We know from the Binomial Theorem that

$$(a-1)^n = \binom{n}{0}a^n - \binom{n}{1}a^{n-1} + \binom{n}{2}a^{n-2} - \cdots + (-1)^n\binom{n}{n}a^0.$$

So $a \cdot f(n) = (a-1)^n - (-1)^n$ and

$$f(n) = \frac{(a-1)^n - (-1)^n}{a} = \frac{3^{\frac{n}{223}} - (-1)^n}{a}.$$

Therefore,

$$f(2007) + f(2008) = \frac{3^{\frac{2007}{223}} + 3^{\frac{2008}{223}}}{a} = 3^{\frac{2007}{223}} \cdot \frac{1 + 3^{\frac{1}{223}}}{a} = 3^{\frac{2007}{223}} = 3^9 = \boxed{19,683}.$$

Solutions for Chapter 2   153

Solution to 2.9 The equation has no solutions when $0 < x < 2$. When $2 \leq x < 3$, $\lfloor x \rfloor = 2$, $\frac{1}{\lfloor x \rfloor} = \frac{1}{2}$. The equation has a solution of $x = 2 + \frac{1}{2}$. When $3 \leq x < 4$, $\lfloor x \rfloor = 3$, $\frac{1}{\lfloor x \rfloor} = \frac{1}{3}$. It has a solution of $x = 3 + \frac{1}{3}$. When $4 \leq x < 5$, $\lfloor x \rfloor = 4$, $\frac{1}{\lfloor x \rfloor} = \frac{1}{4}$. It has a solution of $x = 4 + \frac{1}{4}$. Thus the sum of the three smallest solutions is

$$2 + \frac{1}{2} + 3 + \frac{1}{3} + 4 + \frac{1}{4} = \boxed{\frac{121}{12}}.$$

Solution to 2.10 We use the Binomial Theorem to expand $(4A1)^{1A4}$, and get

$$(4A1)^{1A4} = (4A0+1)^{1A4} = (4A0)^{1A4} + (1A4)(4A0)^{1A3}1^1 + \cdots + (1A4)(4A0)1^{1A3} + 1^{1A4}.$$

Since all the terms before $(1A4)(4A0)1^{1A3}$ have at least two zeros, the only term that affects the tens digit is $(1A4)(4A0)1^{1A3} = (1A4)(4A0)$. Therefore, the tens digit is determined by the units digit of $4 \cdot A$. Since the tens digit is 2, A can only be either 3 or 8. So $\boxed{3 \text{ and } 8}$ are all the possible values for the digit A.

Solution to 2.11 Suppose the arithmetic mean is a two-digit number $10a + b$, for some integers a and b where $1 \leq a \leq 9$ and $0 \leq b \leq 9$. Then

$$x + y = 2(10a + b), \quad \text{and} \quad \sqrt{xy} = 10b + a.$$

Squaring both equations, we get

$$x^2 + 2xy + y^2 = 4(100a^2 + 20ab + b^2),$$
$$xy = 100b^2 + 20ab + a^2.$$

So

$$(x - y)^2 = x^2 + 2xy + y^2 - 4xy = 396(a^2 - b^2).$$

Therefore, $|x - y| = 6\sqrt{11(a^2 - b^2)}$. Since $x - y$ is an integer, $a^2 - b^2 = 11c$ for some perfect square c. Since x and y are distinct, $c \neq 0$. When $c = 1$, $a^2 - b^2 = 11$. We see that $a = 6$ and $b = 5$ is a solution. Then $|x - y| = 6\sqrt{11 \cdot 11} = 66$. When $c = 4$, $a^2 - b^2 = 44$. Since $a + b \leq 18$, we can only have $a + b = 11$ and $a - b = 4$. But, this system has no integer solutions for a and b. Since a is at most 9, c cannot be 9 or higher. Therefore, the only solution is when $c = 1$, $|x - y| = \boxed{66}$.

Solution to 2.12 Let's look at the ratio A_k / A_{k-1}. We see that

$$\frac{A_k}{A_{k-1}} = \frac{\dfrac{1000!}{k!(1000-k)!} \cdot (0.2)^k}{\dfrac{1000!}{(k-1)!(1001-k)!} \cdot (0.2)^{k-1}} = \frac{1001-k}{5k}.$$

Note that for any $1 \le k \le 1000$, the ratio is never zero. The ratio is greater than 1 if and only if $1001 - k > 5k$. That is, if and only if $k < 166.83$. So $A_0 < A_1 < \cdots < A_{166}$ and $A_{166} > A_{167} > \cdots > A_{1000}$. Thus A_k is the largest when $k = \boxed{166}$.

Solution to 2.13 Given any position (s, t) of particle A, let's calculate the expression $s + t$. At the beginning, $s + t = 0$. Next, it is $3 + 4 = 7$. When particle A moves again, the expression becomes $7 + (7 - 1)$. Since no negative values can be added to the expression, when particle A stops at (r, r) we have

$$r + r = 7 + (7-1) + (7-2) + \cdots + (7-6) = 28. \qquad \text{Therefore,} \quad r = \boxed{14}.$$

Solution to 2.14 When $x^2 - 5x + 5 = 1$, $(x^2 - 5x + 5)^{(x^2-7x+12)} = 1$. Let

$$x^2 - 5x + 5 = 1, \qquad \text{we get} \qquad x = 4, \quad \text{or} \quad x = 1.$$

When $x^2 - 5x + 5 \ne 0$ and $x^2 - 7x + 12 = 0$, $(x^2 - 5x + 5)^{(x^2-7x+12)} = 1$. Let

$$x^2 - 7x + 12 = 0, \qquad \text{we get} \qquad x = 4, \quad \text{or} \quad x = 3.$$

Since $4^2 - 5 \cdot 4 + 5 \ne 0$ and $3^2 - 5 \cdot 3 + 5 \ne 0$, both $x = 4$ and $x = 3$ are solutions. When $x^2 - 5x + 5 = -1$ and $x^2 - 7x + 12$ is an even integer, $(x^2 - 5x + 5)^{(x^2-7x+12)} = 1$. Let

$$x^2 - 5x + 5 = -1, \qquad x^2 - 5x + 6 = 0, \qquad \text{we get} \qquad x = 2, \quad \text{or} \quad x = 3.$$

$x^2 - 7x + 12$ is an even integer for both $x = 2$ and $x = 3$. So both $x = 2$ and $x = 3$ are solutions. Therefore, the solutions are: $x = 1, 2, 3$, or 4. Their sum is $\boxed{10}$.

Solution to 2.15 Suppose that they will celebrate in n days, then there exists a positive integer m, such that $520 + n = m \cdot (50 + n)$. Thus

$$mn + 50m = 520 + n, \qquad mn + 50m - n = 520, \qquad (m-1)(n+50) = 470.$$

Since $n + 50 > 50$, n is the smallest when $n + 50 = 47 \cdot 2$ and $m - 1 = 5$. Thus $n = 44$. Therefore, they will celebrate in $\boxed{44 \text{ days}}$.

Solution to 2.16 We first treat $x + 2y - z$ as $(x + 2y) + (-z)$. From the Binomial Theorem, we get

$$(x+2y-z)^8 = (x+2y)^8 + \cdots + \binom{8}{3}(x+2y)^5(-z)^3 + \cdots + (-z)^8.$$

Note that the term $x^3 y^2 z^3$ can only come from the expansion of $\binom{8}{3}(x+2y)^5(-z)^3$. So we expand $(x+2y)^5$ and get

$$(x+2y)^5 = x^5 + \cdots + \binom{5}{2}x^3(2y)^2 + \cdots + (2y)^5.$$

Therefore the coefficient of the term $x^3 y^2 z^3$ in the original expression is

$$\binom{8}{3}(-1)^3 \cdot \binom{5}{2}(2)^2 = \frac{8!}{3! \cdot 5!} \cdot \frac{5!}{2! \cdot 3!} \cdot (-4) = \boxed{-2240}.$$

Solution to 2.17 Suppose Ryan uses x stamps, then the total weight of the letter is $\frac{x}{30} + \frac{9}{10}$ ounces. Since he needs 37 stamps for the first ounce and 23 stamps for each additional ounce, we have

$$37 + 23\lceil \frac{x}{30} + \frac{9}{10} - 1 \rceil = x, \qquad \lceil \frac{x}{30} - \frac{1}{10} \rceil = \frac{x-37}{23}.$$

Here $\lceil a \rceil$ is the ceiling of a. That is, $\lceil a \rceil$ is the least integer greater than or equal to a. Therefore $\frac{x-37}{23}$ is an integer. Thus $x \equiv 14 \pmod{23}$. Since $a \leq \lceil a \rceil$, we have

$$\frac{x-3}{30} \leq \frac{x-37}{23}, \qquad 23(x-3) \leq 30(x-37), \qquad x \geq 149.$$

Since 152 is the smallest integer greater than or equal to 149 which is equal to 14 (mod 23), Ryan should use $\boxed{152}$ stamps.

Solution to 2.18 Since $324 = 4 \cdot 3^4$, we can use $a^4 + 4b^4 = (a^2 - 2ab + 2b^2)(a^2 + 2ab + 2b^2)$ here:

$$n^4 + 324 = n^4 + 4 \cdot 3^4 = (n^2 - 2 \cdot 3n + 2 \cdot 3^2)(n^2 + 2 \cdot 3n + 2 \cdot 3^2) = \left((n-3)^2 + 9\right)\left((n+3)^2 + 9\right).$$

Therefore,

$$\frac{(10^4 + 324)(22^4 + 324) \cdots (58^4 + 324)}{(4^4 + 324)(16^4 + 324) \cdots (52^4 + 324)} = \frac{(7^2 + 9)(13^2 + 9) \cdots (55^2 + 9)(61^2 + 9)}{(1^2 + 9)(7^2 + 9) \cdots (49^2 + 9)(55^2 + 9)}$$

$$= \frac{61^2 + 9}{1^2 + 9} = \boxed{373}.$$

Solution to 2.19 Note that $1, -x, x^2, \ldots, -x^{17}$ is a geometric sequence. So

$$1 - x + x^2 + \cdots + x^{16} - x^{17} = \frac{1 - x^{18}}{1 + x} = \frac{1 - (y-1)^{18}}{y} = \frac{1 - (1-y)^{18}}{y}$$

$$= \frac{1 - \left(1 - \binom{18}{1}y + \binom{18}{2}y^2 - \binom{18}{3}y^3 + \cdots + y^{18}\right)}{y}$$

$$= \binom{18}{1} - \binom{18}{2}y + \binom{18}{3}y^2 - \cdots - y^{17}.$$

So the coefficient of y^2 is $\binom{18}{3} = \boxed{816}$.

Solution to 2.20 Our goal in this problem is to *solve* for $f(x)$, that is, to find a formula for it. Since the original equation gives us a relation between $f(x)$ and $f\left(-\frac{1}{x}\right)$, we would like to get another equation that connects these two terms. So we replace x with $-\frac{1}{x}$ everywhere in the original equation and get

$$f(x) + \frac{1}{x} \cdot f\left(-\frac{1}{x}\right) = 3,$$

$$f\left(-\frac{1}{x}\right) - x \cdot f(x) = 3.$$

Thus, $f\left(-\frac{1}{x}\right) = xf(x) + 3$. Plugging it into the original equation, we get

$$f(x) + \frac{1}{x}(xf(x) + 3) = 3,$$

$$2f(x) = 3 - \frac{3}{x}, \qquad f(2) = \frac{3 - \frac{3}{2}}{2} = \boxed{\frac{3}{4}}.$$

Solution to 2.21 From the original equation, we see that $f(x)$ is negative when x is positive and $f(x)$ is positive when x is negative. Since $f(f(f(x))) = 4$ is positive, $f(f(x))$ is negative and $f(f(x)) = -4$. Now $f(f(x)) = -4$ is negative, so $f(x)$ is positive and $f(x) = \sqrt{4} = 2$. Again, since $f(x) = 2$ is positive, x is negative and $x = \boxed{-2}$.

Solution to 2.22 We recognize that $8x^3 + 36x + \frac{54}{x} + \frac{27}{x^3}$ is the expansion of $\left(2x + \frac{3}{x}\right)^3$ according to the Binomial Theorem. We use AM-GM, which states that for any $a, b \geq 0$, $a + b \geq 2\sqrt{ab}$. Thus

$$\left(2x + \frac{3}{x}\right)^3 \geq \left(2\sqrt{2x \cdot \frac{3}{x}}\right)^3 = \boxed{48\sqrt{6}}.$$

Solution to 2.23 When $x = 1$, $\lfloor 2x \rfloor + \lfloor 4x \rfloor + \lfloor 6x \rfloor + \lfloor 8x \rfloor = 20$. First, let's see how many positive integers from 1 to 20 are expressible in the given form. For any positive integer k, when $x \in (0, 1]$, $\lfloor kx \rfloor$ changes value when $x = \frac{1}{k}, \frac{2}{k}, ..., \frac{k}{k}$. Combining all the value-changing points, we see that in the interval $(0, 1]$, the expression $\lfloor 2x \rfloor + \lfloor 4x \rfloor + \lfloor 6x \rfloor + \lfloor 8x \rfloor$ changes value when $x = \frac{1}{8}, \frac{1}{6}, \frac{1}{4}, \frac{1}{3}, \frac{3}{8}, \frac{1}{2}, \frac{5}{8}, \frac{2}{3}, \frac{3}{4}, \frac{5}{6}, \frac{7}{8}$, or 1. Everytime the expression changes value, we reach a new integer expressible in the given form of $\lfloor 2x \rfloor + \lfloor 4x \rfloor + \lfloor 6x \rfloor + \lfloor 8x \rfloor$. So 12 of the first 20 positive integers are expressible. Next, we notice that for any positive integer n,

$$\lfloor 2(n+x) \rfloor + \lfloor 4(n+x) \rfloor + \lfloor 6(n+x) \rfloor + \lfloor 8(n+x) \rfloor = \lfloor 2x \rfloor + \lfloor 4x \rfloor + \lfloor 6x \rfloor + \lfloor 8x \rfloor + 20n.$$

Thus we can reach the same number of integers when $x \in (0, 1]$ as we can when $x \in (n, n+1]$. Since when $x = 50$, $\lfloor 2x \rfloor + \lfloor 4x \rfloor + \lfloor 6x \rfloor + \lfloor 8x \rfloor = 1000$, the answer is 50 times the number of integers we can reach when $x \in (0, 1]$. That is, $50 \cdot 12 = \boxed{600}$ positive integers are expressible as $\lfloor 2x \rfloor + \lfloor 4x \rfloor + \lfloor 6x \rfloor + \lfloor 8x \rfloor$.

Solutions for Chapter 3

Solution to 3.1 In the original 8 kilograms of solution Y, we have $8 \cdot 30\% = 2.4$ kilograms of liquid X. After the evaporation of 2 kilograms of water, we still have 2.4 kilograms of liquid X. Adding 2 kilograms of solution Y, we get extra $2 \cdot 30\% = 0.6$ kilograms of liquid X. So, the percentage of liquid X in this new solution is

$$\frac{2.4+0.6}{8-2+2} = \boxed{37.5\%}.$$

Solution to 3.2 Let p be the price of one shirt. Let's calculate the cost of buying the least number of shirts at each of the discount levels. Buying 11 shirts costs $9.9p < 10p$. So we get one quantity in the range 1-10, namely 10. Buying 26 shirts costs $22.1p$. Since $\frac{22.1}{0.9} \approx 24.56 < 25$, we get one quantity in the range 11-25, namely 25. Buying 51 shirts costs $40.8p$. Since $\frac{40.8}{0.85} = 48 < 49$, we get 2 quantities in the range 26-50, namely 49 and 50. Buying 101 shirts costs $70.7p$. Since $\frac{70.7}{0.8} \approx 88.38 < 89$, we get 12 quantities in the range 51-100. Buying 251 shirts costs $163.15p$. Since $\frac{163.15}{0.7} \approx 233.07 < 234$, we get 17 quantities in the range 101-250. Therefore, in total we have $1 + 1 + 2 + 12 + 17 = \boxed{33}$ quantities.

Solution to 3.3 Let r be the rate of Alice's car in miles per hour. Let the two-digit number on the first mile marker be $10x + y$, where x and y are single digit positive integers. Then we have

$$r \cdot 1 = 10y + x - (10x + y) = 9(y - x),$$
$$r \cdot 2 = 100x + y - (10x + y) = 90x.$$

Combining the two equations, we get

$$2 \cdot 9(y - x) = 90x, \qquad y = 6x.$$

Since x and y are single digit positive integers, we must have $x = 1$ and $y = 6$. Therefore, the rate $r = 9 \cdot (6 - 1) = \boxed{45 \text{ mph}}$.

Solution to 3.4 Since 330 people can construct 30 km of railway in 9 months, one person can construct

$$\frac{30}{330 \cdot 9} = \frac{1}{99} \text{ km}$$

of railway in one month. Letting x be the number of months needed, we have

$$\frac{1}{99} \cdot 275x = 150, \qquad x = \boxed{54 \text{ months}}.$$

Solution to 3.5 Let's work backwards. Without loss of generality, let's assume that the scores at the end of round 3 were (x, y, z) where $x \geq y \geq z$, with the first player's score x, the second player's score y, and the third player's score z. Since everyone scored 80 at the end of round 4, we must have

$$2z = 80, \quad x - z = 80, \quad y - z = 80.$$

So at the end of round 3, the scores were: $(120, 120, 40)$. Since a different player won each of the final three rounds, let's assume that player 1 won the third round. Then we see that at the end of round 2, the scores were: $(60, 180, 100)$. Next we see that player 2 must win the second round, so at the end of round 1, the scores were: $(150, 90, 190)$. Therefore, the highest score at the end of round 1 was $\boxed{190}$.

Solution to 3.6 Let the weights of the first and the second passenger's checked luggage be x and y kilograms, respectively. Let w kilograms be the airline's permitted maximum weight without charge for each passenger. Let r be the per-kilogram rate for any extra weight. Then we have

$$x + y = 105,$$
$$r(x - w) = 12,$$
$$r(y - w) = 18,$$
$$r(x + y - w) = 78.$$

Adding the middle two equations above, we get $r(x + y - 2w) = 30$. Since $x + y = 105$, we have

$$r(105 - 2w) = 30,$$
$$r(105 - w) = 78.$$

Therefore,

$$\frac{r(105 - 2w)}{r(105 - w)} = \frac{30}{78}, \quad \frac{105 - 2w}{105 - w} = \frac{5}{13}, \quad 13(105 - 2w) = 5(105 - w).$$

So $w = \dfrac{8 \cdot 105}{21} = \boxed{40 \text{ kg}}$.

Solution to 3.7 We see that Abe's speed is $\dfrac{1}{15}$ rm/hr, Bea's speed is $\dfrac{1}{10}$ rm/hr, and Coe's speed is $\dfrac{2}{15}$ rm/hr. After working for one hour and a half, Abe has painted $\dfrac{1}{10}$th of the room. When Bea joins Abe, their combined speed is $\dfrac{1}{15} + \dfrac{1}{10} = \dfrac{1}{6}$ rm/hr. They work together and paint $\dfrac{1}{2} - \dfrac{1}{10} = \dfrac{2}{5}$th of the room. This takes them $\dfrac{2}{5} \cdot 6 = \dfrac{12}{5}$ hours. When Coe joins the other two, their combined speed is

Solutions for Chapter 3

$$\frac{1}{15} + \frac{1}{10} + \frac{2}{15} = \frac{3}{10} \text{ rm/hr.}$$

The three of them paint one half of the room in $\frac{1}{2} \cdot \frac{10}{3} = \frac{5}{3}$ hours. Thus the total number of minutes is

$$60\left(1.5 + \frac{12}{5} + \frac{5}{3}\right) = \boxed{334 \text{ minutes}}.$$

Solution to 3.8 Without loss of generality, let's assume that the volume of Fresh is 1 unit. Then Fresh costs 100 cents. We organize the volume and price information of each brand into a table.

	volume (units)	price (cents)
Fresh	1	100
Bright	$1\frac{1}{3} \cdot 0.75$	$1.6 \cdot 100$
Glow	$1\frac{1}{3}$	$1.6 \cdot 100 \cdot 0.75$

From the table, we see that the number of cents per unit of volume of Glow is

$$\frac{1.6 \cdot 100 \cdot 0.75}{\frac{4}{3}} = \boxed{90 \text{ cents}}.$$

Solution to 3.9 Let W be the width of the river. When the two boats first meet, one boat has traveled 700 yards and the other has traveled $W - 700$ yards. The first boat travels another $W - 700 + 300$ yards and the second boat travels another $700 + W - 300$ yards when they meet the second time. Since each of the boats travels at a constant speed, we have

$$\frac{W-700}{700} = \frac{700+W-300}{W-700+300}, \quad \frac{W}{700} = \frac{2W}{W-400}, \quad W = \boxed{1800 \text{ yards}}.$$

Solution to 3.10 Let's represent various amounts in terms of cents. Suppose Lupe's purchase is $100x + 10y + z$ cents, where x, y, and z are nonnegative single digit integers. Then there are five possible cases for the change amount. They are: $100y + 10x + z$, $100y + 10z + x$, $100z + 10y + x$, $100z + 10x + y$, and $100x + 10z + y$.

Case 1: $100x + 10y + z + 100y + 10x + z = 1000$. We have $110(x+y) + 2z = 1000$. So we must have $z = 5$, and $x + y = 9$. So we get 8 possible amounts of change: 185, 275, 365, 455, 545, 635, 725, and 815.

Case 2: $100x + 10y + z + 100y + 10z + x = 1000$. We have $101x + 110y + 11z = 1000$. Looking at the last digit, we see that it must be true that $x + z = 10$. So $z = 10 - x$ and

$$101x + 110y + 11(10-x) = 1000, \quad 9x + 11y = 89.$$

The only solution is $x = 5$, $y = 4$, and $z = 5$, which is already counted in Case 1.

Case 3: $100x + 10y + z + 100z + 10y + x = 1000$. We have $101x + 20y + 101z = 1000$. Considering the last digit, we must have $x + z = 10$, but then $101 \cdot 10 + 20y > 1000$. So, this case is impossible.

Case 4: $100x + 10y + z + 100z + 10x + y = 1000$. We have $110x + 101z + 11y = 1000$. This case is similar to Case 2, and we get $x = 4$, $y = 5$, and $z = 5$, which is already counted in Case 1.

Case 5: $100x + 10y + z + 100x + 10z + y = 1000$. We have $200x + 11(y + z) = 1000$. We must have $x = 5$ and $y + z = 0$. Since, in this case, the purchase amount is the same as the change amount, it is impossible.

Combining all cases, we see that there are $\boxed{8}$ possible change amounts.

Solution to 3.11 Let's first see if the treasure is in the gold chest. If this were the case, then the inscriptions on all three chests would be wrong, a contradiction. Therefore, the treasure is not in the gold chest. Next, let's see if the treasure is in the silver chest. If this were true, then all three inscriptions must be true, another contradiction. Therefore, the treasure is in the $\boxed{\text{bronze}}$ chest.

Solution to 3.12 Let the length of each train be d miles. Let the speeds of the eastbound train and the westbound train be s_e and s_w, respectively. Since each takes 1 minute to go past Jon, we have

$$\frac{d}{s_e - 20} = \frac{d}{s_w + 20} = \frac{1}{60}.$$

Since the westbound train takes 10 times as long as the eastbound train to go past Steve, we have
$$\frac{10d}{s_e + 20} = \frac{d}{s_w - 20}.$$

Therefore,
$$s_e - 20 = s_w + 20,$$
$$s_e + 20 = 10s_w - 200.$$

Combining the two equations, we get $s_w = \frac{260}{9}$. So

$$d = \frac{s_w + 20}{60} = \frac{\frac{260}{9} + 20}{60} = \boxed{\frac{22}{27} \text{ miles}}.$$

Solution to 3.13 Let the speeds of Ann, Zoe, and the escalator be a, z, and e, respectively. We have $a = 2z$. When Ann walks 27 steps, the escalator goes $n - 27$

Solutions for Chapter 3

steps. Similarly, when Zoe walks 18 steps, the escalator goes $n - 18$ steps. Therefore,

$$\frac{27}{2z} = \frac{n-27}{e},$$
$$\frac{18}{z} = \frac{n-18}{e}.$$

Combining the two equations, we get

$$\frac{27}{2(n-27)} = \frac{18}{n-18}, \quad 3(n-18) = 4(n-27), \quad n = \boxed{54}.$$

Solution to 3.14 Since no problem has three or more answers that are the same, each problem is answered correctly by at most two people. We know that there are 8 correct answers in total. So if only one person got a particular problem correct, then there must be another problem such that at least three people got it correct. But this is not the case. Therefore, exactly two people answer each problem correct. Thus the answer to question 4 must be C and the answer to question 2 must be A. Now that we know John's answers to problems 2 and 4 are correct, his answers to problems 1 and 3 must be wrong. Therefore, the answer to question 1 is A, and the answer to question 3 is D. So the correct answers are $\boxed{A, A, D, C}$.

Solution to 3.15 We first let Alice and Bobby cross. Then Alice comes back with the flashlight. Next time we let Cathy and Doug cross. Then we let Bobby come back. Finally, Alice and Bobby cross one more time. In total, it takes $2 + 1 + 10 + 2 + 2 = \boxed{17 \text{ minutes}}$.

Solution to 3.16 Since there are ten drops, we can test the first egg at the 10th floor. If it breaks, then, starting from the first floor, we can test the second egg from successive floors until the egg either breaks or survives the 9th floor. If the first egg survives the 10th floor, we have 9 drops and two eggs left. By similar reasoning, we can test the first egg again at the $10 + 9 = 19$th floor. Repeating the process, we see that if the first egg survives the $10 + 9 + \cdots + 2 = 54$th floor, then we have 1 drop and two eggs left. So we use the last drop to test any egg from the 55th floor. Thus the tallest building for which we can test every floor has $\boxed{55 \text{ floors}}$.

Solution to 3.17 On the day they buy wine, they can drink one bottle, put 11 bottles in the smaller cupboard, and put the rest in the larger cupboard. Every bottle is exposed to light once on that day. During the next 11 days, they can open the smaller cupboard once and take out one bottle everyday. On the 11th day, the last bottle from the smaller cupboard is exposed to light exactly 12 times and they drink it. The next day, they drink one bottle from the larger cupboard and move 10 bottles from the larger cupboard to the smaller one. Now every remaining bottle is exposed to light twice. Repeating the process, each time when they need to move wine bottles from the larger cupboard, they take out one less bottle. Finally, one day they open the larger cupboard, drink one bottle, and move one bottle to the smaller cupboard. Now every remaining bottle is exposed to light exactly 11 times. The next time they open the larger cupboard, every bottle is exposed to light 12 times. So, the larger cupboard can only have one bottle left, and they drink it. Therefore, in total they can buy at most

$$(1+11) + (1+10) + \cdots + (1+2) + (1+1) + (1+0) = 12 + 11 + 10 + \cdots + 2 + 1 = 78$$

bottles. That is, every $\boxed{78 \text{ days}}$ the Chateau family needs to buy wine.

Solution to 3.18 If the first person were a knight, then both the other two would be liars. Then the answer of the second one would be an honest answer, a contradiction. So the first person is a liar and at least one of the other two is a knight. If the second were a liar, then the third must be a knight. But, again, the answer of the second one would be an honest one, a contradiction. So the second is a knight. Thus the third one must also be a knight and the third would give an honest answer: $\boxed{\text{"One"}}$.

Solution to 3.19 Since the hour hand goes 360 degrees every 12 hours, it goes 0.5 degrees every minute. Because the minute hand goes 360 degrees every hour, it goes 6 degrees every minute. Suppose it is h-hour and m-minute now, then the angle between the hour hand and the 12 o'clock mark is $0.5(60h + m)$ degrees and the angle between the minute hand and the 12 o'clock mark is $6m$ degrees. So at 5:37, the angle between the hour hand and the minute hand is

$$6 \cdot 37 - 0.5(60 \cdot 5 + 37) = 53.5 \text{ degrees.}$$

After 5:37, the angle between the two hands gets larger and larger until it reaches 180 degrees. Then it gets smaller and eventually at some time, say x minutes, after 6 o'clock it is 53.5 degrees again. Therefore,

$$0.5(60 \cdot 6 + x) - 6x = 53.5, \qquad x = 23.$$

Thus, $\boxed{6:23}$ is the next time the two hands will be the same as it is now.

Solution to 3.20 Let the speed of the bus be v and the speed of Kyle be k. Let d be the distance between any two successive buses traveling in the same direction. Then, the required interval is just $\frac{d}{v}$. If we look at things from Kyle's perspective, thus letting Kyle be stationary, we get

$$\frac{d}{v-k} = 12,$$
$$\frac{d}{v+k} = 4.$$

Therefore,

Solutions for Chapter 3

$$\frac{d}{v} = \frac{d}{\frac{v-k}{2} + \frac{v+k}{2}} = \frac{1}{\frac{v-k}{2 \cdot d} + \frac{v+k}{2 \cdot d}}$$

$$= \frac{1}{\frac{1}{24} + \frac{1}{8}} = \boxed{6 \text{ minutes}}.$$

Solution to 3.21 With a total of 100 students, 90 of them solved the first problem and 80 solved the second problem. So, at least 70 students solved both the first and second problems. Similarly, since 70 students solved the third problem and 60 solved the fourth problem, at least 30 students solved both the third and fourth problems. Since no one solved all four problems, the number of students who solved both the third and fourth problems cannot be greater than $100 - 70 = 30$. Therefore, $\boxed{30 \text{ students}}$ solved both the third and fourth problems.

Solution to 3.22 Suppose R_s judges voted for Rooster, R_v judges voted for Raven, and C_k judges voted for Cuckoo. Since each count is at most 13 off, we have

$$59 - 13 \le R_s + R_v + C_k \le 59 + 13, \qquad 46 \le R_s + R_v + C_k \le 72.$$

Similarly, we add up the other three counts and get

$$15 + 18 + 20 - 3 \cdot 13 \le 2(R_s + R_v + C_k) \le 15 + 18 + 20 + 3 \cdot 13, \qquad 7 \le R_s + R_v + C_k \le 46.$$

Combining the two inequalities, we get $R_s + R_v + C_k = 46$. Furthermore, we see that Woodpecker counted 13 less in each of his last three counts. In particular, he counted 13 less when he counted the number of judges who voted for Cuckoo or Rooster. That is, $R_s + C_k = 20 + 13$ in reality. Therefore, the number of judges who voted for Raven is

$$R_v = (R_s + R_v + C_k) - (R_s + C_k) = 46 - (20 + 13) = \boxed{13 \text{ judges}}.$$

Solution to 3.23 Let n be the number of steps on the escalator. Let the speeds of Al, Bob, and the escalator be a, b, and e, respectively. We have $a = 3b$. When Bob walks 75 steps, the escalator goes $n - 75$ steps. So we have

$$\frac{75}{b} = \frac{n-75}{e}, \qquad b = \frac{75e}{n-75}.$$

When Al walks 150 steps, from the perspective of an observer at the bottom of the escalator, Al's speed is $3b - e$, and Al goes n steps. Therefore,

$$\frac{150}{3b} = \frac{n}{3b-e}, \qquad b = \frac{50e}{150-n}.$$

Combining the two equations, we get $3(150 - n) = 2(n - 75)$. So $n = \boxed{120 \text{ steps}}$.

Solutions for Chapter 4

Solution to 4.1 The sum of the coefficients of a polynomial $P(x)$ is the value of the polynomial when $x = 1$. Therefore, letting $x = 1$, we get

$$1 + 23 - 18 - 24 + 108 = (1 - 3 - 2 + 9) \cdot P(1), \qquad P(1) = \frac{90}{5} = \boxed{18}.$$

Solution to 4.2 For any polynomial $P(x)$ and any number a, the remainder of $P(x)$ divided by $x - a$ is $P(a)$. So the remainder is $(-1)^{51} + 51 = \boxed{50}$.

Solution to 4.3 Since $P(x)$ has remainder 99 when divided by $x - 19$, $P(19) = 99$. Since it has remainder 19 when divided by $x-99$, $P(99) = 19$. The remainder when $P(x)$ is divided by $(x-19)(x-99)$ is a linear polynomial $ax+b$. So $P(x) = Q(x)(x-19)(x-99) + ax+b$ for some polynomial $Q(x)$. Plugging in $x = 19$ and $x = 99$, we get

$$19a + b = 99, \quad \text{and} \quad 99a + b = 19.$$

Solving the system, we get $a = -1$ and $b = 118$. So the remainder is $\boxed{-x + 118}$.

Solution to 4.4 Since the y-intercept of the graph of $y = P(x)$ is 2, $c = 2$. By Vieta's Formulas, we have

$$\frac{-a}{3} = -c = 1 + a + b + c.$$

Because $c = 2$, we get $a = 6$ and $b = -1 - a - 2c = -1 - 6 - 4 = \boxed{-11}$.

Solution to 4.5 Since $P\left(\frac{x}{3}\right) = x^2 + x + 1$, $P(3x) = P\left(\frac{9x}{3}\right) = (9x)^2 + 9x + 1$. Thus,

$$81x^2 + 9x + 1 = 7, \qquad 81x^2 + 9x - 6 = 0, \qquad 27x^2 + 3x - 2 = 0.$$

By Vieta's Formulas, the sum of all roots of the equation is $\frac{-3}{27} = \boxed{-\frac{1}{9}}$.

Solution to 4.6 Let the roots of $4x^3 - 12x^2 + cx + d = 0$ be r, $-r$, and s. We have

$$r + (-r) + s = 3,$$
$$rs + (-r)s + r(-r) = \frac{c}{4},$$
$$r(-r)s = -\frac{d}{4}.$$

Therefore, $s = 3$, $c = -4r^2$, and $d = 12r^2$. So $\dfrac{d}{c} = \dfrac{12r^2}{-4r^2} = \boxed{-3}$.

Solution to 4.7 Since r, s, and t are roots of $x^3 - 6x^2 + 5x - 7 = 0$, $\frac{1}{r}$, $\frac{1}{s}$, and $\frac{1}{t}$ are roots of
$$\left(\frac{1}{x}\right)^3 - 6\left(\frac{1}{x}\right)^2 + 5\left(\frac{1}{x}\right) - 7 = 0, \qquad -7x^3 + 5x^2 - 6x + 1 = 0.$$
That is, they are the roots of $7x^3 - 5x^2 + 6x - 1 = 0$. By Newton's Sums, we have
$$\frac{1}{r^2} + \frac{1}{s^2} + \frac{1}{t^2} = \left(\frac{1}{r} + \frac{1}{s} + \frac{1}{t}\right)^2 - 2\left(\frac{1}{rs} + \frac{1}{st} + \frac{1}{tr}\right) = \left(\frac{5}{7}\right)^2 - 2\left(\frac{6}{7}\right) = \boxed{-\frac{59}{49}}.$$

Solution to 4.8 Let r and s be the two roots of $x^2 - x - 1 = 0$. We have $rs = -1$. Since $x^2 - x - 1$ is a factor of $ax^3 + bx^2 + 1$, r and s are roots of $ax^3 + bx^2 + 1 = 0$ as well. Let t be the third root of $ax^3 + bx^2 + 1 = 0$. We see that $rst = -\frac{1}{a}$. So $t = \frac{1}{a}$. Thus, $x - \frac{1}{a}$ is another factor of $ax^3 + bx^2 + 1$. Since the leading coefficient of $ax^3 + bx^2 + 1$ is a, we have
$$ax^3 + bx^2 + 1 = a(x^2 - x - 1)(x - \frac{1}{a}) = (x^2 - x - 1)(ax - 1) = ax^3 - (1+a)x^2 + (1-a)x + 1.$$
Comparing the coefficients of both sides, we get $a = 1$ and $b = -(1+a) = \boxed{-2}$.

Solution to 4.9 The roots of $x^3 - x = 0$ are 1, -1, and 0. Let $ax^2 + bx + c$ be the remainder when $x^{81} + x^{49} + x^{25} + x^9 + x$ is divided by $x^3 - x$. When $x = 1$, $x^{81} + x^{48} + x^{25} + x^9 + x = 5$. When $x = -1$, $x^{81} + x^{49} + x^{25} + x^9 + x = -5$. When $x = 0$, $x^{81} + x^{49} + x^{25} + x^9 + x = 0$. Therefore,
$$a(1) + b(1) + c = 5,$$
$$a(-1)^2 + b(-1) + c = -5,$$
$$a(0) + b(0) + c = 0.$$
So $a = 0$, $b = 5$ and $c = 0$. Thus, the remainder is $\boxed{5x}$.

Solution to 4.10 By Vieta's Formulas, we have $r + s + t = -a$, $rs + st + tr = b$, and $rst = -c$. By Newton's Sums, we have
$$r^2 + s^2 + t^2 = (r+s+t)^2 - 2(rs+st+tr) = a^2 - 2b,$$
$$r^2s^2 + s^2t^2 + t^2r^2 = (rs+st+tr)^2 - 2rst(s+t+r) = b^2 - 2ac.$$
Thus,
$$(rs+t)(st+r)(tr+s) = (rs^2t + r^2s + +st^2 + tr)(tr+s)$$
$$= r^2s^2t^2 + rs^3t + r^3st + r^2s^2 + rst^3 + s^2t^2 + t^2r^2 + rst$$
$$= c^2 - c(r^2 + s^2 + t^2 + 1) + r^2s^2 + s^2t^2 + t^2r^2$$
$$= c^2 - c(a^2 - 2b + 1) + b^2 - 2ac = \boxed{(b+c)^2 - c(a+1)^2}.$$

Solution to 4.11 Let r, s, t, and u be the four zeros of the equation with $rs = -32$. Since $rs \cdot tu = -1984$, $tu = \dfrac{-1984}{-32} = 62$. Since $r + s + t + u = 18$, $r + s = 18 - t - u$. By Vieta's Formulas, we have

$$rst + rsu + rtu + stu = -200, \qquad -32(t+u) + (r+s)tu = -200,$$

$$-32(t+u) + 62(18 - t - u) = -200, \qquad t + u = \dfrac{62 \cdot 18 + 200}{32 + 62} = 14.$$

So $r + s = 18 - t - u = 4$. By Vieta's Formulas again,

$$k = rs + rt + ru + st + su + tu = -32 + (r+s)(t+u) + 62 = -32 + 4 \cdot 14 + 62 = \boxed{86}.$$

Solution to 4.12 Since a is a root, $a^4 - a^3 = a^2 + 1$. So

$$p(a) = a^2(a^4 - a^3 - a - 1) - a = a^2(a^2 + 1 - a - 1) - a = a^4 - a^3 - a = a^2 - a + 1.$$

Similarly, $p(b) = b^2 - b + 1$, $p(c) = c^2 - c + 1$, and $p(d) = d^2 - d + 1$. Since a, b, c, and d are roots of $x^4 - x^3 - x^2 - 1 = 0$, by Vieta's Formulas, we have

$$a + b + c + d = 1, \quad \text{and} \quad ab + ac + ad + bc + bd + cd = -1.$$

By Newton's Sums, we get

$$a^2 + b^2 + c^2 + d^2 = (a+b+c+d)^2 - 2(ab+ac+ad+bc+bd+cd) = 1 + 2 = 3.$$

Thus,

$$p(a) + p(b) + p(c) + p(d) = a^2 + b^2 + c^2 + d^2 - (a+b+c+d) + 4 = 3 - 1 + 4 = \boxed{6}.$$

Solution to 4.13 By Vieta's Formulas,

$$a + b + c = \dfrac{14}{3}, \qquad ab + bc + ac = \dfrac{1}{3}, \quad \text{and} \quad abc = -\dfrac{62}{3}.$$

Therefore,

$$\dfrac{1}{a+3} + \dfrac{1}{b+3} + \dfrac{1}{c+3} = \dfrac{(b+3)(c+3) + (a+3)(c+3) + (a+3)(b+3)}{(a+3)(b+3)(c+3)}$$

$$= \dfrac{(ab+bc+ac) + 6(a+b+c) + 27}{abc + 3(ab+ac+bc) + 9(a+b+c) + 27}$$

$$= \dfrac{\dfrac{1}{3} + 2 \cdot 14 + 27}{-\dfrac{62}{3} + 1 + 3 \cdot 14 + 27} = \boxed{\dfrac{83}{74}}.$$

Solutions for Chapter 4

Solution to 4.14 We have $a^3 + b^3 = (a+b)(a^2 + b^2 - ab) = (a+b)(5 - ab)$ and $a^2 + b^2 = (a+b)^2 - 2ab$. So let $a + b = x$ and $ab = y$. Then

$$x(5 - y) = 7,$$
$$x^2 - 2y = 5.$$

From the last equation, we get $y = \dfrac{x^2 - 5}{2}$. Plugging it into the first equation, we have

$$x(5 - \dfrac{x^2 - 5}{2}) = 7, \qquad x(15 - x^2) = 14, \qquad x^3 - 15x + 14 = 0.$$

Note that $x = 1$ is a root of $x^3 - 15x + 14 = 0$. Using long division, we get

$$x^3 - 15x + 14 = (x - 1)(x^2 + x - 14).$$

By the quadratic formula, the roots of $x^2 + x - 14 = 0$ are $x = \dfrac{-1 \pm \sqrt{57}}{2}$. Thus

$$x^3 - 15x + 14 = (x - 1)(x^2 + x - 14) = (x - 1)\left(x - \dfrac{-1 + \sqrt{57}}{2}\right)\left(x - \dfrac{-1 - \sqrt{57}}{2}\right).$$

Therefore, the largest possible value of $a + b$ is the largest root of $x^3 - 15x + 14 = 0$, which is $\boxed{\dfrac{-1 + \sqrt{57}}{2}}$.

Solution to 4.15 We see that $(x - 1)f(x) = (x - 1)(x^4 + x^3 + x^2 + x + 1) = x^5 - 1$. Therefore $x^5 = (x - 1)f(x) + 1$.

$$f(x^5) = (x^5)^4 + (x^5)^3 + (x^5)^2 + x^5 + 1$$
$$= \bigl((x - 1)f(x) + 1\bigr)^4 + \bigl((x - 1)f(x) + 1\bigr)^3 + \bigl((x - 1)f(x) + 1\bigr)^2 + (x - 1)f(x) + 1 + 1.$$

Expanding the last expression, we see that all the terms have a factor of $f(x)$ except for the five constant terms. Therefore, the remainder when $f(x^5)$ is divided by $f(x)$ is $1 + 1 + 1 + 1 + 1 = \boxed{5}$.

Solution to 4.16 Note that $x^{60} - 1 = (x^3)^{20} - 1 = \bigl((x^3 - 2) + 2\bigr)^{20} - 1$. Expanding it, we see that all the terms have a factor of $x^3 - 2$ except for the constant term. Therefore, the remainder when $x^{60} - 1$ is divided by $x^3 - 2$ is $\boxed{2^{20} - 1}$.

Solution to 4.17 Letting $x = -1$, we get $p(0) = 0$. Letting $x = 0$ and get $p(1) = 0$. We keep on doing this and get $p(2) = p(3) = \cdots = p(10) = 0$. So $0, 1, ..., 10$ are all roots of $p(x)$. Since $p(x)$ is an 11th degree polynomial, it has only 11 roots. So the sum of the roots of $p(x)$ is $0 + 1 + 2 + \cdots + 10 = \boxed{55}$.

Solution to 4.18 Letting $f(x) = x^4 + x^3 + x^2 + x + 1$, we see that $(x-1)f(x) = (x-1)(x^4 + x^3 + x^2 + x + 1) = x^5 - 1$. So $x^5 = (x-1)f(x) + 1$. Thus,

$$x^{44} + x^{33} + x^{22} + x^{11} + 1 = (x^5)^8 \cdot x^4 + (x^5)^6 \cdot x^3 + (x^5)^4 \cdot x^2 + (x^5)^2 \cdot x + 1$$
$$= \big((x-1)f(x) + 1\big)^8 \cdot x^4 + \big((x-1)f(x) + 1\big)^6 \cdot x^3$$
$$+ \big((x-1)f(x) + 1\big)^4 \cdot x^2 + \big((x-1)f(x) + 1\big)^2 \cdot x + 1.$$

Expanding the last expression, we see that the only terms that do not have the factor $f(x)$ are $1 \cdot x^4$, $1 \cdot x^3$, $1 \cdot x^2$, $1 \cdot x$, and 1. Their sum is $f(x)$. Therefore, the remainder when $x^{44} + x^{33} + x^{22} + x^{11} + 1$ is divided by $x^4 + x^3 + x^2 + x + 1$ is $\boxed{0}$.

Solution to 4.19 Let $q(x) = (x+1)p(x) - x$. Clearly $q(x)$ is a polynomial with degree $n+1$. Furthermore, $q(0) = q(1) = \cdots = q(n) = 0$. So

$$q(x) = (x+1)p(x) - x = ax(x-1)(x-2)\cdots(x-n) \tag{$*$}$$

for some constant a. Letting $x = -1$, we get

$$1 = a(-1)(-2)(-3)\cdots(-n-1), \qquad a = (-1)^{n+1}\frac{1}{(n+1)!}.$$

Plugging $x = n+1$ into $(*)$, we get

$$(n+2)p(n+1) - (n+1) = (-1)^{n+1}\frac{1}{(n+1)!} \cdot (n+1) \cdot n \cdot (n-1) \cdots (n+1-n),$$

$$(n+2)p(n+1) = (-1)^{n+1} + (n+1), \qquad p(n+1) = \boxed{\frac{(-1)^{n+1} + n + 1}{n+2}}.$$

Solution to 4.20 Expanding the two given equations, we get

$$x^4 - x^2 + 2x - 1 = 2y^3 - 4\sqrt{5} - 2, \tag{$**$}$$
$$y^4 - y^2 + 2y - 1 = 2x^3 + 4\sqrt{5} - 2.$$

Adding the two equations above, we have

$$(x^4 - 2x^3 - x^2 + 2x + 1) + (y^4 - 2y^3 - y^2 + 2y + 1) = 0.$$

That is, $(x^2 - x - 1)^2 + (y^2 - y - 1)^2 = 0$. Since the value of a perfect square is greater than or equal to zero, we get both $x^2 - x - 1 = 0$ and $y^2 - y - 1 = 0$. Plugging $x^2 = x + 1$ and $y^2 = y + 1$ into $(**)$, we get $x = y - \sqrt{5}$. So $x < y$ and x and y are the two roots of the quadratic equation $u^2 - u - 1 = 0$. Therefore, $x = \dfrac{1 - \sqrt{5}}{2}$, $y = \dfrac{1 + \sqrt{5}}{2}$, and

$$8x^2 + 4y^3 = 8 \cdot \frac{1 - 2\sqrt{5} + 5}{4} + 4 \cdot \frac{1 + 3\sqrt{5} + 3 \cdot 5 + 5\sqrt{5}}{8} = \boxed{20}.$$

Solutions for Chapter 5

Solutions for Chapter 5

Solution to 5.1 The triangular numbers are numbers of the form $\frac{n(n+1)}{2}$ for integers $n \geq 1$. We multiply each number of the sequence by 7 and write the new numbers in this form and get

$$\frac{(7-1) \cdot 7}{2}, \quad \frac{7 \cdot (7+1)}{2}, \quad \frac{(2 \cdot 7 - 1) \cdot 2 \cdot 7}{2}, \quad \frac{2 \cdot 7(2 \cdot 7 + 1)}{2}, \quad \ldots$$

Therefore, the 100th term of this sequence is

$$\frac{\frac{50 \cdot 7(50 \cdot 7 + 1)}{2}}{7} = \boxed{8775}.$$

Solution to 5.2 Let's write the first a few terms of the sequence in the form $2^a 3^b$. We have

$$2^1 3^0, \quad 2^1 3^1, \quad 2^2 3^1, \quad 2^3 3^2, \quad 2^5 3^3, \quad \ldots$$

Note that the summations of a and b form a Fibonacci sequence: 1, 2, 3, 5, 8, 13, 21, 34, ... Therefore, for the ninth term, $a + b = \boxed{55}$.

Solution to 5.3 We see that

$$a_3 = \frac{1}{2}(a_1 + a_2),$$
$$a_4 = \frac{1}{3}(a_1 + a_2 + a_3) = \frac{1}{2}(a_1 + a_2),$$
$$a_5 = \frac{1}{4}(a_1 + a_2 + a_3 + a_4) = \frac{1}{2}(a_1 + a_2),$$
$$\vdots$$

By induction, we see that for all $n > 2$, $a_n = \frac{1}{2}(a_1 + a_2)$. In particular, $a_9 = \frac{a_1 + a_2}{2}$. So $a_2 = 2a_9 - a_1 = \boxed{179}$.

Solution to 5.4 Since $a_1 = 2$ and $a_{n+1} = a_n + 2n$ for $n \geq 1$, we have

$$a_{100} = a_{99} + 2 \cdot 99$$
$$= a_{98} + 2 \cdot 98 + 2 \cdot 99$$
$$\vdots$$
$$= a_1 + 2 \cdot 1 + \cdots + 2 \cdot 99$$
$$= 2 + 2 \cdot 1 + \cdots + 2 \cdot 99 = 2 + 2 \cdot \frac{99 \cdot 100}{2} = \boxed{9902}.$$

Solution to 5.5 We see that this increasing sequence of positive integers can be represented in terms of a_1 and a_2:

$$a_1,\ a_2,\ a_1+a_2,\ a_1+2a_2,\ 2a_1+3a_2,\ 3a_1+5a_2,\ 5a_1+8a_2,\ 8a_1+13a_2,\ \ldots$$

Since $a_7 = 120 = 5a_1 + 8a_2$, we have $5a_1 = 8(15 - a_2)$. Since 5 and 8 are relatively prime, 8 is a factor of a_1. When $a_1 = 8$, $a_2 = 10$. When $a_1 \geq 2 \cdot 8$, $a_2 \leq 5$. But, this is impossible because $a_1 \leq a_2$. Thus $a_1 = 8$ is the only solution. Therefore,

$$a_8 = 8a_1 + 13a_2 = 8 \cdot 8 + 13 \cdot 10 = \boxed{194}.$$

Solution to 5.6 The first sequence is $a_{n+1} = 1+3n$ for all $n \geq 1$. We see that $a_{2004} = 6010$. The second sequence is $b_{n+1} = 9+7n$ for all $n \geq 1$. We see that $b_{2004} = 14030$. The smallest common term of the two sequences is 16. The common terms of the two sequences form an arithmetic sequence $\{c_n\}$ with $c_{n+1} = 16+21n$ for all $n \geq 1$. The largest number in this new sequence that is in S is

$$c_{286} = 16 + 21 \cdot 285 = 6001.$$

Therefore, by the principle of inclusion-exclusion, the number of distinct numbers in S is $2004 + 2004 - 286 = \boxed{3722}$.

Solution to 5.7 The characteristic equation of $f(n) = 3f(n-2) - 2f(n-1)$ is

$$\lambda^2 + 2\lambda - 3 = 0.$$

So $(\lambda+3)(\lambda-1) = 0$. $\lambda = -3$ or $\lambda = 1$. Thus $f(n) = A \cdot (1)^n + B \cdot (-3)^n$ for some real numbers A and B. Plugging in $f(1)$ and $f(2)$, we have

$$A + (-3)B = -1,$$
$$A + (-3)^2 B = 3.$$

Solving the system, we get $A = 0$ and $B = \frac{1}{3}$. Therefore,

$$f(n) = \frac{(-3)^n}{3}, \qquad f(9) = \frac{(-3)^9}{3} = \boxed{-6561}.$$

Solution to 5.8 Since $a_n = 4a_{n-1} - 4a_{n-2}$, its characteristic equation is

$$\lambda^2 = 4\lambda - 4, \qquad (\lambda-2)^2 = 0.$$

Since the characteristic equation has two repeated roots, we have $a_n = A \cdot 2^n + B \cdot n \cdot 2^n$, for some real numbers A and B. Plugging in $a_1 = 0$ and $a_2 = 4$, we get

$$2A + 2B = 0,$$
$$4A + 4 \cdot 2B = 4.$$

Solving the system of equations, we get $A = -1$ and $B = 1$. So $a_n = (n-1)2^n$. Since the largest power of 2 that is under 100 is 2^6, we have

$$n - 1 = 2^6, \qquad n = 2^6 + 1 = \boxed{65}.$$

Solution to 5.9 From the solution of Example 5.5, we know that when the sequence of second differences is a constant sequence, a_n is quadratic in terms of n. So

$$a_n = an^2 + bn + c$$

for some real numbers a, b, and c. Since $a_{19} = a_{92} = 0$, $n = 19$ and $n = 92$ are the roots of the equation $an^2 + bn + c = 0$. Therefore,

$$a_n = a(n-19)(n-92).$$

Since $(a_3 - a_2) - (a_2 - a_1) = 1$, we have

$$a(3-19)(3-92) - 2a(2-19)(2-92) + a(1-19)(1-92) = 1, \qquad a = \frac{1}{2}.$$

Therefore, $a_1 = \frac{1}{2}(1-19)(1-92) = \boxed{819}$.

Solution to 5.10 Since the general term of an arithmetic sequence is a linear function in terms of n, multiplying the corresponding terms of two arithmetic sequences gives us a sequence whose general term is a quadratic function $a_n = an^2 + bn + c$, for some real numbers a, b, and c. Plugging in a_1, a_2, and a_3, we get

$$a + b + c = 1440,$$
$$4a + 2b + c = 1716,$$
$$9a + 3b + c = 1848.$$

Solving the system of equations, we get $a = -72$, $b = 492$ and $c = 1020$. Therefore,

$$a_8 = -72 \cdot 8^2 + 492 \cdot 8 + 1020 = \boxed{348}.$$

Solution to 5.11 We see that after every nine terms, the next term is generated by adding a leading digit "1" to this ninth term. So after 9 it is 19; after 99 it is 199, and so on. Thus the number of digits of a term is increased by 1 after every nine terms. Since $100 = 9 \cdot 11 + 1$, the 100th term has $11 + 1 = \boxed{12}$ digits.

Solution to 5.12 Note that for all n, $(n+1)^2 - (n+1) + 1 = n^2 + n + 1$. we can use this identity to cancel infinitely many terms in the given infinite product.

$$\prod_{n=2}^{\infty} \frac{n^3-1}{n^3+1} = \prod_{n=2}^{\infty} \frac{(n-1)(n^2+n+1)}{(n+1)(n^2-n+1)}$$
$$= \frac{1 \cdot 7}{3 \cdot 3} \cdot \frac{2 \cdot 13}{4 \cdot 7} \cdot \frac{3 \cdot 21}{5 \cdot 13} \cdot \frac{4 \cdot 31}{6 \cdot 21} \cdots = \boxed{\frac{2}{3}}.$$

Solution to 5.13 Since each number is either a power of 3 or is the sum of distinct powers of 3, we see that, when we represent the sequence in base 3, the numbers of the sequence have a one-to-one correspondence with those ternary numbers whose digits are either 1 or 0. Consequently, the numbers of the sequence have a one-to-one correspondence with all the binary numbers. That is, the 100th term of the sequence is the one whose ternary representation is the same as the binary representation of 100. Since $100_{10} = 1100100_2$, the 100th term of sequence is

$$1100100_3 = 3^6 + 3^5 + 3^2 = \boxed{981}.$$

Solution to 5.14 When we write out the first a few terms of the sequence, we have

$$4, 7, 1, 8, 9, 7, 6, 3, 9, 2, 1, 3, 4, 7, \ldots$$

Thus the sequence has a period of 12 and a sum of

$$4+7+1+8+9+7+6+3+9+2+1+3 = 60$$

for every 12 terms. Since $10,000 = 166 \cdot 60 + 40$, and $166 \cdot 12 = 1992$, we have

$$S_{1992} = 60 \cdot 166 = 9960.$$

Since $S_{1998} = 9960 + 4 + 7 + 1 + 8 + 9 + 7 = 9996$ and $S_{1999} = 9996 + 6 > 10,000$, the smallest value of n is $\boxed{1999}$.

Solution to 5.15 Let $a_n = \left(2+\sqrt{3}\right)^n + \left(2-\sqrt{3}\right)^n$. Note that this looks like the closed form of some homogeneous recurrence relation. So we would like to see if we could find such a recurrence relation. Let $\lambda_1 = 2+\sqrt{3}$ and $\lambda_2 = 2-\sqrt{3}$. The equation with λ_1 and λ_2 as roots is $x^2 - 4x + 1 = 0$. So the recurrence relation is $a_{n+2} = 4a_{n+1} - a_n$ with initial conditions $a_0 = 2$ and $a_1 = 4$.

Observing the units digit of a_n starting with $n = 0$, we get 2, 4, 4, 2, 4, 4, ..., which has a period of 3. Since $2016 \equiv 0 \pmod{3}$, the units digit of a_{2016} is the same as that of a_0, which is $\boxed{2}$.

Solution to 5.16 From Problem 5.15, we know that the units digit of the expression $\left(2+\sqrt{3}\right)^{2016} + \left(2-\sqrt{3}\right)^{2016}$ is 2. Since $0 < 2-\sqrt{3} < \frac{1}{2}$,

$$0 < (2-\sqrt{3})^{2016} < \frac{1}{2^{2016}} < \frac{1}{2^{2000}} < \frac{1}{10^{200}}.$$

Solutions for Chapter 5

Thus the units digit of $(2 + \sqrt{3})^{2016}$ must be 1 and the digit immediately to the right of the decimal point must be $\boxed{9}$ so as to make a units digit of 2 after adding a very small positive number.

Solution to 5.17 Note that

$$1 + \frac{1}{n^2} + \frac{1}{(n+1)^2} = \frac{n^4 + 2n^3 + 3n^2 + 2n + 1}{n^2(n+1)^2} = \frac{(n^2 + n + 1)^2}{n^2(n+1)^2} = \left(1 + \frac{1}{n(n+1)}\right)^2.$$

Thus,

$$S = \left(1 + \frac{1}{1 \cdot 2}\right) + \left(1 + \frac{1}{2 \cdot 3}\right) + \cdots + \left(1 + \frac{1}{1999 \cdot 2000}\right)$$

$$= 1999 + \left(1 - \frac{1}{2}\right) + \left(\frac{1}{2} - \frac{1}{3}\right) + \cdots + \left(\frac{1}{1999} - \frac{1}{2000}\right)$$

$$= 1999 + 1 - \frac{1}{2000} = \boxed{\frac{3,999,999}{2000}}.$$

Solution to 5.18 Let $a_1 = a$ and $a_2 = b$. Let's calculate the first a few terms of the sequence:

$$a_3 = \frac{b+1}{a},$$

$$a_4 = \frac{a_3 + 1}{a_2} = \frac{a+b+1}{ab},$$

$$a_5 = \frac{a_4 + 1}{a_3} = \frac{\frac{a+b+1}{ab} + 1}{\frac{b+1}{a}} = \frac{a+1}{b},$$

$$a_6 = \frac{a_5 + 1}{a_4} = \frac{\frac{a+1}{b} + 1}{\frac{a+b+1}{ab}} = a,$$

$$a_7 = \frac{a_6 + 1}{a_5} = \frac{a+1}{\frac{a+1}{b}} = b.$$

We see that the sequence has a period of 5. Thus,

$$a_{2014} = a_4 = \frac{a+b+1}{ab} = \frac{1}{a} + \frac{1}{b} + \frac{1}{ab}.$$

Since a and b are positive integers, a_{2014} has the maximum possible value when $a = b = 1$. Then a_{2014} has the maximum value of $\boxed{3}$.

Solution to 5.19 With partial fraction decomposition, we get

$$\frac{1}{(n+2)^2 + n} = \frac{1}{n^2 + 5n + 4} = \frac{1}{3}\left(\frac{1}{n+1} - \frac{1}{n+4}\right).$$

Therefore,
$$S = \frac{1}{3}\left(\frac{1}{2} - \frac{1}{5} + \frac{1}{3} - \frac{1}{6} + \frac{1}{4} - \frac{1}{7} + \frac{1}{5} - \frac{1}{8} + \cdots\right) = \frac{1}{3}\left(\frac{1}{2} + \frac{1}{3} + \frac{1}{4}\right) = \boxed{\frac{13}{36}}.$$

Solution to 5.20 We have
$$a_{n+1}a_{n-1} = a_n^2 + 2016,$$
$$a_n a_{n-2} = a_{n-1}^2 + 2016.$$

Subtracting the two equations, we get
$$a_{n-1}(a_{n+1} + a_{n-1}) = a_n(a_n + a_{n-2}),$$
$$\frac{a_{n+1} + a_{n-1}}{a_n} = \frac{a_n + a_{n-2}}{a_{n-1}}.$$

That is, $\frac{a_{n+1} + a_{n-1}}{a_n}$ is an invariant. Since $a_0 = a_1 = 3$, $a_2 a_0 = a_1^2 + 2016$, we have $a_2 = 675$. Next we show that $a_0, a_1, a_2, \ldots$ is an increasing sequence. We see that $a_2 > a_1$. Given $a_n > a_{n-1}$, since $a_{n+1}a_{n-1} = a_n^2 + 2016$, we have

$$a_{n+1} = \frac{a_n^2}{a_{n-1}} + \frac{2016}{a_{n-1}} = a_n\left(\frac{a_n}{a_{n-1}}\right) + \frac{2016}{a_{n-1}} > a_n.$$

Because $\frac{a_{n+1} + a_{n-1}}{a_n}$ is an invariant,

$$\frac{a_{n+1} + a_{n-1}}{a_n} = \frac{a_2 + a_0}{a_1} = \frac{675 + 3}{3} = 226, \qquad a_{n+1} = 226 a_n - a_{n-1}.$$

Combining the results, we see that $a_{n+1} = 226 a_n - a_{n-1} > 226 a_n - a_n = 225 a_n$. Therefore, $a_n \geq 2016$ for all $n \geq 3$ because $a_3 > 225 a_2 > 2016$. Thus,

$$\frac{a_{2015}^2 + a_{2016}^2}{a_{2015} \cdot a_{2016}} = \frac{a_{2016}}{a_{2015}} + \frac{a_{2015}}{a_{2016}} = \frac{226 a_{2015} - a_{2014}}{a_{2015}} + \frac{a_{2015}}{a_{2016}}$$
$$= 226 + \frac{a_{2015}^2 - a_{2014} a_{2016}}{a_{2015} \cdot a_{2016}} = 226 - \frac{2016}{a_{2015} \cdot a_{2016}}.$$

Since $a_n \geq 2016$ for all $n \geq 3$, $\frac{2016}{a_{2015} \cdot a_{2016}} < 1$. So the largest integer that does not exceed $\frac{a_{2015}^2 + a_{2016}^2}{a_{2015} \cdot a_{2016}}$ is $\boxed{225}$.

Solutions for Chapter 6

Solution to 6.1 Plugging $x = y = 1$ in the original equation, we get $f(2) = 4(f(1))^2$. Plugging $x = 1$ and $y = 2$ in the original equation, we get

$$32 = f(3) = 4f(1) \cdot f(2) = 16(f(1))^3, \qquad f(1) = \boxed{\sqrt[3]{2}}.$$

Solution to 6.2 The original equation can be written as

$$f\left(\frac{x+1}{x}\right) = x - \frac{1}{x} + \frac{1}{1 + \frac{1}{x}}.$$

Letting $y = \frac{x+1}{x}$, we get $yx = x+1$, $x = \frac{1}{y-1}$. Plugging it into the equation above, we have

$$f(y) = \frac{1}{y-1} - (y-1) + \frac{1}{y} = \frac{-y^3 + 2y^2 + y - 1}{y^2 - y}.$$

Replacing y by x, we get

$$\boxed{f(x) = \frac{-x^3 + 2x^2 + x - 1}{x^2 - x}}.$$

Solution to 6.3 Since $2002 = 2048 - 46 = 2^{11} - 46$, we have $f(2002) + f(46) = 11^2$. Since $46 = 64 - 18$, we have $f(46) + f(18) = 6^2$. Since $18 = 32 - 14$, we have $f(18) + f(14) = 5^2$. Since $14 = 16 - 2$, we have $f(14) + f(2) = 4^2$. Letting $a = b = 2$ in the original equation, we get $2f(2) = 2^2$. So $f(2) = 2$. Now

$$f(14) = 4^2 - 2 = 14, \qquad f(18) = 25 - 14 = 11,$$
$$f(46) = 36 - 11 = 25, \qquad f(2002) = 121 - 25 = \boxed{96}.$$

Solution to 6.4

$$f(5,2) = 5 + f(4,3) = 5 + 4 + f(3,1) = 5 + 4 + 3 + f(2,2) = 5 + 4 + 3 + 2 + f(1,0) = \boxed{19}.$$

Solution to 6.5 Plugging $x = 1$ in the second equation, we get $f(1) = \frac{1}{2}$. Notice that for any positive integer n,

$$f(2^n) = 2f(2^{n-1}) = 2^2 f(2^{n-2}) = \cdots = 2^n f(1) = 2^{n-1}.$$

Similarly,

$$2^n f(\frac{1}{2^n}) = 2^{n-1} f(\frac{1}{2^{n-1}}) = \cdots = 2^{n-n} f(\frac{1}{2^{n-n}}) = f(1) = 2^{-1}.$$

So we have $f(2^{-n}) = 2^{-n-1}$. But from the second given equation, we also have $f(2^{-n}) = 1 - f(2^n) = 1 - 2^{-n-1}$. Thus,

$$2^{-n-1} = 1 - 2^{-n-1}.$$

But, no positive integer n satisfies the equation above. Thus $\boxed{\text{no such function}}$ exists.

Solution to 6.6 Let c be the constant term of $P(x)$. Since $P(x)$ is an odd function, $P(-0) = c = -P(0) = -c$. So $c = 0$. So $P(x) = xP_1(x)$ for some polynomial $P_1(x)$ and the sum of the coefficients of $P_1(x)$ is the same as the sum of the coefficients of $P(x)$. That is, $P_1(1) = P(1) = 1988$. Now

$$P(-x) = (-x)P_1(-x) = -P(x) = -xP_1(x), \qquad P_1(-x) = P_1(x).$$

So $P_1(x)$ is an even function and $P_1(1) = P_1(-1) = 1988$. Let $P_1(x) = Q(x)(x^2 - 1) + ax + b$. Then

$$P_1(1) = a + b = 1988,$$
$$P_1(-1) = -a + b = 1988.$$

So $a = 0$ and $b = 1988$. Therefore, $P(x) = xP_1(x) = Q(x)(x^3 - x) + 1988x$. The remainder when $P(x)$ is divided by $x^3 - x$ is $\boxed{1988x}$.

Solution to 6.7 Let n be the degree of f. Then $f(x^2)$ has degree $2n$, $(f(x))^2$ has degree $2n$, and $f(f(x))$ has degree n^2. Since $n \geq 1$, $2n = n^2$ gives us $n = 2$. So $f(x) = ax^2 + bx + c$ for some constants a, b, and c, where $a \neq 0$. Now

$$f(x^2) = ax^4 + bx^2 + c = (ax^2 + bx + c)^2 = a^2x^4 + 2abx^3 + 2acx^2 + b^2x^2 + 2bcx + c^2.$$

Comparing the coefficients, we get $a^2 = a$, $b^2 + 2ac = b$, and $ab = 0$. Since $a \neq 0$, $a = 1$ and $b = 0$. Then we have $c = 0$. Therefore, only $\boxed{1}$ function, namely, $f(x) = x^2$, satisfies the given equation.

Solution to 6.8 If $P(x)$ is an nth degree polynomial, then $P(x+1) - P(x)$ has degree $n-1$. Since $P(x+1) - P(x)$ is a quadratic polynomial, $P(x) = ax^3 + bx^2 + cx + d$ for some real numbers a, b, c, and d. Therefore,

$$a(x+1)^3 - ax^3 + b(x+1)^2 - bx^2 + c(x+1) - cx + d - d = 3x^2 + 3x + 1,$$
$$3ax^2 + (3a + 2b)x + a + b + c = 3x^2 + 3x + 1.$$

Comparing the coefficients, we get $a = 1$, $b = c = 0$, and d can be any real number. Therefore, $\boxed{P(x) = x^3 + \text{a constant}}$.

Solutions for Chapter 6

Solution to 6.9 We see that

$$f(94) = 94^2 - f(93) = 94^2 - 93^2 + f(92)$$
$$= 94^2 - 93^2 + 92^2 - 91^2 + \cdots + 20^2 - f(19)$$
$$= (94 + 93 + \cdots + 21) + 20^2 - 94 = \frac{94 + 21}{2} \cdot 74 + 306 = 4561.$$

When 4561 is divided by 1000, the remainder is $\boxed{561}$.

Solution to 6.10 Let $d = P(1) - P(0)$. We can rewrite the original equation as

$$P(x+1) - P(x) = P(x) - P(x-1).$$

In particular, for any positive integer n, we have

$$P(n) = P(n) - P(n-1) + P(n-1) - P(n-2) + \cdots + P(1) - P(0) + P(0) = d \cdot n + P(0).$$

Let $Q(x) = P(x) - dx - P(0)$. Since every positive integer is its root, $Q(x)$ is a constant function. So $P(x) = dx + c$ for some constant c and the degree of $P(x)$ is $\boxed{1}$.

Solution to 6.11 The given equation is $f(x) + f\left(\frac{x-1}{x}\right) = 1 - x$. Replacing x with $\frac{x-1}{x}$ in the original equation, we get

$$f\left(\frac{x-1}{x}\right) + f\left(-\frac{1}{x-1}\right) = \frac{1}{x}.$$

Replacing x with $-\frac{1}{x-1}$ in the original equation, we get

$$f\left(-\frac{1}{x-1}\right) + f(x) = 1 + \frac{1}{x-1}.$$

Adding all these three equations together and dividing by 2, we get

$$f(x) + f\left(\frac{x-1}{x}\right) + f\left(-\frac{1}{x-1}\right) = 1 - \frac{x}{2} + \frac{1}{2x} + \frac{1}{2x-2}.$$

Therefore,

$$f(x) = 1 - \frac{x}{2} + \frac{1}{2x} + \frac{1}{2x-2} - f\left(\frac{x-1}{x}\right) - f\left(-\frac{1}{x-1}\right) = 1 - \frac{x}{2} + \frac{1}{2x} + \frac{1}{2x-2} - \frac{1}{x}.$$

Thus, $\boxed{f(x) = \frac{-x^3 + 3x^2 - 2x + 1}{2x^2 - 2x}}$.

Solution to 6.12 Letting $x = -1$, we get $-1 \cdot f(-2) = 0$. So -2 is a root of $f(x)$. Letting $x = -2$, we get $-2f(-3) = 0$ because $f(-2) = 0$. So -3 is a root of $f(x)$. Repeating the process, we see that $f(x)$ has infinitely many roots $-2, -3, -4, \ldots$. So

$f(x)$ is a constant polynomial and $f(x) = c$ for some constant c. Now $x \cdot c = (x+1) \cdot c$ gives us $c = 0$. Therefore, $\boxed{f(x) = 0}$.

Solution to 6.13 Letting $m = n = 1$, we get $f(1) = (f(1))^2$. Since f is a function from positive integers to positive integers, we have $f(1) = 1$. Note that $f(2) = 2$. Now suppose there is a positive integer k such that for all $1, 2, ..., 2k$, we have $f(n) = n$ for all positive integer $n \le k$. Then when $n = 2k + 2$, we get

$$f(2k+2) = f(2) \cdot f(k+1) = 2(k+1) = 2k+2.$$

Since f is strictly increasing, $f(2k) = 2k$ and $f(2k+2) = 2k+2$, we must have $f(2k+1) = 2k+1$. Therefore by induction, for all $n \in \mathbb{Z}^+$, $\boxed{f(n) = n}$.

Solution to 6.14 We have

$$P_n(x) = P_{n-1}(x-n) = P_{n-2}(x-n-(n-1)) = \cdots$$
$$= P_0(x-n-(n-1)-\cdots-2-1) = P_0\left(x - \frac{1}{2}n(n+1)\right).$$

So $P_{20}(x) = P_0\left(x - \frac{1}{2} \cdot 20 \cdot 21\right) = P_0(x-210) = (x-210)^3 + 313(x-210)^2 - 77(x-210) - 8$. Thus the coefficient of x is $3(210)^2 - 313 \cdot 2 \cdot 210 - 77 = \boxed{763}$.

Solution to 6.15 We need to reduce $f(14, 52)$ to something of the form $f(x, x)$. By using $(x+y)f(x, y) = yf(x, x+y)$ repeatedly, we get

$$f(14, 52) = f(14, 14 + 38) = \frac{52}{38} f(14, 38)$$
$$= \frac{52}{38} f(14, 14 + 24) = \frac{52}{24} f(14, 24) = \frac{52}{10} f(10, 14)$$
$$= \frac{52}{10} \cdot \frac{14}{4} f(4, 10) = \frac{91}{5} f(4, 10) = \frac{91}{3} f(4, 6)$$
$$= 91 f(2, 4) = 91 \cdot 2 f(2, 2) = 91 \cdot 2 \cdot 2 = \boxed{364}.$$

Solution to 6.16 Letting $y = 1$, we get $f(x) = xf(x) + f(1)$. Thus $(1-x)f(x) = f(1)$. Letting $x = 1$, we see that $f(1) = 0$. When $x \ne 1$, $f(x) = \frac{f(1)}{1-x}$. So $f(x) = 0$ for all $x \ne 1$. Combining the two cases, we see that $\boxed{f(x) = 0}$ for all $x \in \mathbb{R}$.

Solution to 6.17 Since for all n, $f(2n) = f(n)$ and $f(2n+1) = f(n) + 1$, we see by induction that $f(n)$ is the $\boxed{\text{sum of the digits of } n \text{ in base 2}}$.

Solution to 6.18 Let's use $f^{(k)}(n)$ to represent $f(f(\cdots(f(n))\cdots))$, where there are k f's. Then the original equation can be written as $f^{(1)}(n) - n = 2(f^{(2)}(n) - f^{(1)}(n))$. Replacing n with $f(n)$, we get $f^{(2)}(n) - f^{(1)}(n)) = 2(f^{(3)}(n) - f^{(2)}(n))$. Similarly,

$$f^{(1)}(n) - n = 2(f^{(2)}(n) - f^{(1)}(n)) = 2^2(f^{(3)}(n) - f^{(2)}(n))$$
$$= \cdots = 2^k(f^{(k+1)}(n) - f^{(k)}(n)) = \cdots.$$

Since each expression $f^{(k+1)}(n) - f^{(k)}(n)$ is an integer, 2^k must divide $f^{(1)}(n) - n$ evenly for all k. This is possible only when $f^{(1)}(n) - n = 0$. Thus $\boxed{f(n) = n}$ for all n.

Solution to 6.19 We first prove the following statement (S): for any positive integers m and n, if $m \geq n$, then $f(m) \geq n$. Clearly S is true when $n = 1$. Suppose it is true when $n = k$. That is, for positive integers m and k such that $m \geq k$, we have $f(m) \geq k$. Now when $m \geq k+1$, $m-1 \geq k$. So $f(m-1) \geq k$ and $f(f(m-1)) \geq k$ by our induction hypothesis. Thus, $f(m) > f(f(m-1)) \geq k$. So $f(m) \geq k+1$. Therefore by induction, the statement S is true for all positive integers m and n.

In particular, when we let $m = n$, we get that $f(n) \geq n$ for all n. Thus,

$$f(n+1) > f(f(n)) \geq f(n).$$

That is, $f(n)$ is a strictly increasing function. Next we show that $f(n) = n$ for all n using proof by contradiction. Suppose there were a k such that $f(k) \neq k$. Then $f(k) \geq k+1$ and $f(f(k)) \geq f(k+1)$ because f is a strictly increasing function. Thus,

$$f(k+1) > f(f(k)) \geq f(k+1).$$

Since the above inequality is impossible, we have $\boxed{f(n) = n}$ for all n.

Solution to 6.20 First we show that f is injective. This is true because if $f(n_1) = f(n_2)$, then

$$f(f(n_1)) = f(f(n_2)), \qquad n_1 + 1987 = n_2 + 1987, \qquad n_1 = n_2.$$

Since $f(f(\mathbb{N}))$ contains all the positive integers greater than or equal to 1987, the set $\mathbb{N} - f(f(\mathbb{N})) = \{0, 1, 2, \ldots, 1986\}$ is a finite set. So its subset $\mathbb{N} - f(\mathbb{N})$ is also a finite set. Suppose that $\mathbb{N} - f(\mathbb{N})$ has r distinct elements $k_1, k_2, \ldots, k_r$. Now let's consider $f(k_1), f(k_2), \ldots, f(k_r)$. These r elements are distinct because f is injective. We see that for each $1 \leq i \leq r$, $f(k_i) \notin f(f(\mathbb{N}))$ because $k_i \notin f(\mathbb{N})$. Thus for each $k_i \in \mathbb{N} - f(\mathbb{N})$, we have $f(k_i) \in f(\mathbb{N}) - f(f(\mathbb{N}))$. That is, $f(\mathbb{N} - f(\mathbb{N})) \subseteq f(\mathbb{N}) - f(f(\mathbb{N}))$.

On the other hand, if $f(a) \in f(\mathbb{N}) - f(f(\mathbb{N}))$ for some $a \in \mathbb{N}$, then for any $b \in \mathbb{N}$, $f(a) \neq f(f(b))$. Note that $f(a) \neq f(f(b))$ implies $a \neq f(b)$. Thus $a \in \mathbb{N} - f(\mathbb{N})$ and $f(a) \in f(\mathbb{N} - f(\mathbb{N}))$. That is, $f(\mathbb{N}) - f(f(\mathbb{N})) \subseteq f(\mathbb{N} - f(\mathbb{N}))$.

Combining our results, we see that $f(\mathbb{N} - f(\mathbb{N})) = f(\mathbb{N}) - f(f(\mathbb{N}))$, and f is a one-to-one correspondence from $\mathbb{N} - f(\mathbb{N})$ to $f(\mathbb{N}) - f(f(\mathbb{N}))$. So $\mathbb{N} - f(f(\mathbb{N}))$, the union of the two disjoint sets $\mathbb{N} - f(\mathbb{N})$ and $f(\mathbb{N}) - f(f(\mathbb{N}))$, has $r + r = 2r$ elements. But the set $\mathbb{N} - f(f(\mathbb{N})) = \{0, 1, 2, \ldots, 1986\}$ has an odd number of elements, a contradiction. Therefore, $\boxed{\text{no such } f \text{ exists}}$.

Solutions for Chapter 7

Solution to 7.1 Without loss of generality, let $AB = 1$. Then EI, the height of the equilateral triangle BCE, is $\frac{\sqrt{3}}{2}$. So

$$EG = EI - GI = \frac{\sqrt{3}}{2} - (1 - \frac{\sqrt{3}}{2}) = \sqrt{3} - 1.$$

Since EG is a diagonal of square $EFGH$, the side length EF of the square $EFGH$ is $\frac{\sqrt{3}-1}{\sqrt{2}}$. Therefore,

$$\frac{[EFGH]}{[ABCD]} = \left(\frac{\sqrt{3}-1}{\sqrt{2}}\right)^2 = \boxed{2 - \sqrt{3}}.$$

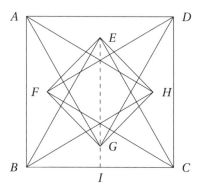

Solution to 7.2 Let the side length of the square be x. We see that

$$\triangle AXW \sim \triangle WBZ \sim \triangle ZYC \sim \triangle ABC.$$

So $AX = \frac{3}{4}x$ and $YC = \frac{4}{3}x$. Therefore,

$$\frac{3}{4}x + x + \frac{4}{3}x = 5. \quad \text{So} \quad x = \boxed{\frac{60}{37}}.$$

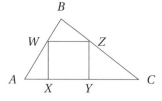

Solution to 7.3 Let the width and the height of the central rectangle be x and y, respectively.

Solutions for Chapter 7

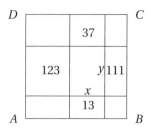

Without loss of generality, we can move the three rectangles at the top underneath the three rectangles at the bottom, as shown in the left diagram below. Next, we can move the right most rectangles to the left of the left most rectangles, as shown in the right diagram below. Now we have

$$(23 - x) \cdot y = 234,$$
$$x \cdot (23 - y) = 50.$$

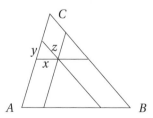

So $23(y-x) = 184$, $y = x+8$. Thus, $x \cdot (15-x) = 50$, $x = 5$ or $x = 10$. We see that $x = 10$ gives us the largest possible value of xy. The largest area is $10 \cdot (10+8) = \boxed{180}$.

Solution to 7.4 Note that these three smaller triangles are all similar to $\triangle ABC$ because they have the same angle measures. Let x, y, and z be the lengths of the three sides of the triangle with area 1. We see that the triangle with area 4 has three corresponding sides with lengths $2x$, $2y$, and $2z$. Similarly, the triangle with area 9 has three corresponding sides with lengths $3x$, $3y$, and $3z$. Thus $AC = 3y + y + 2y = 6y$ and $AB = x + 3x + 2x = 6x$. So $[ABC] = 6^2 \cdot 1 = \boxed{36}$.

Solution to 7.5 We will use $[ABC] = \frac{1}{2}ab\sin \angle C$ to solve this problem. Since $AX = \frac{3}{4}AB$, $AZ = \frac{1}{6}AC$, and $\triangle ABC$ and $\triangle AXZ$ share a common angle, $\angle A$,

$$[AXZ] = \frac{3}{4} \cdot \frac{1}{6}[ABC] = \frac{1}{8}[ABC].$$

Similarly, $BX = \frac{1}{4}AB$, $BY = \frac{4}{5}BC$, and we have $[BYX] = \frac{1}{5}[ABC]$. Also $YC = \frac{1}{5}BC$, $ZC = \frac{5}{6}AC$, so $[ZYC] = \frac{1}{6}[ABC]$. Therefore,

$$[XYZ] = [ABC] - \frac{1}{8}[ABC] - \frac{1}{5}[ABC] - \frac{1}{6}[ABC] = 240 - 30 - 48 - 40 = \boxed{122}.$$

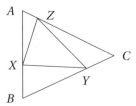

Solution to 7.6 Let $E = (x, y)$. First, we use Pick's Theorem to find the area of quadrilateral $ABCD$. We have 5 interior "horses" and 7 "fenceposts", so $[ABCD] = \frac{1}{2} \cdot 7 + 5 - 1 = \frac{15}{2}$. So $[ADE] = \frac{15}{4} = \frac{1}{2} \cdot y \cdot AD$. Since $AD = 4$, we have $y = \frac{15}{8}$.

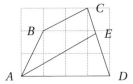

The equation of line CD is $y = -3(x - 4)$. Plugging in $y = \frac{15}{8}$, we have

$$\frac{15}{8} = -3(x-4). \quad \text{So} \quad x = \frac{27}{8}.$$

Since $\gcd(27, 8) = 1$ and $\gcd(15, 8) = 1$, $p + q + r + s = 27 + 8 + 15 + 8 = \boxed{58}$.

Solution to 7.7 Let D be the midpoint of BC. We see that $D = (0.5, -0.5)$. Since $\triangle ABC$ is isosceles with $AB = AC$, A' is on the extension of line segment AD and $A'D = DA$. Let $A' = (x, y)$. Since D is the midpoint of AA', we have

$$0.5 = \frac{1}{2}(x+2),$$
$$-0.5 = \frac{1}{2}(y+7).$$

So $A' = (-1, -8)$ and the slope of $A'C$ is $\frac{7}{4}$. After two more reflections, we see that $\triangle A''CB'$ is a reflection of $\triangle ACB$ over line $A'C$. Therefore, $A''A \perp A'C$. So the slope of $A''A$ is $\boxed{-\frac{4}{7}}$.

Solutions for Chapter 7

Solution to 7.8 We use the Shoelace Theorem to solve this problem. We have

$$[ABCD] = \frac{1}{2}|(1\cdot 11 + 1\cdot 4 + 8\cdot 4 + 4\cdot 7) - (1\cdot 7 + 8\cdot 11 + 4\cdot 4 + 1\cdot 4)| = \boxed{20}.$$

Solution to 7.9 Since $\triangle ABC$ is scalene, $BC \neq 9$ and $BC \neq 6$. By the Law of Cosines, $\triangle ABC$ is acute if and only if for any sides x, y, and z, $x^2 + y^2 > z^2$. Since $\sqrt{9^2 + 6^2} < 11$, $BC < 11$. Since $\sqrt{9^2 - 6^2} > 6$, $BC > 6$. So the possible positive integer side lengths of BC are 7, 8, and 10. Their sum is $\boxed{25}$.

Solution to 7.10 Since $\sin 15° = \frac{\sqrt{6}-\sqrt{2}}{4}$ and $\cos 15° = \frac{\sqrt{6}+\sqrt{2}}{4}$, we have

$$\tan 15° = \frac{\sin 15°}{\cos 15°} = \frac{\sqrt{6}-\sqrt{2}}{\sqrt{6}+\sqrt{2}} = 2 - \sqrt{3}.$$

Therefore, $EC = BC \tan 15° = 20 - 10\sqrt{3}$ and $DE = 20 - EC = 10\sqrt{3}$. By the Pythagorean Theorem,

$$AE = \sqrt{AD^2 + DE^2} = \sqrt{100 + 300} = \boxed{20}.$$

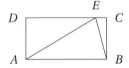

Solution to 7.11 Let $CD = x$ and $BC = y$. Let C be the origin $(0,0)$. We have $A = (\sqrt{11}, y)$, $B = (0, y)$, and $D = (x, 0)$. The slope of line AC is $\frac{y}{\sqrt{11}}$ and the slope of line BD is $-\frac{y}{x}$. Since $AC \perp BD$, we have

$$\frac{y}{\sqrt{11}} \cdot \left(-\frac{y}{x}\right) = -1.$$

So $y^2 = x\sqrt{11}$. By the Pythagorean Theorem, we have

$$y^2 + (x - \sqrt{11})^2 = 1001,$$
$$x\sqrt{11} + x^2 - 2x\sqrt{11} - 990 = 0,$$
$$(x - 10\sqrt{11})(x + 9\sqrt{11}) = 0.$$

So $x = 10\sqrt{11}$. Therefore, $BC^2 = y^2 = x\sqrt{11} = \boxed{110}$.

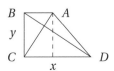

Solution to 7.12 We reflect point A over line $y = 5$ and get point $A' = (0, 10)$. Similarly, we reflect point B over line $x = 6$ and get point $B' = (8, -5)$. The original problem is equivalent to finding the shortest distance between A' and B'. Since the straight line gives us the shortest distance between two points, we see the shortest distance has length $A'B' = \sqrt{8^2 + 15^2} = \boxed{17}$.

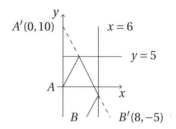

Solution to 7.13 Let x be the distance from the tip of the angle to the second vertical line. Let y be the distance between two adjacent parallel lines. Since the ratio of the areas of two similar triangles is equal to the square of the ratio of the lengths of the corresponding sides (heights) of the two triangles, we have

$$\frac{(x+4y)^2 - (x+3y)^2}{(x+2y)^2 - (x+y)^2} = \frac{11}{5},$$

$$\frac{2x+7y}{2x+3y} = \frac{11}{5}.$$

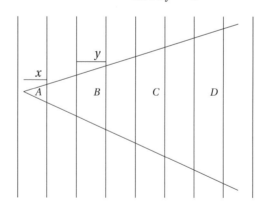

Therefore, $y = 6x$. The ratio we need to find is:

$$\frac{(x+6y)^2 - (x+5y)^2}{x^2} = \frac{y(2x+11y)}{x^2} = 6 \cdot 68 = \boxed{408}.$$

Solution to 7.14 Since no matter where the bridge is located, it always takes 1 km to go across the bridge, let's ignore this distance and treat the river as a line with

Solutions for Chapter 7

no width. Then the shortest distance is $\sqrt{3^2 + 4^2} = 5$, when the route is a straight line. Adding back the 1 km bridge, we get that the shortest distance is $\boxed{6 \text{ km}}$.

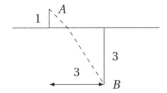

Solution to 7.15 We construct an equilateral triangle FDB as shown. Since $FD = BD$, $ED = CD$, and $m\angle FDE = 60° - m\angle EDB = m\angle BDC$, $\triangle FDE \cong \triangle BDC$ by SAS. Therefore $FE = BC = AB$. Since $m\angle ABC = 120°$ and $m\angle FBD = 60°$, $m\angle ABF + m\angle DBC = 60°$. We see that $m\angle BFE = 60° - m\angle DFE = 60° - m\angle DBC = m\angle ABF$, so $FE \parallel AB$. Since $FE = AB$, $FEBA$ is a parallelogram, and $\triangle AGB \cong \triangle EGF$. Thus, $[ABCDE] = [FDB] = \frac{1}{2} \cdot 2 \cdot \sqrt{3} = \boxed{\sqrt{3}}$.

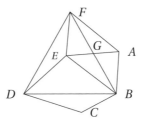

Solution to 7.16 Point P divides the square into four rectangles as shown. By the Pythagorean Theorem, we have

$$a^2 + c^2 = 1,$$
$$a^2 + d^2 = 25,$$
$$b^2 + d^2 = 49.$$

Since $2 \cdot 25 = 1 + 49$, we have

$$2a^2 + 2d^2 = a^2 + c^2 + b^2 + d^2,$$
$$d^2 - c^2 = b^2 - a^2,$$
$$(d-c)(d+c) = (b-a)(b+a).$$

Since $a+b = c+d$, we have

$$d - c = b - a,$$
$$d + c = b + a.$$

Therefore, $d = b$ and $a = c$. So $a = c = \frac{\sqrt{2}}{2}$ and $b = d = \frac{7\sqrt{2}}{2}$. Thus, the square has side length $a + b = 4\sqrt{2}$ and its area is $\boxed{32}$.

Solution to 7.17 Since $ABCD$ is a trapezoid, $\triangle CED \sim \triangle AEB$. We see that $\sin \angle CAB = \sin \angle DCE = \frac{4}{5}$. So both $\triangle CED$ and $\triangle AEB$ are 3-4-5 right triangles with

$$CE : DE : DC = AE : BE : BA = 3 : 4 : 5.$$

So we let $CE = 3x$ and $AE = 3y$. Since $AC = 5$, we have $3x + 3y = 5$. So $x + y = \frac{5}{3}$. We see that $DC = 5x$ and $AB = 5y$. Therefore,

$$[ABCD] = \frac{1}{2} \cdot 4(DC + AB) = 2(5x + 5y) = 10 \cdot \frac{5}{3} = \boxed{\frac{50}{3}}.$$

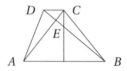

Solution to 7.18 Let H be the midpoint of BD. Since F is the midpoint of DE, $HF \parallel BE$. Since $AB = AC$ and D is the midpoint of BC, we have $AD \perp BC$ and $m\angle BAD = m\angle DAE$. Note that $DE \perp AC$, so $\triangle ABD \sim \triangle ADE$. Since H is the midpoint of BD and F the midpoint of DE, $\triangle ABH \sim \triangle ADF$. So $m\angle BAH = m\angle DAF$. Adding angle $\angle HAD$ to both sides of the previous equation, we get $m\angle BAD = m\angle HAF$. Note that

$$\frac{AB}{AH} = \frac{AD}{AF}.$$

Therefore $\triangle BAD \sim \triangle HAF$. Thus $m\angle AFH = m\angle ADB = 90°$. Since $HF \parallel BE$,

$$m\angle AGE = 180° - m\angle AGB = 180° - m\angle AFH = \boxed{90°}.$$

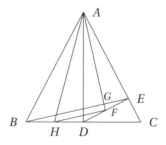

Solution to 7.19 Let F be a point on the extension of AB such that $CF \perp AB$. Similarly, let G be on DE such that $CG \perp DE$. Since $m\angle DCE = 20°$ and $m\angle DEC = 80°$, we have $m\angle EDC = 80°$. So, $EG = GD$. We see that both $\triangle CFB$ and $\triangle CGE$ are $10° - 80° - 90°$ triangles and $BC = 2EC$. Thus,

$$\triangle CFB \sim \triangle CGE \quad \text{and} \quad [CFB] = 4[CGE] = 2[CDE].$$

Therefore,

$$[ABC] + 2[CDE] = [ABC] + [CFB] = [AFC]$$

$$= \frac{1}{2} AF \cdot AC \cdot \sin 60° = \boxed{\frac{\sqrt{3}}{8}}.$$

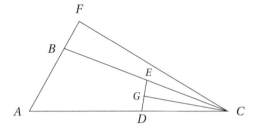

Solution to 7.20 From F, we draw line FH parallel to DA and line FI parallel to CB. Let H and I be the intersection points of FH and FI with line AB, respectively. We see that both $AHFD$ and $IBCF$ are parallelograms. Thus,

$$AH = DF = FC = IB = \frac{1}{2} DC.$$

Since $m\angle DAB + m\angle CBA = 90°$, we have $m\angle FHI + m\angle FIH = 90°$. So $\triangle HFI$ is a right triangle. Since E is the midpoint of AB and $AH = IB$, E is also the midpoint of HI. So

$$EF = \frac{1}{2} HI = \frac{1}{2}(AB - DC) = \frac{1}{2}(20 - 8) = \boxed{6}.$$

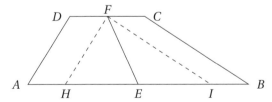

Solution to 7.21 Suppose $AB = a$ and $AC = d$. Let F be the intersection of AC and BD. First, we compute d in terms of a. We see that $AC \parallel DE$ and $BD \parallel EA$. So $AFDE$ is a parallelogram, a rhombus, to be exact. Therefore $BF = BD - FD = d - a$. Note that isosceles triangles $\triangle BCF$ and $\triangle DBC$ share the same angle, $\angle CBF$, so $\triangle BCF \sim \triangle DBC$. Thus,

$$\frac{FB}{BC} = \frac{CD}{DB}, \qquad \frac{d-a}{a} = \frac{a}{d}, \qquad d^2 - ad - a^2 = 0, \qquad d = \frac{1+\sqrt{5}}{2}a.$$

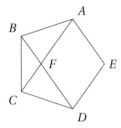

Next we extend BA and DE, and let them meet at G. Since $BG \parallel CE$ and $CA \parallel DG$, $ACEG$ is a parallelogram and a rhombus. So $AG = EG = d$. We extend BM and let it meet DG at point K. Since M is the midpoint of AE and $CA \parallel DG$, $\triangle AZM \cong \triangle EKM$. Thus $EK = ZA = 3$. In triangle BKG, since $ZA \parallel KG$, we have

$$\frac{ZA}{KG} = \frac{BA}{BG}, \qquad \frac{3}{d-3} = \frac{a}{a+d}.$$

Recall that if $\dfrac{a}{b} = \dfrac{c}{d}$, then $\dfrac{a}{b} = \dfrac{a-c}{b-d}$. Thus,

$$\frac{a}{a+d} = \frac{a-3}{(a+d)-(d-3)} = \frac{a-3}{a+3}.$$

Since $d = \dfrac{1+\sqrt{5}}{2}a$, we have

$$\frac{a}{a+d} = \frac{1}{1 + \dfrac{1+\sqrt{5}}{2}} = \frac{2}{3+\sqrt{5}} = \frac{a-3}{a+3}, \qquad (\sqrt{5}+1)a = 15 + 3\sqrt{5}, \qquad a = \boxed{3\sqrt{5}}.$$

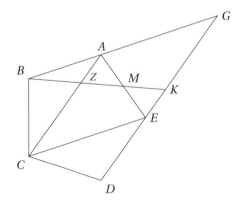

Solutions for Chapter 8

Solution to 8.1 We can rotate the shaded semi-circle with radius 1, the one with diameter PR, 100° counterclockwise to let it fill the unshaded semi-circle with radius 1. As a result, we see that the shaded region is $\frac{360-100}{360}$ th of the circle with radius 2. So its area is

$$\frac{260}{360} \cdot 4\pi = \boxed{\frac{26}{9}\pi}.$$

Solution to 8.2 Since arc $\widehat{AED}$ has its center at B, $AB = DB$. Since $AD = DB = 20$, triangle ABD is an equilateral triangle with side length 20 and its area is $\frac{20^2\sqrt{3}}{4} = 100\sqrt{3}$. So the unshaded region below arc $\widehat{AED}$ and above chord AD has area

$$\frac{60}{360} \cdot 20^2\pi - 100\sqrt{3} = \frac{200\pi}{3} - 100\sqrt{3}. \qquad (*)$$

Since C is the center of arc $\widehat{AFD}$, $AC = DC$. Since $m\angle ACD = 2(m\angle ABD) = 120°$, C is the centroid of $\triangle ABD$ and $CD = \frac{2}{3} \cdot \frac{\sqrt{3}}{2} \cdot 20 = \frac{20\sqrt{3}}{3}$. So the area of triangle ACD is one-third the area of triangle $ABD = \frac{100\sqrt{3}}{3}$. Thus, the area below arc $\widehat{AFD}$ and above chord AD has area

$$\frac{120}{360} \cdot \left(\frac{20\sqrt{3}}{3}\right)^2 \pi - \frac{100\sqrt{3}}{3} = \frac{400}{9}\pi - \frac{100\sqrt{3}}{3}. \qquad (**)$$

Therefore, the shaded region has area $(**) - (*)$, which is

$$\frac{400}{9}\pi - \frac{100\sqrt{3}}{3} - \left(\frac{200\pi}{3} - 100\sqrt{3}\right) = \frac{200\sqrt{3}}{3} - \frac{200\pi}{9} \approx \boxed{46\text{ in}^2}.$$

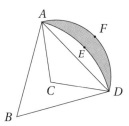

Solution to 8.3 We see that circle O has radius 2 because circle A, which passes through its center, has diameter 2. Let r be the radius of circle B. Let the extension of AO meet BC at D. We see that $AD \perp BC$ and $OB = 2 - r$. By the Pythagorean Theorem, $OD = \sqrt{(2-r)^2 - r^2} = \sqrt{4-4r}$. In right triangle ABD, $AB = 1 + r$. So $AD = \sqrt{(1+r)^2 - r^2} = \sqrt{1+2r}$. Since $AD = AO + OD$, we have

$$\sqrt{1+2r} = 1 + \sqrt{4-4r},$$
$$1 + 2r = 1 + 2\sqrt{4-4r} + 4 - 4r,$$
$$3r - 2 = \sqrt{4-4r},$$
$$9r^2 - 12r + 4 = 4 - 4r,$$
$$r = \boxed{\frac{8}{9}}.$$

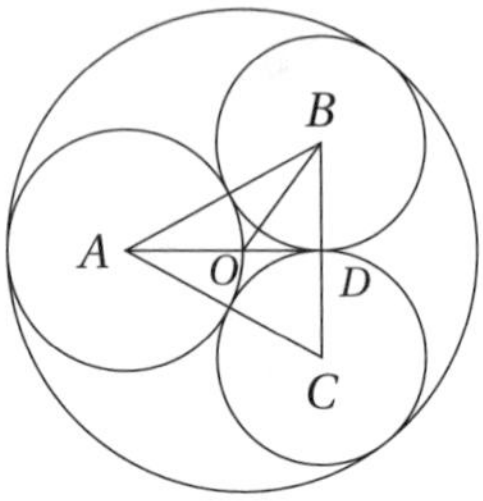

Solution to 8.4 Since AD bisects $\angle BAC$, $\angle BAD = \angle DAC$. So $BD = CD$. By Ptolemy's Theorem, $AC \cdot BD + AB \cdot CD = AD \cdot BC$. Thus,

$$8 \cdot BD + 7 \cdot CD = 9 \cdot AD,$$
$$\frac{AD}{CD} = \boxed{\frac{5}{3}}.$$

Solution to 8.5 Since the cardboard is 6 cm long, we can line up three circles A, B, and C, each 2 cm in diameter, along one edge. As shown in the diagram, to minimize the width of the cardboard, circle D must be tangent to circles A and B, and circle E must be tangent to circles B and C. So the minimum width of the cardboard is 2 times the radius of each circle plus the height of equilateral $\triangle ABD$. That is, the width is

$$2 + \frac{\sqrt{3}}{2} \cdot 2 = \boxed{2 + \sqrt{3} \text{ cm}}.$$

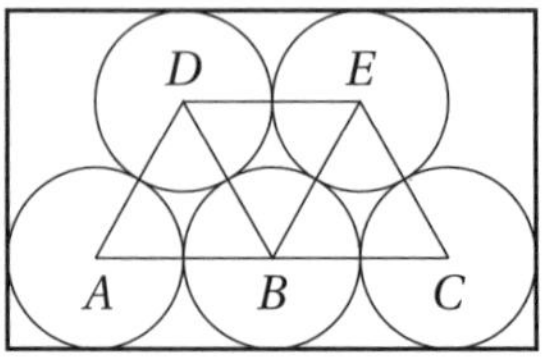

Solutions for Chapter 8

Solution to 8.6 Without loss of generality, let the coordinates of the four vertices of the rectangle be $A = (0,0)$, $B = (4,0)$, $C = (4,3)$, and $D = (0,3)$. Then the intersection of the two diagonals is at point $E = (2, 1.5)$. The diagonal that passes through AC has the equation $y = \frac{3}{4}x$. The center of the circle that passes through AC is on the line perpendicular to AC and through E. The equation of this line is

$$y - 1.5 = -\frac{4}{3}(x-2), \qquad 8x + 6y - 25 = 0.$$

Next we use the Point-Line Distance Formula to calculate the distance from any vertex of the rectangle to the line $8x + 6y - 25 = 0$. We see that vertices B and D give us the least possible distance:

$$\frac{|8 \cdot 4 + 6 \cdot 0 - 25|}{\sqrt{8^2 + 6^2}} = \frac{|8 \cdot 0 + 6 \cdot 3 - 25|}{\sqrt{8^2 + 6^2}} = \boxed{\frac{7}{10}} \text{ in}.$$

Solution to 8.7 Let h be the radius of the circle with center B that is tangent to AC. Since $m\angle ABC = 30°$, the measure of the central angle $\angle AOC$ is $60°$. So, $\triangle OAC$ is an equilateral triangle and $AC = OA = 12$. Thus the area of $\triangle ABC$ is $\frac{1}{2} \cdot 12h = 6h$. The overlapping region of circle B and $\triangle ABC$ has area $\frac{30}{360} \cdot \pi \cdot h^2$. So we must maximize

$$6h - \frac{1}{12}\pi h^2 = -\frac{\pi}{12}\left(h^2 - \frac{12 \cdot 6}{\pi}h\right)$$
$$= -\frac{\pi}{12}\left(h - \frac{36}{\pi}\right)^2 + \frac{3 \cdot 36}{\pi}.$$

This happens when $h = \frac{36}{\pi}$. Then the area of the desired region has a maximum value of

$$0 + \frac{3 \cdot 36}{\pi} = \boxed{\frac{108}{\pi}}.$$

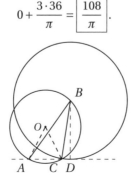

Solution to 8.8 By Power of a Point, $PA \cdot PB = PC \cdot PD$. That is, $2 \cdot 10 = 4 \cdot (4 + CD)$, so $CD = 1$. Since $ABDC$ is a cyclic quadrilateral, $\triangle CDE \sim \triangle ABE$. Since $CD : AB = 1 : 8$, we have $64[CDE] = [ABE]$. Note that $[APD] = \frac{1}{2} AP \cdot PD \cdot \sin \angle P$ and $[CPB] = \frac{1}{2} CP \cdot PB \cdot \sin \angle P$. We have,

$$\frac{[APD]}{[CPB]} = \frac{2 \cdot 5}{4 \cdot 10} = \frac{[CDE] + [PAEC]}{[ABE] + [PAEC]},$$

$$\frac{1}{4} = \frac{\frac{1}{64}[ABE] + [PAEC]}{[ABE] + [PAEC]},$$

$$\frac{[PAEC]}{[ABE]} = \boxed{\frac{5}{16}}.$$

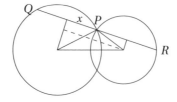

Solution to 8.9 From the centers of the circles, we draw line segments perpendicular to QR. Let $x = \frac{1}{2} PQ$. By the Pythagorean Theorem, we have

$$\sqrt{12^2 - (2x)^2} = \sqrt{8^2 - x^2} - \sqrt{6^2 - x^2},$$
$$12^2 - 4x^2 = 8^2 - x^2 - 2\sqrt{(8^2 - x^2) \cdot (6^2 - x^2)} + 6^2 - x^2,$$
$$x^2 - 22 = \sqrt{(8^2 - x^2) \cdot (6^2 - x^2)},$$
$$x^4 - 44x^2 + 22^2 = x^4 - 10^2 x^2 + 8^2 \cdot 6^2,$$
$$2x^2 = 65.$$

Therefore, $PQ = 2x = \boxed{\sqrt{130}}$.

Solution to 8.10 Since $ABCD$ is a cyclic quadrilateral, $\triangle AXB \sim \triangle CXD$. Since $2AB = CD$, we have

$$2BX = DX = 5 + AX,$$
$$2AX = CX = 11 + BX.$$

Solutions for Chapter 8

So $AX = 9$ and $BX = 7$. By Heron's Formula,

$$[XAB] = \sqrt{10(10-9)(10-7)(10-4)} = \boxed{6\sqrt{5}}.$$

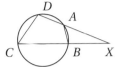

Solution to 8.11 Let C be a point on OD such that $AC \perp OD$. We see that $CD = 1 - \frac{\sqrt{3}}{2}$ because $\triangle OAC$ is a $30°-60°-90°$ triangle. Let's use R to denote the region bounded by AC, CD, and arc $\widehat{AD}$. We have

$$[R] = \frac{30}{360}\pi - \frac{1}{2} \cdot \frac{1}{2} \cdot \frac{\sqrt{3}}{2} = \frac{\pi}{12} - \frac{\sqrt{3}}{8}.$$

We need to find the length OX such that $[OBX] + [AXC] + [R] = \frac{1}{8}\pi$. That is,

$$\frac{1}{2} \cdot OX \cdot 1 + \frac{1}{2} \cdot \frac{1}{2}\left(\frac{\sqrt{3}}{2} - OX\right) + \frac{\pi}{12} - \frac{\sqrt{3}}{8} = \frac{\pi}{8},$$

$$\frac{OX}{4} = \frac{\pi}{8} - \frac{\pi}{12}, \qquad OX = \boxed{\frac{\pi}{6}}.$$

Solution to 8.12 Let's connect F and P. Since $m\angle PAF = m\angle PDF = 45°$, $APFD$ is cyclic. So $m\angle APF = 90°$. Thus, $\triangle APF$ is a $45°-45°-90°$ triangle and $AF = AP\sqrt{2}$. Similarly, we can connect Q and E and see that $\triangle AEQ$ is a $45°-45°-90°$ triangle and $AE = AQ\sqrt{2}$. Since $\triangle APQ$ and $\triangle AEF$ share a common angle, $\angle PAQ$, we have

$$\frac{[AEF]}{[APQ]} = \frac{AE \cdot AF}{AP \cdot AQ} = \frac{AQ\sqrt{2} \cdot AP\sqrt{2}}{AP \cdot AQ} = \boxed{2}.$$

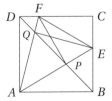

Solution to 8.13 We see that line segment PF divides the right triangle PBC into two smaller right triangles, PBF and PFC. So $m\angle BPF = m\angle BCP$ and $m\angle PBF = m\angle CPF$. Since $ABCD$ is cyclic, $m\angle BCP = m\angle PDE$ and $m\angle PBF = m\angle EAP$. In triangle EPD, we see that $m\angle PDE = m\angle BCP = m\angle BPF = m\angle EPD$. So $\triangle EPD$ is isosceles and $ED = EP$. Similarly, in triangle EAP, we have $m\angle EAP = m\angle PBF = m\angle CPF = m\angle APE$. So $\triangle EAP$ is isosceles and $EA = EP$. Thus,

$$AE = EP = ED = \frac{1}{2}AD = \boxed{3}.$$

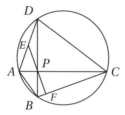

Solution to 8.14 Let O' be the circumcircle of triangle ADE. Since $DA = DB$,

$$m\angle ADB = 180° - 2m\angle DBA = 180° - 2m\angle ACB = m\angle ABC.$$

Since $AEBC$ is cyclic, $m\angle ABC = m\angle AEC = m\angle ADE + m\angle DAE$. Thus, $m\angle ADB = m\angle ADE + m\angle DAE$. So $m\angle EDF = m\angle DAE$. Therefore DF is tangent to circle O'. By Power of a Point, $DF^2 = FE \cdot FA$. Since FB is tangent to circle O, we have $BF^2 = FE \cdot FA$. Therefore, $BF = DF = \frac{1}{2}DB = \boxed{12}$.

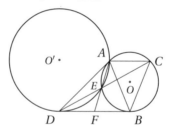

Solution to 8.15 Since $m\angle ABC = 60°$, $m\angle AOC = 180° - \frac{1}{2}m\angle A - \frac{1}{2}m\angle C = 120°$. So $BDOE$ is cyclic. Thus $m\angle OED = m\angle OBD$ and $m\angle ODE = m\angle EBO$. Since O is the incenter of $\triangle ABC$, $m\angle EBO = m\angle OBD = 30°$. Thus $m\angle OED = m\angle ODE$ and $\triangle OED$ is isosceles. Therefore, $OE = OD = \boxed{5}$.

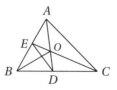

Solutions for Chapter 8

Solution to 8.16 Let E be a point on the extension of BA such that $m\angle ECA = 40°$. Extend BD and let G be its intersection with EC. Extend ED and let F be its intersection with BC. We see that $m\angle AEG = 60°$ and that D is the incenter of $\triangle EBC$. From the solution of 8.15, we see that $AD = DG$. Since $\triangle BCG$ is a $20° - 80° - 80°$ triangle, $BG = BC$. Therefore, $AD = DG = BC - BD = \boxed{y - z}$.

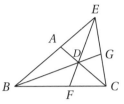

Solution to 8.17 Let $AB = x$ and $AC = y$. We have

$$x^2 + y^2 = 25^2,$$
$$2xy = 2 \cdot 2 \cdot 150.$$

Subtracting the two equations, we get $(x - y)^2 = 25$. Since $AB > AC$, $x = y + 5$. So $(y + 5)y = 300$. Thus $y = 15 = AC$ and $x = 20 = AB$. So s, the semiperimeter of $\triangle ABC$, is 30. Let N be the point of tangency of AB with circle I. From $[ABC] = r \cdot s$, we get the radius of the incircle I is 5. So $BM = \sqrt{5^2 + 20^2} = 5\sqrt{17}$ and $BN = AB - 5 = 15$. By Power of a Point, $BN^2 = BL \cdot BM$. So

$$BL = \frac{15^2}{5\sqrt{17}} = \boxed{\frac{45\sqrt{17}}{17}}.$$

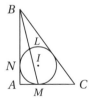

Solution to 8.18 Let I be the incenter of quadrilateral $ABCD$. Let E, F, G, and H be points of tangency of circle I with AB, BC, CD, and DA, respectively.

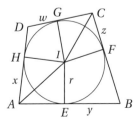

We have

$$x + y = 130, \quad y + z = 110,$$
$$z + w = 70, \quad w + x = 90.$$

Since $ABCD$ is cyclic, $m\angle A + m\angle C = 180°$. Since $AEIH$ is cyclic, $m\angle A + m\angle EIH = 180°$ as well. Thus $m\angle C = m\angle EIH$ and $\triangle AIE \sim \triangle ICF$. So $r^2 = x \cdot z$. Similarly, $r^2 = y \cdot w$. That is, $x \cdot z = y \cdot w$. Solving the following system of equations

$$x + y = 130,$$
$$(110 - y)x = y(90 - x),$$

we get $x = \frac{117}{2}$ and $y = \frac{143}{2}$. Their positive difference is $\boxed{13}$.

Solution to 8.19 Let a be the side length of equilateral $\triangle ABC$. Since $ABPC$ is cyclic, $\triangle CQP \sim \triangle AQB$. So $CP : AB = PQ : QB$. That is, $5 : a = PQ : QB$. Also, $\triangle AQC \sim \triangle BQP$. So $AC : PB = CQ : PQ$. That is, $a : 3 = CQ : PQ$. Since $CQ + QB = a$, we have

$$a = \frac{a \cdot PQ}{5} + \frac{a \cdot PQ}{3},$$
$$PQ = \frac{1}{\frac{1}{5} + \frac{1}{3}} = \boxed{\frac{15}{8}}.$$

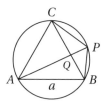

Solution to 8.20 From D, we draw a line parallel to CP. From A, we draw a line parallel to BP. Let P' be the intersection of these two lines. Let E be the intersection of $P'P$ and AD. Since $AD = BC$ and $AD \parallel BC$, we see that $\triangle P'DA \cong \triangle PCB$. So $P'D = PC$ and $P'PCD$ is a parallelogram. Since $DC \perp DA$, $P'P \perp DA$. So $m\angle AEP' = 90°$. Since $m\angle DP'A + m\angle APD = 180°$, $APDP'$ is cyclic. Thus, $m\angle ADP = m\angle AP'P$. Therefore, $m\angle ADP + m\angle PBC = m\angle AP'E + m\angle P'AE = \boxed{90°}$.

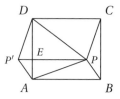

Solutions for Chapter 9

Solution to 9.1 Since any vertex of a regular dodecahedron is associated with three faces, we can glue the open edges together whenever we see that a vertex is connected with three faces already. So A_1 and A_2 are the same vertex. We keep on doing this, treating the glued-together vertices as one vertex. Then we can see that A_3 is the same vertex as A_1 and A_2. Similarly, we can see that B_1, B_2, and B_3 are the same vertex; and that C_1, C_2, and C_3 are the same vertex.

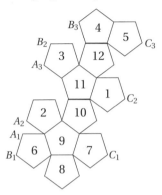

The sum of the numbers adjacent to A_1, A_2, A_3 is $6 + 2 + 3 = 11$. The sum of the numbers adjacent to B_1, B_2, B_3 is $6 + 3 + 4 = 13$. The sum of the numbers adjacent to C_1, C_2, C_3 is $7 + 1 + 5 = 13$. The sums of the numbers adjacent to other vertices are all too big to be the minimum. So, the minimum sum is $\boxed{11}$.

Solution to 9.2 Below are two grids. The grid to the left shows an arrangement that satisfies both views and has the largest possible unit cubes. The grid to the right shows an arrangement that satisfies both views and has the least possible unit cubes. Therefore, $N - n = 26 - 8 = \boxed{18}$.

2	1	2	1	2
1	1	1	1	1
2	1	2	1	2
1	1	1	1	1

0	0	2	0	2
0	0	0	1	0
2	0	0	0	0
0	1	0	0	0

Solution to 9.3 Let's count the blocks with exactly two sides painted one by one.

3	2	2
2	1	1
1	2	3

We see that the following blocks have exactly two sides painted: the bottom and the middle blocks in the "3" pile of the left column, the bottom and the middle blocks in the "3" pile of the right column, the block in the "1" pile of the right column, and the bottom block in the "2" pile of the right column. Therefore, there are $\boxed{6}$ such blocks.

Solution to 9.4 Let r be the radius and O be the center of the sphere. Connect OA, OB, OC, and OD. We see that the tetrahedron is divided into four pyramids with triangular bases ABC, ABD, ACD, and BCD, and with height r. So, the sum of the volumes of the four pyramids is the volume of the tetrahedron.

The volume of the tetrahedron is one-third the area of its base times the height, i.e. $\frac{1}{3} \cdot \frac{1}{2} \cdot 6 \cdot 4 \cdot 2 = 8$. $[ACD] = \frac{1}{2} \cdot 6 \cdot 2 = 6$. $[ABD] = \frac{1}{2} \cdot 6 \cdot 4 = 12$. $[BCD] = \frac{1}{2} \cdot 4 \cdot 2 = 4$. We see that $AB = 2\sqrt{13}$, $BC = 2\sqrt{5}$, $AC = 2\sqrt{10}$. By Heron's Formula, we have

$[ABC]$
$= \sqrt{(\sqrt{13}+\sqrt{10}+\sqrt{5})(\sqrt{10}+\sqrt{5}-\sqrt{13})(\sqrt{13}+\sqrt{10}-\sqrt{5})(\sqrt{13}+\sqrt{5}-\sqrt{10})}$
$= \sqrt{(10\sqrt{2}+2)(10\sqrt{2}-2)} = \sqrt{196} = 14.$

Since a triangular pyramid is a tetrahedron, we have

$$\frac{1}{3}(6+12+4+14)r = 8, \qquad r = \frac{2}{3}.$$

So $m+n = 2+3 = \boxed{5}$.

Solution to 9.5 When folded, the solid has five triangular faces on the top, five triangular faces on the bottom, and five square faces in the middle. So vertex A is the same as vertices A_1 and A_2. By the Pythagorean Theorem, the shortest distance is

$$AB = A_2 B = \sqrt{\left(\frac{1}{2}\right)^2 + \left(1+\frac{\sqrt{3}}{2}\right)^2} = \sqrt{2+\sqrt{3}}$$
$$= \boxed{\frac{\sqrt{6}+\sqrt{2}}{2}}.$$

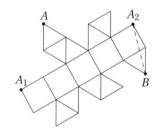

Solutions for Chapter 9

Solution to 9.6 The original solid has $2 \cdot 3 \cdot 4 = 24$ unit cubes. One arrangement to minimize the number of cubes on the top layer and preserve the three views is as follows:

1	1	2
1	1	2
2	1	1
1	2	1

Therefore, at most $\boxed{8}$ unit cubes can be removed.

Solution to 9.7 The three sides of the triangle have lengths 34, 30, and $8\sqrt{13}$. So the four faces of the triangular pyramid are congruent triangles with side lengths 17, 15, and $4\sqrt{13}$.

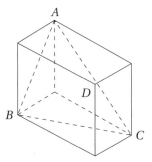

Now look at the triangular pyramid $ABCD$ inside a right rectangular prism as shown. It has four congruent triangular faces. This means that we can embed our pyramid inside a right rectangular prism with three edges a, b, and c satisfying the following equations:

$$a^2 + b^2 = 17^2,$$
$$b^2 + c^2 = 15^2,$$
$$a^2 + c^2 = 16 \cdot 13.$$

Solving this system of equations, we get $a^2 = 136$, $b^2 = 153$, and $c^2 = 72$. We see that the right rectangular prism consists of our embedded pyramid and four congruent pyramids each with a volume of $\frac{1}{6}abc$. Therefore, the volume of our pyramid is

$$abc - 4 \cdot \frac{1}{6}abc = \frac{1}{3}abc = \frac{1}{3}\sqrt{136 \cdot 153 \cdot 72} = \boxed{408}.$$

Solution to 9.8 The triangular prism has a 5-12-13 right triangular base and height 15. So its volume is $\frac{1}{2} \cdot 5 \cdot 12 \cdot 15 = \boxed{450 \text{ cubic units}}$.

Solution to 9.9 A regular octahedron can be considered as two square based pyramids glued together. It has four pairs of parallel faces. When one such pyramid is glued to a tetrahedron, the resulting solid has 5 faces. Note that this solid has two faces, call them F_1 and F_2, that are parallel, where F_1 is from the pyramid and F_2 is from the tetrahedron. Adding a second pyramid, its face, call it F_3, that is parallel to F_1 of the first pyramid has a common edge with face F_2. Since F_2 is parallel to F_3, F_2 and F_3 are coplanar. So the final solid has $5+5-2-1 = \boxed{7 \text{ faces}}$.

Solution to 9.10 We can split the polyhedron into two parts along the thick dashed line. The bottom portion is a regular triangular prism with height 4. Its base is an equilateral triangle with side length 4. So its volume is

$$4 \cdot \frac{4^2 \sqrt{3}}{4} = 16\sqrt{3}.$$

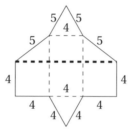

The top portion is wedge-shaped polyhedron with a 3 by 4 rectangular base.

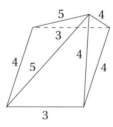

Note that each of the rectangle's sides with length 3 is perpendicular to two sides of the equilateral triangle with side length 4. It is perpendicular to one side because of the 3-4-5 right triangle. It is perpendicular to another side because of the 3 by 4 rectangle. Therefore the dihedral angle between the 3 by 4 rectangular base and the equilateral triangle is 90°. Thus the height of this polyhedron is the height of the equilateral triangle, which is $4\frac{\sqrt{3}}{2} = 2\sqrt{3}$. So the volume of the polyhedron is

$$\frac{1}{3} \cdot 3 \cdot 4 \cdot 2\sqrt{3} = 8\sqrt{3}.$$

Adding the two parts, we see that the total volume of the polyhedron is $16\sqrt{3} + 8\sqrt{3} = \boxed{24\sqrt{3} \text{ in}^3}$.

Solutions for Chapter 9

Solution to 9.11 We see that the intersection of the plane with the tetrahedron is a square with side length 1. It cuts the tetrahedron into two congruent parts. Therefore, the surface area of one of the pieces is one-half the surface area of the tetrahedron plus the area of the square. That is,

$$\frac{1}{2} \cdot 4 \cdot \frac{1}{2} \cdot 2 \cdot \sqrt{3} + 1 \cdot 1 = \boxed{1 + 2\sqrt{3}}.$$

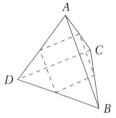

Solution to 9.12 Let's look at the horizontal part of the staircase, disregarding the height of 10 feet for now. When the staircase turns 270°, it goes

$$\frac{270}{360} \cdot 2\pi \cdot \frac{7}{\pi} = \frac{21}{2} \text{ feet}.$$

Since it also rises 10 feet, the length of the handrail is

$$\sqrt{10^2 + \left(\frac{21}{2}\right)^2} = \boxed{\frac{29}{2}} \text{ feet}.$$

Solution to 9.13 Extend AH and BG and let C be the intersection of the two lines. Extend AE and BF and let D be their intersection. We see that $ABCD$ is a regular tetrahedron with side length $2s$. So the volume of our solid is one-half the volume of a tetrahedron with side length $2s$. Since the volume of a tetrahedron with side length s is $\dfrac{s^3 \sqrt{2}}{12}$, the required volume is

$$\frac{1}{2} \cdot \frac{\sqrt{2}}{12} (2s)^3 = \frac{\sqrt{2}}{3} \cdot (6\sqrt{2})^3 = \boxed{288}.$$

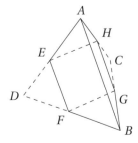

Solution to 9.14 The polyhedron is a unit cube with one corner missing. The missing part is a tetrahedron with volume $\frac{1}{3} \cdot \frac{1}{2} \cdot 1^3 = \frac{1}{6}$. Therefore, the volume of the polyhedron is $1 - \frac{1}{6} = \boxed{\frac{5}{6}}$.

Solution to 9.15 Let the perpendicular distance from D to plane ABC be x. We see that $BC = 4\sqrt{2}$, $AB = AC = 5$. So the height of $\triangle ABC$ is $\sqrt{17}$, and $[ABC] = \frac{1}{2} \cdot 4\sqrt{2} \cdot \sqrt{17} = 2\sqrt{34}$. The volume of tetrahedron $ABCD$ is $\frac{1}{3} \cdot \frac{1}{2} \cdot 4 \cdot 4 \cdot 3 = 8$. We see that the volume of tetrahedron $ABCD$ is also equal to one-third of x times the area of triangle ABC. Therefore,

$$\frac{1}{3} \cdot 2\sqrt{34} x = 8, \qquad x = \boxed{\frac{6\sqrt{34}}{17}}.$$

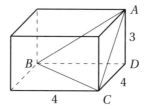

Solution to 9.16 Let M be the midpoint of AB and N the midpoint of CD. We see that MN is a median in triangle CMD. Using Stewart's Theorem in triangle CAB, we have

$$7^2 \cdot \frac{41}{2} + 36^2 \cdot \frac{41}{2} = CM^2 \cdot 41 + \frac{1}{4} \cdot 41^3.$$

Solving the equation, we get $CM = \frac{\sqrt{1009}}{2}$. Similarly, using Stewart's Theorem in triangle ABD, we get

$$18^2 \cdot \frac{41}{2} + 27^2 \cdot \frac{41}{2} = DM^2 \cdot 41 + \frac{1}{4} \cdot 41^3.$$

Solving the equation, we get $DM = \frac{\sqrt{425}}{2}$. Now we know the three sides of triangle CMD, so we can find d using Stewart's Theorem again.

$$\frac{425}{4} \cdot \frac{13}{2} + \frac{1009}{4} \cdot \frac{13}{2} = d^2 \cdot 13 + \frac{1}{4} \cdot 13^3.$$

Solutions for Chapter 9

Solving the equation, we get $d^2 = \boxed{137}$.

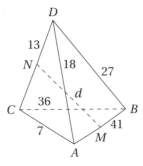

Solution to 9.17 The equation of the first ball is

$$x^2 + y^2 + \left(z - \frac{21}{2}\right)^2 \leq 36.$$

The equation of the second ball is

$$x^2 + y^2 + (z-1)^2 \leq \frac{81}{4}.$$

First we let $x = y = 0$ in order to check the range of z. From the first equation, we get $\frac{21}{2} - 6 \leq z \leq \frac{21}{2} + 6$. From the second equation, we get $1 - \frac{9}{2} \leq z \leq 1 + \frac{9}{2}$. So the only possible integer value of z is 5. Plugging $z = 5$ into the two equations, we get:

$$x^2 + y^2 \leq \frac{23}{4},$$
$$x^2 + y^2 \leq \frac{17}{4}.$$

We only need to consider the second equation because the region described by the first equation is larger. We see that $|x| \leq 2$, and $|y| \leq 2$. If $x = \pm 2$, then $y = 0$. This gives us two points. If $x = \pm 1$, then $y = -1$, $y = 0$, or $y = 1$ work. This gives us 6 points. If $x = 0$, then y can be $-2, -1, 0, 1,$ or 2. This gives us 5 points. Therefore, in total, there are $\boxed{13}$ lattice points.

Solution to 9.18 Let h be the desired height. When the container is held with its point down, the liquid is 9 inches deep, so its volume is $(\frac{9}{12})^3 = \frac{27}{64}$th that of the container. When the container is held with its point up, we have a cone of air with volume $(1 - \frac{27}{64})$th that of the container and height $12 - h$. Therefore,

$$\left(\frac{12-h}{12}\right)^3 = 1 - \frac{27}{64}, \qquad h = \boxed{12 - 3\sqrt[3]{37} \text{ inches}}.$$

Solution to 9.19 Since one square, one hexagon, and one octagon meet at each vertex, the polyhedron has $4 \cdot 12 = 48$ vertices. Since each vertex is associated with 3 edges, the polyhedron has $\frac{48 \cdot 3}{2} = 72$ edges. Now let's count diagonals that are on the faces of the polyhedron. Every square has two diagonals. A hexagon has 9 diagonals. An octagon has 20 diagonals. Therefore, the number of interior diagonals is

$$\binom{48}{2} - 72 - 12 \cdot 2 - 8 \cdot 9 - 6 \cdot 20 = \boxed{840}.$$

Solution to 9.20 We flatten the icosahedron into a net and calculate the length of the straight line NS. By the Pythagorean Theorem,

$$NS = \sqrt{\left(\frac{1}{2}\right)^2 + \left(3 \cdot \frac{\sqrt{3}}{2}\right)^2} = \boxed{\sqrt{7}}.$$

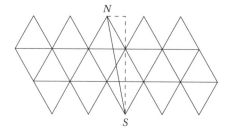

Solution to 9.21 Let r be the radius of any one of the marbles. We first cut a cross section through the centers of two diagonally opposite marbles.

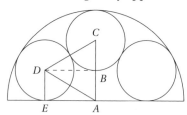

In right triangle BCD, since the length of the hypotenuse is $2r$ and the length of one leg is r, $\triangle BCD$ is a $30°-60°-90°$ triangle. Note that $\triangle BCD \cong \triangle EDA$. In triangle EDA, $DE = r$ and $DA = 1 - r$. So $r = \frac{1}{2}(1 - r)$. Thus, $r = \frac{1}{3}$. We see that the height of the pyramid is r. The length of the diagonal of the square base of the pyramid is $2DB = 2 \cdot \frac{\sqrt{3}}{2} \cdot 2r = 2r\sqrt{3}$. So the area of the square base is $6r^2$. Therefore, the volume of the pyramid is

$$V = \frac{1}{3} \cdot 6r^2 \cdot r = 2r^3 = \boxed{\frac{2}{27}}.$$

Solutions for Chapter 10

Solutions for Chapter 10

Solution to 10.1 Let $m\angle BAC = x$. Since $AX = XY$, $m\angle BXY = 2x$. Since $XY = BY$, $m\angle XBY = 2x$. So $m\angle BYC = 2x + x = 3x$. Since $BY = BC$, we have

$$m\angle ABC = 120° = 2x + m\angle YBC = 2x + 180° - 2 \cdot 3x.$$

Therefore, $m\angle BAC = x = \boxed{15°}$.

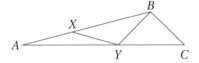

Solution to 10.2 Since $m\angle A = 30°$, we have that $m\angle B + m\angle C = 180° - 30° = 150°$. So

$$m\angle BPC = 180° - m\angle PBC - m\angle PCB = 180° - \frac{2}{3}m\angle B - \frac{2}{3}m\angle C = 180° - 100° = \boxed{80°}.$$

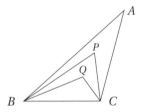

Solution to 10.3 Since $AB = BC$, $m\angle BAC = \frac{1}{2}(180° - 40°) = 70°$. Since $AD = DC$, $m\angle DAC = \frac{1}{2}(180° - 140°) = 20°$. So $m\angle BAD = m\angle BAC - m\angle DAC = \boxed{50°}$.

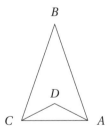

Solution to 10.4 We circumscribe the five-pointed star with a pentagon and label the angles as shown. The sum of the measures of the pentagon's interior angles is 540°. That is,

$$m\angle 1 + 180° - a + m\angle 2 + 180° - b + m\angle 3 + 180° - c + m\angle 4 + 180° - d + m\angle 5 + 180° - e = 540°.$$

Therefore, $a + b + c + d + e - (m\angle 1 + m\angle 2 + m\angle 3 + m\angle 4 + m\angle 5) = \boxed{360°}$.

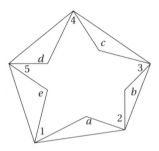

Solution to 10.5 In triangle ABT, $m\angle TAB = 30°$, $m\angle TBA = 45°$. So $m\angle ATC = 30° + 45° = 75°$.

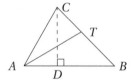

Since $m\angle ACB = 180° - 60° - 45° = 75° = m\angle ATC$, $\triangle ATC$ is an isosceles triangle and $AC = AT = 24$. Let D be the foot of the perpendicular from C to AB. We see that $AB = AD + DB = \dfrac{24}{2} + 24 \cdot \dfrac{\sqrt{3}}{2} = 12(\sqrt{3} + 1)$. Thus,

$$[ABC] = \frac{1}{2} AC \cdot AB \cdot \sin CAB = \frac{1}{2} \cdot 24 \cdot 12(\sqrt{3}+1) \cdot \frac{\sqrt{3}}{2} = 72(3 + \sqrt{3}) = 216 + 72\sqrt{3}.$$

Therefore, $a + b + c = 216 + 72 + 3 = \boxed{291}$.

Solution to 10.6 We see that $m\angle ABC = m\angle BCA = \dfrac{1}{2}(180° - 100°) = 40°$ because $\triangle ABC$ is isosceles. Since $BD = AB$, triangle ABD is an isosceles triangle. Since $m\angle ABD = 40° + 20° = 60°$, $\triangle ABD$ is an equilateral triangle. So $m\angle DAC = m\angle BAC - m\angle BAD = 100° - 60° = 40°$. Since $AD = AB = AC$, triangle DAC is isosceles. So $m\angle ACD = \dfrac{1}{2}(180° - 40°) = 70°$. Therefore, $m\angle BCD = m\angle DCA - m\angle BCA = 70° - 40° = \boxed{30°}$.

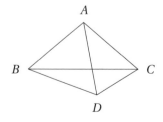

Solution to 10.7 We see that $m\angle RSU = m\angle R + m\angle T = 78°$. Since $RUSV$ is a cyclic quadrilateral, $m\angle RVU = m\angle RSU = 78°$. Therefore,

$$m\angle RQV = 180° - m\angle VRQ - m\angle RVQ = 180° - 36° - 78° = \boxed{66°}.$$

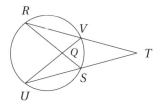

Solution to 10.8 Let $m\angle PCA = x$. Since $\triangle ABC$ is isosceles, $m\angle CBA = m\angle BCA = \frac{1}{2}(180° - 82°) = 49°$. Since $\triangle ABP$ is isosceles, $m\angle BAP = m\angle BPA = \frac{1}{2}(180° - 38°) = 71°$. Therefore $m\angle PBC = 49° - 38° = 11°$ and $m\angle CAP = 82° - 71° = 11°$. Let D be a point on BC such that $BD = AP$. Since $BP = BA = CA$, $\triangle DPB \cong \triangle PCA$ by SAS. Therefore $m\angle DPB = m\angle PCA = x$ and $PD = PC$. Thus $\triangle PDC$ is isosceles and $m\angle PDC = m\angle PCD$. That is, $x + 11° = 49° - x$. Therefore, $m\angle PCA = x = \boxed{19°}$.

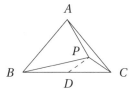

Solution to 10.9 Let $m\angle ACF = \alpha$. Since $\triangle CEF$ is equilateral, $m\angle CFE = 60° = m\angle CAF + \alpha$. So $m\angle CAF = 60° - \alpha$. Therefore $m\angle CAB = 60° - \alpha + \alpha = 60°$. Next we use the Law of Cosines in triangle ABC and get

$$CB^2 = AC^2 + AB^2 - 2AC \cdot AB \cdot \cos 60°,$$
$$CB^2 = AC^2 + 4AC^2 - 2AC \cdot 2AC \cdot \frac{1}{2},$$
$$CB^2 = 3AC^2.$$

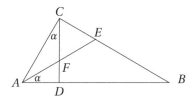

So $CB = AC\sqrt{3}$, and the sides of triangle ABC are in the ratio of $2 : \sqrt{3} : 1$. Thus, triangle ABC is a $30° - 60° - 90°$ right triangle. Therefore $m\angle ACB = \boxed{90°}$.

Solution to 10.10 We see that

$$\triangle ABC \sim \triangle DBA \sim \triangle EDA.$$

Therefore, $m\angle ADE = m\angle ABC = \boxed{27°}$.

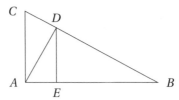

Solution to 10.11 Let F and G be the midpoints of BC and AD, respectively. Without loss of generality, we may assume that the square has a side length of 2. Then

$$EF = BF \cdot \tan 15° = \frac{\sqrt{6}-\sqrt{2}}{\sqrt{6}+\sqrt{2}} = 2-\sqrt{3}.$$

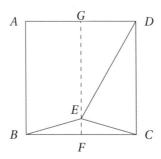

So $GE = 2-(2-\sqrt{3}) = \sqrt{3}$ and $\tan \angle EDA = \frac{GE}{GD} = \sqrt{3}$. Thus $m\angle EDA = \boxed{60°}$.

Solution to 10.12

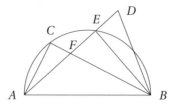

Since AB is the diameter, $m\angle ACB = m\angle AEB = 90°$. Since $DE = EF$, $\triangle BFE \cong \triangle BDE$. So

$$m\angle BDE = m\angle BFE = m\angle AFC = 180° - 90° - 20° = 70°.$$

Since $AB = AD$, $m\angle BAD = 180° - 2 \cdot m\angle ADB = \boxed{40°}$.

Solutions for Chapter 10

Solution to 10.13 Sometimes it's better to use an indirect approach when we need to solve a problem. Since triangle CDP looks nice, let's construct an equilateral triangle CDP' inside the regular pentagon. Since the degree measure of each interior angle of a regular pentagon is $108°$, we have $m\angle BCP' = 108° - 60° = 48°$. Since $BC = P'C$, triangle BCP' is isosceles. So $m\angle CBP' = \frac{1}{2}(180° - 48°) = 66°$. Thus $m\angle P'BA = 108° - 66° = 42°$. Similarly, we can show that $m\angle P'EA = 42°$. Thus P and P' are the same point. So $m\angle CPD = \boxed{60°}$.

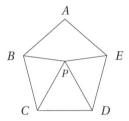

Solution to 10.14 Let $m\angle ADB = x$ and $m\angle CAD = y$. Since $CA = CD$, $m\angle CDB = y - x$ and $m\angle ACD = 180° - 2y$. Since $\triangle BAC$ is equilateral, $m\angle BCA = 60°$. Since $BC = CD$, triangle BDC is isosceles. In $\triangle BDC$, we have

$$2(y-x) + 60° + 180° - 2y = 180°.$$

So $2x = 60°$. Therefore, $m\angle ADB = \boxed{30°}$.[1]

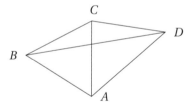

Solution to 10.15 Let $\overset{\frown}{AB} = x$ and $\overset{\frown}{AD} = y$. Since the arcs of a circle sum to $360°$, we have $3x + y = 360°$. Since $m\angle E = \frac{1}{2}(\overset{\frown}{BC} - \overset{\frown}{AD})$, we have $x - y = 80°$. Solving the system of equations, we get $y = 30°$. Thus $m\angle ACD = \frac{1}{2} \cdot 30° = \boxed{15°}$.

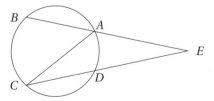

---

[1] The condition $AD = 13$ is not used. Note the similarity between this problem and Problem 10.6.

Solution to 10.16 We draw a line parallel to AB passing through point Y and see that $m\angle XYZ = 45° + 25° = 70°$. Since $XY = YZ$, $\triangle XYZ$ is an isosceles triangle. So $m\angle YXZ = \frac{1}{2}(180° - 70°) = \boxed{55°}$.

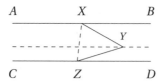

Solution to 10.17 First let's see if $ABCD$ is cyclic, that is, if $m\angle ABC + m\angle ADC = 180°$. Let F be a point on AD such that $AF = AB$. Since AC is the angle bisector of $\angle BAF$, $\triangle ABC \cong \triangle AFC$. So $m\angle AFC = m\angle ABC$ and $CF = CB = CD$. Therefore, $\triangle CFD$ is an isosceles triangle and $m\angle CFD = m\angle CDF$. Thus,

$$m\angle ABC + m\angle ADC = m\angle AFC + m\angle CFD = 180°$$

and $ABCD$ is cyclic. Therefore, $m\angle ADC = 180° - 130° = 50°$. Since $CD = ED$, triangle CDE is isosceles. So $m\angle CED = \frac{1}{2}(180° - 50°) = 65°$. Therefore, $m\angle ACE = m\angle CED - m\angle CAE = 65° - 20° = \boxed{45°}$.

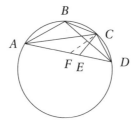

Solution to 10.18 Let $m\angle PCA = x$. Since

$$m\angle ACB = 180° - 22° - 22° - 8° - 30° = 98°,$$

we have $m\angle PCB = 98° - x$. By Trig Ceva, we have

$$\frac{\sin x}{\sin(98° - x)} \cdot \frac{\sin 22°}{\sin 22°} \cdot \frac{\sin 30°}{\sin 8°} = 1.$$

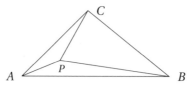

So $\sin x = 2\sin 8° \cdot \sin(98° - x)$. Since $\sin\alpha \sin\beta = \frac{1}{2}\big(\cos(\alpha - \beta) - (\cos(\alpha + \beta)\big)$, we have

Solutions for Chapter 10

$$\sin x = \cos(x - 90°) - \cos(106° - x) = \sin x - \cos(106° - x).$$

So $\cos(106° - x) = 0$. Thus, $106° - x = 90°$ and $m\angle PCA = x = \boxed{16°}$.

Solution to 10.19 With angle chasing, we see that $m\angle CBA = 18°$, $m\angle BAE = 21°$, $m\angle CEA = 39°$, $m\angle CFA = 69°$ and $m\angle ECD = 30°$. Since $m\angle ADC = m\angle ACD = 48°$, $AD = AC$. Let G be on BC such that $m\angle CAG = 24°$. Then $m\angle CGA = 180° - 78° - 24° = 78°$. So $\triangle ACG$ is an isosceles triangle and $AG = AC = AD$. We see that $m\angle GAD = 84° - 24° = 60°$. So isosceles triangle AGD is an equilateral triangle and $GD = GA$. Since

$$m\angle EAG = m\angle EAC - m\angle GAC = 63° - 24° = 39° = m\angle GEA,$$

$\triangle GEA$ is an isosceles triangle and so $GE = GA = GD$. Thus $\triangle GED$ is an isosceles triangle. Since $m\angle EGD = 180° - 60° - 78° = 42°$, $m\angle GED = \frac{1}{2}(180° - 42°) = 69°$. So $m\angle FED = 69° - 39° = 30°$. Therefore, $m\angle CDE = 180° - 30° - 69° = \boxed{81°}$.

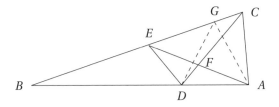

Solution to 10.20 Let G be a point on AC such that BG is the angle bisector of $\angle ABD$. Connect D with G and D with F. Since $m\angle DAG = m\angle GBD = 30°$, quadrilateral $AGDB$ is cyclic. So $m\angle ADG = m\angle ABG = 30°$. So triangle AGD is isosceles. Thus $AG = DG$ and $m\angle DGC = 60°$. Therefore $\triangle GCD$ is a right triangle and $DG = \frac{1}{2}GC$. Since $DG + GC = AG + GC = AC$, we have $AG = \frac{1}{3}AC$ and so points G and F trisect AC. So $DG = GF$ and $\triangle DGF$ is an equilateral triangle. Therefore $m\angle FDC = 90° - 60° = 30°$. Let H be the midpoint of DC. Since E is the midpoint of BC and F the midpoint of GC, we see that $EH \parallel BD$, $HF \parallel DG$ and $EF \parallel BG$. So $\triangle EFH \sim \triangle BGD$ and thus $m\angle FEH = m\angle GBD = 30° = m\angle FDH$. Therefore, $DFHE$ is a cyclic quadrilateral. Since H is the midpoint of DC in isosceles triangle DFC with $DF = FC$, $m\angle DHF = 90°$. So $m\angle DEF = m\angle DHF = \boxed{90°}$.

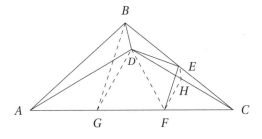

Solutions for Chapter 11

Solution to 11.1 Since $AE : EB = 2 : 3$, we assign weights of 3 to A and 2 to B. So, $5E$ is the balance point of AB. Since $AD : DC = 2 : 1$, we assign a weight of 6 to C. So, $9D$ is the balance point of AC. We see that $3A$, $2B$, and $6C$ are balanced by $6C$ and $5E$. They are also balanced by $2B$ and $9D$. Thus K, the intersection of CE and BD, is the center of mass of $3A$, $2B$, and $6C$. So $9DK = 2KB$ and $DK : KB = \boxed{2:9}$.

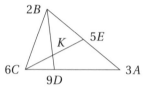

Solution to 11.2 The area of the right triangle ABC is $\frac{1}{2} \cdot 4 \cdot 7 = 14$. The area of the right triangle ACF is $\frac{1}{2} \cdot 4 \cdot 3 = 6$. So the area of $\triangle AFB$ is $14 - 6 = 8$.

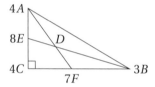

To find the area of $\triangle ABD$, let's use mass points to get the ratio $AD : DF$. To use F to balance CB, we assign a weight of 3 to B and a weight of 4 to C. To use E to balance AC, we assign a weight of 4 to A. So E has a weight of 8 and F has a weight of 7. We see that D, the intersection of AF and EB, is the center of mass of $4A$, $3B$, and $4C$. So $AD : DF = 7 : 4$. So the area of triangle ABD is:

$$\frac{7}{7+4} \cdot 8 = \boxed{\frac{56}{11}}.$$

Solution to 11.3 We first use mass points to find the ratio $PQ : PA$. To use M to balance AC, we assign a weight of 3 to C and a weight of 1 to A. To use P to balance BC, we assign a weight of 6 to B. We see that the three mass points $1A$, $6B$, and $3C$ are balanced by $1A$ and $9P$. They are also balanced by $6B$ and $4M$.

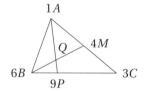

Solutions for Chapter 11

So Q, the intersection of BM and AP, is the center of mass and $9PQ = 1QA$. So $PQ = \frac{1}{10}PA$. Since the area of $\triangle BPQ$ is 1, the area of $\triangle ABP$ is $10 \cdot 1 = 10$. Finally, the area of $\triangle ABC$ is $3 \cdot 10 = \boxed{30 \text{ in}^2}$.

Solution to 11.4 We see that $\triangle FCY$ and $\triangle BAY$ are similar. So $CY : YA = 2 : 3$ and $FY : YB = 2 : 3$. We use mass points in $\triangle ABC$ to find the ratio $YX : YB$. To use Y to balance AC, we assign a weight of 3 to C and a weight of 2 to A. To use E to balance BC, we assign a weight of 1.5 to B. The three mass points $2A$, $1.5B$, and $3C$ are balanced by $2A$ and $4.5E$. They are also balanced by $5Y$ and $1.5B$. So X, the intersection of BY and AE, is the center of mass of triangle ABC. Thus $5YX = 1.5XB$. Therefore,

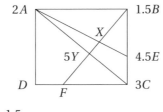

$$YX = \frac{1.5}{5+1.5}YB, \quad \text{and} \quad XB = \frac{5}{5+1.5}YB.$$

So
$$FY : YX : XB = \frac{2}{3} : \frac{1.5}{6.5} : \frac{5}{6.5} = \frac{2}{3} : \frac{3}{13} : \frac{10}{13} = 26 : 9 : 30.$$

Since $\gcd(26, 9, 30) = 1$, $a + b + c = 26 + 9 + 30 = \boxed{65}$.

Solution to 11.5 We will first find the ratio $GC : AC$. After that, we will find the ratio $AH : AC$. Since AD is a median, the centroid of $\triangle ABC$ is on AD. Note that the centroid of a triangle divides each median in the ratio $2 : 1$. Since $AE : ED = 2 : 1$, E is the centroid of $\triangle ABC$. So BG is also a median. Thus $GC = GA = \frac{1}{2}AC$.

Next we assign masses to A, B, and C so that F is the center of mass. We assign a weight of 1 to C and a weight of 1 to B. So D has a weight of 2. Since $AF : FD = 1 : 2$, we assign a weight of 4 to A. Since F, the center of mass of $4A$, $1B$, and $1C$, lies on BH, H is the balance point of $4A$ and $1C$. So $AH = \frac{1}{4}HC = \frac{1}{5}AC$. Therefore,
$HG = AC - AH - GC = AC - \frac{1}{5}AC - \frac{1}{2}AC = \frac{3}{10}AC = \boxed{21}$.

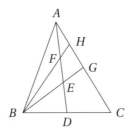

Solution to 11.6 Since the three sides of $\triangle ABC$ are 13, 14, and 15, its semi-perimeter s is $\dfrac{13+14+15}{2} = 21$. By Heron's Formula,

$$[ABC] = \sqrt{21 \cdot (21-13) \cdot (21-14) \cdot (21-15)} = 84.$$

Since $\frac{1}{2} \cdot 14 \cdot BD = [ABC]$, we have $BD = 12$. Since $\triangle ABD$ is a right triangle, $AD = \sqrt{13^2 - 12^2} = 5$ and $DC = 9$.

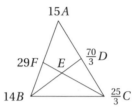

Since CF is the angle bisector of $\angle C$, $AF : FB = AC : BC = 14 : 15$. To use F to balance AB, we assign a weight of 15 to A and a weight of 14 to B. To use D to balance AC, we assign a weight of $\frac{25}{3}$ to C. The three mass points $15A$, $14B$, and $\frac{25}{3}C$ are balanced by $\frac{25}{3}C$ and $29F$. They are also balanced by $14B$ and $\frac{70}{3}D$. So E is the center of mass. Thus, $CE : EF = 29 : \frac{25}{3} = \boxed{87 : 25}$.

Solution to 11.7 Since M, N, P, and Q are the points of tangency of AB, BC, CD, and DA with the circle, respectively, $QA = AM = a$, $MB = BN = b$, $NC = CP = c$, and $PD = DQ = d$. We choose positive real numbers x, y, z, and w such that

$$ax = by = cz = dw.$$

Note that such positive numbers x, y, z, and w always exist. We assign weights x, y, z, and w to points A, B, C, and D, respectively. We see that M is the balance point of AB, N is the balance point of BC, P is the balance point of CD, and Q is the balance point of AD.

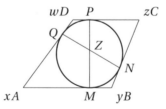

The four mass points xA, yB, zC, and wD are balanced by $(x+y)M$ and $(z+w)P$. They are also balanced by $(y+z)N$ and $(x+w)Q$. Therefore, Z, the intersection of MP and NQ, is the center of mass. Thus, $(x+y)MZ = (z+w)ZP$. So

$$\frac{MZ}{ZP} = \frac{z+w}{x+y} = \frac{\frac{d}{c} \cdot w + w}{\frac{d}{a} \cdot w + \frac{d}{b} \cdot w} = \boxed{\frac{ab(c+d)}{cd(a+b)}}.$$

Solutions for Chapter 11

Solution to 11.8 By the Law of Sines, we have

$$\frac{BC}{\sin \angle A} = \frac{AB}{\sin \angle C}. \quad \text{So} \quad \frac{5BC}{4} = \frac{25AB}{24}.$$

Thus $BC : AB = 5 : 6$. Since BD is the bisector of $\angle B$, we have $CD : DA = 5 : 6$ by the Angle Bisector Theorem. Now we use mass points. To use D to balance AC, we assign weights of 6 to C and 5 to A. Since M is the midpoint of BC, we assign a weight of 6 to B. The three mass points $5A$, $6B$, and $6C$ are balanced by $5A$ and $12M$. They are also balanced by $6B$ and $11D$. Therefore, E, the intersection of BD and AM, is the center of mass. Thus, $12EM = 5AE$ and $AE : EM = \boxed{12:5}$.

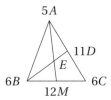

Solution to 11.9 Applying the Angle Bisector Theorem twice, we get $CE : EA = 3 : 7$ and $BD : DC = 7 : 5$. Next we assign masses so that P is the center of mass. To use D to balance BC, we assign weights of 5 to B and 7 to C. To use E to balance AC, we assign a weight of 3 to A. We see that $3A$, $5B$, and $7C$ are balanced by $3A$ and $12D$. They are also balanced by $5B$ and $10E$. Thus, P, the intersection of AD and BE, is the center of mass. Therefore, $5x = 10y$ and $x : y = \boxed{2:1}$.

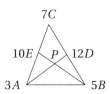

Solution to 11.10 Since $\triangle FPA$ and $\triangle BPF$ share a common height, $AF : FB = 4 : 3$. Since $\triangle BDP$ and $\triangle BPA$ share a common height, $DP : PA = 1 : 2$.

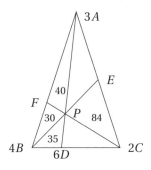

Next we assign masses to A, B, and C to make P the center of mass. To use F to balance AB, we assign weights of 3 to A and 4 to B. Since $AP:PD = 2:1$, D must have a weight of 6. This means that C has a weight of 2 and $BD:DC = 1:2$. So $[ABC] = 3 \cdot [ABD] = 3 \cdot (30 + 40 + 35) = \boxed{315}$.

Solution to 11.11 Without loss of generality, let's assume that $\triangle BDF$ has an area of 1. We assign masses to A, B, and C to make F the center of mass. Since E is the midpoint of AC, we assign weights of 1 to A and 1 to C. Since $BD:DC = 1:2$, we assign a weight of 2 to B. We see that the three mass points $1A$, $2B$, and $1C$ are balanced by $2B$ and $2E$. They are also balanced by $1A$ and $3D$. So F, the intersection of AD and BE, is the center of mass. So $BF = FE$ and $AF = 3FD$. Therefore, the area of $\triangle ABF$ is 3 and the area of $\triangle AFE$ is also 3. Since $\triangle ABE$ and $\triangle EBC$ have the same area, we have

$$[FDCE] = [BCE] - [BDF] = [ABE] - 1 = 3 + 3 - 1 = 5.$$

Thus, the ratio of the area of $\triangle BDF$ to that of quadrilateral $FDCE$ is $\boxed{1:5}$.

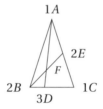

Solution to 11.12 Let O be the intersection of AC and BD. Since $ABCD$ is a parallelogram, $AO = OC$. Let's assign masses to A, B, and D to make P the center of mass of $\triangle ABD$. Since MN is a transversal, A will have a split mass $A_B + A_D$. Since $AM:AB = 17:1000$, we assign a weight of 17 to B and a weight of $1000 - 17 = 983$ to A_B. Then, M is the balance point of $A_B B$ and has a weight of 1000. Since O is the midpoint of BD, we assign a weight of 17 to D. Since $AN:AD = 17:2009$, we assign a weight of $2009 - 17 = 1992$ to A_D. Then, N is the balance point of $A_D D$ and has a weight of 2009. So A has a total weight of $983 + 1992 = 2975$. We see that the three mass points $2975A$, $17B$, and $17D$ are balanced by $2975A$ and $34O$. They are also balanced by $1000M$ and $2009N$. Therefore, P, the intersection of AO and MN, is the center of mass. So $2975AP = 34PO$.

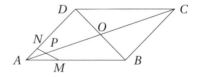

Thus,

$$\frac{AP}{AO} = \frac{34}{34 + 2975} = \frac{2}{177}. \quad \text{So,} \quad \frac{AC}{AP} = \frac{2AO}{AP} = \boxed{177}.$$

Solutions for Chapter 11   217

Solution to 11.13 We connect B and F and use mass points in $\triangle ABF$ to make E the center of mass. Since $AD : DB = 3 : 2$, we assign weights of 2 to A and 3 to B. So D has a weight of 5. Since $BE : EC = 3 : 2$, to make E the center of mass, C must be the balance point of AF and have a weight of $\frac{9}{2}$. Thus, F must have a weight of $\frac{9}{2} - 2 = \frac{5}{2}$.

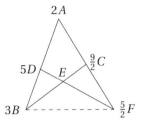

We see that the three mass points $2A$, $3B$, and $\frac{5}{2}F$ are balanced by $5D$ and $\frac{5}{2}F$. Therefore,

$$5DE = \frac{5}{2}EF. \qquad DE : EF = \boxed{1:2}.$$

Solution to 11.14 We can choose weights x, y, and z and assign them to A, B, and C, respectively, so that O is the center of mass. Then A' has a weight of $y + z$; B' has a weight of $x + z$; and C' has a weight of $x + y$. Since $\dfrac{AO}{OA'} + \dfrac{BO}{OB'} + \dfrac{CO}{OC'} = 92$, we have

$$\frac{y+z}{x} + \frac{x+z}{y} + \frac{x+y}{z} = 92.$$

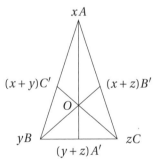

Therefore,

$$\frac{AO}{OA'} \cdot \frac{BO}{OB'} \cdot \frac{CO}{OC'} = \frac{y+z}{x} \cdot \frac{x+z}{y} \cdot \frac{x+y}{z}$$

$$= \frac{2xyz + y^2z + z^2y + x^2z + z^2x + x^2y + y^2x}{xyz}$$

$$= 2 + \frac{y+z}{x} + \frac{x+z}{y} + \frac{x+y}{z} = \boxed{94}.$$

Solution to 11.15 We can assign weights x, y, and z to points A, B, and C, respectively, so that P is the center of mass of xA, yB, and zC. We see that points D, E, and F have weights $y+z$, $x+z$, and $x+y$, respectively. Since $(x+y+z)P$ is balanced by xA and $(y+z)D$, by yB and $(x+z)E$, and by zC and $(x+y)D$, we have:

$$d(y+z) = ax,$$
$$d(x+z) = by,$$
$$d(x+y) = cz.$$

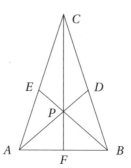

So
$$\frac{x}{x+y+z} = \frac{1}{1+\frac{y+z}{x}} = \frac{1}{1+\frac{a}{d}} = \frac{d}{a+d}.$$

Similarly,
$$\frac{y}{x+y+z} = \frac{d}{b+d}, \quad \text{and} \quad \frac{z}{x+y+z} = \frac{d}{c+d}.$$

Therefore,
$$\frac{d}{a+d} + \frac{d}{b+d} + \frac{d}{c+d} = \frac{x+y+z}{x+y+z} = 1.$$

Since $d = 3$, we have:
$$\frac{3}{a+3} + \frac{3}{b+3} + \frac{3}{c+3} = 1.$$

Thus,
$$3(bc+3b+3c+9) + 3(ac+3a+3c+9) + 3(ab+3a+3b+9)$$
$$= abc + 3ab + 3ac + 3bc + 9a + 9b + 9c + 27.$$

So $abc = 9(a+b+c) + 54$. Since $a+b+c = 43$, $abc = 9 \cdot 43 + 54 = \boxed{441}$.[2]

Solution to 11.16 Let A_1, B_1, and C_1 be points on BC, CA, and AB such that AA_1, BB_1, and CC_1 are angle bisectors of $\angle A$, $\angle B$, and $\angle C$, respectively. Let O be the

---

[2] This problem can also be solved using the result from Problem 11.14.

Solutions for Chapter 11

center of the inscribed circle of $\triangle ABC$. Then AA_1, BB_1, and CC_1 are concurrent cevians intersecting at point O. By the Angle Bisector Theorem, $BA_1 : A_1C = 21 : 22$, $CB_1 : B_1A = 20 : 21$, and $AC_1 : C_1B = 22 : 20$. So we assign weights of 20 to A, 22 to B, and 21 to C. We see that O is the center of mass of $20A$, $22B$, and $21C$. Thus, $42C_1O = 21OC$ and $41B_1O = 22OB$.

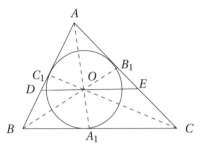

Since $DO \parallel BC$, $DO : BC = C_1O : C_1C = 21 : (42 + 21)$. Since $OE \parallel BC$, $OE : BC = B_1O : B_1B = 22 : (41 + 22)$. Therefore,

$$DE : BC = (DO + OE) : BC = (21 + 22) : 63.$$

So $DE = \dfrac{43}{63} \cdot 20 = \dfrac{860}{63}$. Since $\gcd(860, 63) = 1$, $m + n = 860 + 63 = \boxed{923}$.

Solution to 11.17 Let's assign masses to $\triangle ABC$ to make P the center of mass. Let's assign weights of 1 to C, x to A, and y to B. Then E has a weight of $1 + x$ and D has a weight of $1 + y$. Therefore,

$$3(1 + x) = 9y,$$
$$6(1 + y) = 6x.$$

So $x = 2$ and $y = 1$. Thus F has a weight of 3 and $3FP = 1PC$. Since $FC = 20$, we have $FP = 5$ and $PC = 15$. Furthermore, since $2D$ is the balance point of $1B$ and $1C$, $BD = DC$.

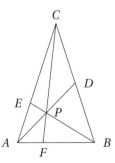

In $\triangle PBC$, $PB = 9$, $PC = 15$, and the cevian $PD = 6$. We want to find the length of BD. Let's call it t. By Stewart's Theorem, we have

$$9^2 t + 15^2 t = 6^2(2t) + (2t)t^2,$$
$$234t = 2t^3,$$
$$t = 3\sqrt{13}.$$

Since $9^2 + 6^2 = (3\sqrt{13})^2$, $\triangle PBD$ is a right triangle and $[PBD] = \frac{1}{2} \cdot 6 \cdot 9 = 27$. Since $AP = PD$, $[APC] = [PDC] = [PBD] = [PAB]$. Therefore,

$$[ABC] = 4 \cdot [PBD] = \boxed{108}.$$

Solution to 11.18 Since $\triangle ABC$ is an equilateral triangle, we assign a weight of 12 to each of A, B, and C. Here we use 12 instead of 1 to simplify calculations. Then M, the centroid of $\triangle ABC$, is the center of mass of $12A$, $12B$, and $12C$, and has a weight of 36.

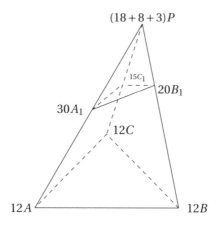

We would like to use A_1 to balance AP, B_1 to balance BP, and C_1 to balance CP. This means P has a split mass of $P_A + P_B + P_C$. Since $PA_1 : A_1 A = 2:3$, P_A has a weight of 18. Since $PB_1 : B_1 B = 3:2$, P_B has a weight of 8. Since $PC_1 : C_1 C = 4:1$, P_C has a weight of 3. So P has a total weight of $18 + 8 + 3 = 29$. We see that the four mass points $29P$, $12A$, $12B$, and $12C$ are balanced by $29P$ and $36M$. They are also balanced by $30A_1$, $20B_1$, and $15C_1$. So M_1, the intersection of PM with plane α is the center of mass of these four mass points. Therefore,

$$29PM_1 = 36M_1 M. \qquad PM_1 : M_1 M = \boxed{36:29}.$$

Solution to 11.19 We assign a weight of 1 to A, a weight of -1 to B, and a weight of 1 to C. By Theorem 11.3, we see that D is the balance point of $1A$, $(-1)B$, and $1C$, and has a weight of 1. Because S is associated with each of the points A, B, and C, S has a split mass of $S_A + S_B + S_C$. Since $SA_1 : SA = 1:3$, we assign a weight of 2 to S_A. We see that $3A_1$ is the balance point of $S_A A$. Since $SB_1 : SB = 1:5$, we assign a weight of -4 to B. We see that $(-5)B_1$ is the balance point of $S_B B$. Since

Solutions for Chapter 11

$SC_1 : SC = 1 : 4$, we assign a weight of 3 to S_C. We see that $4C_1$ is the balance point of $S_C C$. So the total weight of S is $2 - 4 + 3 = 1$.

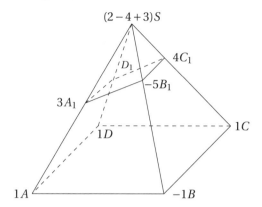

We see that the four mass points $1S$, $1A$, $(-1)B$, and $1C$ are balanced by $1S$ and $1D$. These four mass points are also balanced by $3A_1$, $(-5)B_1$, and $4C_1$. So D_1, the intersection of SD and plane α, is the center of these four mass points. Therefore, $1SD_1 = 1D_1 D$. So $SD_1 : SD = \boxed{1 : 2}$.

Solution to 11.20 We first assign masses to A, B, and C to make P the center of mass. Since $BA_1 : A_1 C = 1 : 3$, we assign a weight of 1 to C and a weight of 3 to B. Since $BC_1 : C_1 A = 3 : 1$, we assign a weight of 9 to A.

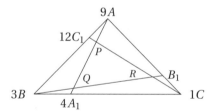

We see that the three mass points $9A$, $3B$, and $1C$ are balanced by $9A$ and $4A_1$. They are also balanced by $12C_1$ and $1C$. So P, the intersection of $C_1 C$ and AA_1, is the center of mass. So $C_1 P : PC = 1 : 12$. So $[AC_1 P] = \dfrac{1}{13}[AC_1 C]$. Thus,

$$[APC] = \frac{12}{13}[AC_1 C] = \frac{12}{13} \cdot \frac{1}{4}[ABC] = \frac{3}{13} S.$$

With similar arguments, we see that $[ABQ] = \dfrac{3}{13} S$ and $[BCR] = \dfrac{3}{13} S$. Therefore,

$$[RQR] = S - 3 \cdot \frac{3}{13} S = \boxed{\frac{4}{13} S}.$$

Solutions for Chapter 12

Solution to 12.1 Since gcd(6, 9) = 3, let's first consider the largest number of Mc-Nuggets that cannot be purchased with quantities of 3 and 20. By the Chicken McNugget Theorem, $3 \cdot 20 - 3 - 20 = 37$ pieces cannot be purchased with 3 and 20, so 37 pieces cannot be purchased with 6, 9, and 20. Since **38** = 20+18, **39** = 9+5·6, **40** = 2·20, **41** = 20+12+9, and **42** = 6·7, these quantities are all purchasable. Next, we show that 43 is not purchasable. First of all, 43 is not a multiple of 3, so it is not purchasable with 6 and 9 alone. Using one 20 does not help because 43 − 20 = 23 is not a multiple of 3. Using two 20s does not help either because 43 − 2·20 = 3 is not purchasable with 6 and 9. Therefore, 43 is not purchasable.

To check that every number after 43 is purchasable, we note that **44** = 20 + 24, **45** = 5·9, **46** = 40 + 6, **47** = 20 + 27, **48** = 6·8, and **49** = 40 + 9. We then note that every number after 49 is a multiple of 6 plus one of the numbers from 44 to 49. So the answer is $\boxed{43}$.

Solution to 12.2 If n is a three-digit number in base-10, then

$$10^2 \le n \le 10^3 - 1, \qquad 100 \le n \le 999.$$

If n is a three-digit number in base-9, then

$$9^2 \le n \le 9^3 - 1, \qquad 81 \le n \le 728.$$

If n is a three-digit number in base-11, then

$$11^2 \le n \le 11^3 - 1, \qquad 121 \le n \le 1330.$$

Therefore, if $121 \le n \le 728$, then n is a three-digit number in base-9, base-10, and base-11. So there are $728 - 121 + 1 = \boxed{608}$ such numbers.

Solution to 12.3 We find the base (-2) representation of 34 by repeated division by -2 and recording nonnegative remainders.

$$
\begin{array}{ll}
34/-2 = -17, & \text{remainder } 0 \\
-17/-2 = 9, & \text{remainder } 1 \\
9/-2 = -4, & \text{remainder } 1 \\
-4/-2 = 2, & \text{remainder } 0 \\
2/-2 = -1, & \text{remainder } 0 \\
-1/-2 = 1, & \text{remainder } 1 \\
1/-2 = 0, & \text{remainder } 1 \\
\end{array}
$$

Therefore, 34_{10} is $\boxed{1,100,110_{(-2)}}$.

Solution to 12.4 By the Chicken McNugget Theorem, the largest number that cannot be expressed with 5 and 7 is $5 \cdot 7 - 5 - 7 = 23$. So, we only need to find the largest number ≤ 23 that cannot be expressed with 5, 7, and 11. We see that $23 = 5+7+11$, $22 = 2 \cdot 11$, $21 = 3 \cdot 7$, $20 = 4 \cdot 5$, $19 = 5+2 \cdot 7$, $18 = 7+11$, $17 = 2 \cdot 5 + 7$, $16 = 11+5$, $15 = 3 \cdot 5$, and $14 = 2 \cdot 7$. However we cannot express 13 with 5, 7, and 11. Therefore, the answer is $\boxed{13}$.

Solution to 12.5 First we see that, for every group of 12 answers, the student will get the same number of them right. To determine this constant number, we will line up his answers with the correct answers as follows:

Correct: F F F T F F F T F F F T
Student: T T F T T F T T F T T F

We see that answer numbers 3, 4, 6, 8, and 9 are all correct for the student. Since there are 8 whole groups of 12 in 100, the number of correct answers is at least $8 \cdot 5 = 40$. Since 100 divided by 12 leaves a remainder of 4, we need to consider the first 4 answers of the next group of 12. Of these, answer numbers 3 and 4 are correct. Therefore, the total number of correct answers is $40 + 2 = \boxed{42}$.

Solution to 12.6 Let $n = p_1^{e_1} p_2^{e_2} \cdots p_k^{e_k}$. We see that n has $(1+e_1)(1+e_2) \cdots (1+e_k)$ factors. An odd number clearly does not have any even factors, so it doesn't satisfy the requirements. If $n \equiv 2 \pmod 4$, then each of its odd factors t can be paired with its even factor $2t$. So, n has the same number of odd factors as even factors. If $n \equiv 0 \pmod 4$, then again each of its odd factors t can be paired with $2t$. But note that factors such as $4t$ are not paired with any other factors. So, it has more even factors than odd factors. Therefore, the only natural numbers that have the same number of odd factors as even factors are those that are even but not divisible by 4. From 100 to 1000, there are 451 even numbers and 225 of those are not divisible by 4. Therefore, the answer is $\boxed{225}$.

Solution to 12.7 First we find the base (-4) representation of 33 by repeated division by -4 and recording nonnegative remainders.

$$33/(-4) = -8, \quad \text{remainder } 1,$$
$$-8/(-4) = 2, \quad \text{remainder } 0,$$
$$2/(-4) = 0, \quad \text{remainder } 2.$$

Thus, $33 = 201_{-4}$. Next, let's work on the $\frac{1}{3}$ part. Note that among all rational numbers representable as $0.a_1 a_2 \cdots$ in base (-4), the largest is $0.030303\cdots_{-4} = \frac{1}{5}$ and the smallest is $0.303030\cdots_{-4} = -\frac{4}{5}$. Here the period in the expression is the base (-4) radix point. Since $\frac{1}{3} > \frac{1}{5}$, the base (-4) representation of $\frac{1}{3}$ must start with a 1 before the radix point. That is, we must write $\frac{1}{3}$ as $1 - \frac{2}{3}$. We find the base (-4) representation of $-\frac{2}{3}$ by repeated multiplication by -4 and recording nonnegative quotients. Note that the corresponding remainders must be between $-\frac{4}{5}$ and $\frac{1}{5}$.

$$-4 \cdot (-\frac{2}{3}) = 3, \quad \text{remainder } -\frac{1}{3},$$
$$-4 \cdot (-\frac{1}{3}) = 2, \quad \text{remainder } -\frac{2}{3}.$$

Therefore, $\frac{1}{3} = 1.\overline{32}_{(-4)}$. Combining the two parts, we see that $33\frac{1}{3} = \boxed{202.\overline{32}_{(-4)}}$.

Solution to 12.8 Since $C(256) = C(0) = 0$, we can treat 256 as 0. We represent each number from 0 to 255 as an 8-digit binary string. For example, we write 0 as 00000000. Since the numbers from 0 to 255 range over all the 8-digit binary strings, we only need to count how many consecutive 1's we have from 00000000 to 11111111. Note that any two adjacent digits can either be 00, 01, 10, or 11. So $\frac{1}{4}$ of the time, we get a pair of adjacent 1's. When we count from right to left, an 8-digit binary string has 7 pairs of adjacent digits. So we have

$$C(1) + C(2) + \cdots C(256) = C(0) + C(1) + \cdots + C(255) = 2^8 \cdot 7 \cdot \frac{1}{4} = \boxed{448}.$$

Solution to 12.9 The problem is equivalent to finding the largest positive integer that cannot be expressed in the form $1 + 7m + 11n$ for nonnegative integers m and n. By the Chicken McNugget Theorem, the largest positive integer that cannot be expressed in the form $7m + 11n$ is $7 \cdot 11 - 7 - 11 = 59$. So the answer is $\boxed{60}$.

Solution to 12.10 Since $\gcd(7, 100) = 1$ and $\phi(100) = 40$, $7^{40} \equiv 1 \pmod{100}$ by Euler's Theorem. Thus if $7^{7^7} \equiv x \pmod{40}$, then $7^{7^{7^7}} \equiv 7^x \pmod{100}$. Since $\phi(40) = 16$ and $\gcd(7, 40) = 1$, $7^{16} \equiv 1 \pmod{40}$. Similarly, if $7^7 \equiv y \pmod{16}$, then $7^{7^7} \equiv 7^y \pmod{40}$. We see that

$$7^7 \equiv 49^3 \cdot 7 \equiv (3 \cdot 16 + 1)^3 \cdot 7 \equiv 7 \pmod{16}.$$

Thus,

$$7^{7^7} \equiv 7^7 \equiv 7 \cdot (40 + 9)^3 \equiv 7 \cdot 9^3 \equiv 7 \cdot 9 \cdot (80 + 1) \equiv 7 \cdot 9 \equiv 23 \pmod{40}.$$

Therefore, $7^{7^{7^7}} \equiv 7^{23} \pmod{100}$. Since $7^4 \equiv (50-1)^2 \equiv 1 \pmod{100}$, $7^{23} \equiv 7^3 \equiv (50-1) \cdot 7 \equiv 50 - 7 \equiv 43 \pmod{100}$. Thus the last two digits of $7^{7^{7^7}}$ are $\boxed{43}$.

Solution to 12.11 We know that the two numbers have the same number of digits. Since the new number starts with a 6 and the old number is $\frac{1}{4}$ of the new one, we divide 6 by 4 and see that the old number must start with a 1. Therefore, the new number starts with 61. We divide 61 by 4 and see that the old number must start with 15. So the new number starts with 615. We divide 615 by 4 and see that the old number must start with 153. Thus the new number starts with 6153. We divide 6153 by 4 and see that the old number must start with 1538. Hence the new

Solutions for Chapter 12

number starts with 61538. We divide 61538 by 4 and see that the old number must start with 15384. We divide 615384 by 4 and see that the old number is $\boxed{153{,}846}$.

Solution to 12.12 Note that any whole-number weight of an object from 1 to 40 pounds can be weighed using weights 1, 2, 4, 8, 16, and 32 by placing the weights on one side of the scale and the object on the other side of the scale. Since we are allowed to place the weights on both sides of the scale, we can do better. Since $2 \equiv -1 \pmod{3}$, we can prove by induction that any whole number can be expressed as the difference of two base-3 positive integers each has only 0 and 1 as its digits. Therefore, using a set of four weights 1, 3, 9, and 27, we can weigh any whole-number weight of an object from 1 to 40 pounds. This set contains the minimum number of weights. The greatest weight in this set is $\boxed{27}$.

Solution to 12.13 Clearly, $\gcd(a,b) = 1$. Otherwise, infinitely many scores would be unattainable. By the Chicken McNugget Theorem,

$$\frac{1}{2}(a-1)(b-1) = 35, \qquad (a-1)(b-1) = 70.$$

Since $a > b$ and $\gcd(a,b) = 1$, we have either $(a,b) = (71,2)$, or $(a,b) = (11,8)$. Since $58 = 2 \cdot 29$ is attainable with $(71,2)$, we only have $(11,8)$ left. Now we show that 58 is unattainable with $(11,8)$. 11 is clearly attainable with $(11,8)$. By the Chicken McNugget Theorem, $(11 \cdot 8 - 11 - 8) - 11 = 58$ is not attainable with $(11,8)$. Thus, the desired pair is $\boxed{(11,8)}$.

Solution to 12.14 The set $\{1,2,3,...,50\}$ has 8 numbers that are congruent to 1 (mod 7), and 7 numbers each that are congruent to 0, 2, 3, 4, 5, or 6 (mod 7). First we put one number that is congruent to 0 (mod 7) to S. To maximize the number of elements in S, we next put all 8 numbers that are congruent to 1 (mod 7) to S, and put all numbers that are congruent to either 2 or 3 (mod 7) to S. We cannot put in any more. So, the maximum number of elements is $1 + 8 + 7 + 7 = \boxed{23}$.

Solution to 12.15 Since the given fraction is reducible, $\gcd(n-13, 5n+6) > 1$. By the Euclidean Algorithm, we have

$$\gcd(5n+6, n-13) = \gcd(5n+6-5(n-13), n-13) = \gcd(71, n-13).$$

Since 71 is a prime number, $n-13$ must be a non-zero multiple of 71. So the least n occurs when $n - 13 = 71$, $n = \boxed{84}$.

Solution to 12.16 Let $n = p_1^{e_1} p_2^{e_2} ... p_k^{e_k}$. Then we have

$$(1+e_1)(1+e_2) \cdots (1+e_k) = 75 = 3 \cdot 5^2.$$

We see that n can have at most three distinct prime factors and that these three prime factors must be 2, 3, and 5 in order to make n as small as possible. So $n =$

$2^{e_1}3^{e_2}5^{e_3}$ where $e_2 \geq 1$ and $e_3 \geq 2$. To minimize n, we want 5 to be raised to the least power. So the smallest n is $2^4 \cdot 3^4 \cdot 5^2$. So $\dfrac{n}{75} = 2^4 \cdot 3^3 = \boxed{432}$.

Solution to 12.17 This odometer simply uses base 9 except that it uses 5, 6, 7, 8, and 9 to represent 4, 5, 6, 7, and 8, respectively. So the actual number of miles traveled is $2004_9 = 2 \cdot 9^3 + 4 = \boxed{1462 \text{ miles}}$.

Solution to 12.18 Let's rewrite the number as a sequence $\{1, 2, 3, 4, ..., 200\}$. After the first pass, the new sequence is $\{3, 3\cdot 2, 3\cdot 3, 3\cdot 4, ..., 3\cdot 66\}$. After the second pass, the new sequence is $\{3^2, 3^2 \cdot 2, 3^2 \cdot 3, 3^2 \cdot 4, ..., 3^2 \cdot 22\}$. After the third pass, the new sequence is $\{3^3, 3^3 \cdot 2, 3^3 \cdot 3, 3^3 \cdot 4, ..., 3^3 \cdot 7\}$. After the fourth pass, the new sequence is $\{3^4, 3^4 \cdot 2\}$. Note that the number $3^4 = 81$ corresponds to the digit 9 and the number $3^4 \cdot 2 = 162$ corresponds to the digit 8 in the original 200-digit number. So, the resulting two-digit number is $\boxed{98}$.

Solution to 12.19 We see that there is a one-to-one correspondence between integers whose base three representation does not contain the digit 2 and integers in base 2. Since $1992_{10} = 2201210_3$, the largest integer less than or equal to 1992 that does not contain the digit 2 is 1111111_3. Therefore, there are $1111111_2 = 2^7 - 1 = \boxed{127}$ such integers.

Solution to 12.20 We see that $\phi(100) = 40$. Since $\gcd(33, 100) = 1$, Euler's Theorem tells us that $33^{40} \equiv 1 \pmod{100}$. Therefore,

$$3^3 \cdot 33^{33} \cdot 333^{333} \cdot 3333^{3333}$$
$$\equiv 3^3 \cdot 33^{33} \cdot 33^{333} \cdot 33^{3333} \pmod{100}$$
$$\equiv 3^3 \cdot 33^{3699} \pmod{100}$$
$$\equiv 3^3 \cdot 33^{19} \pmod{100}$$

Using the Binomial Theorem, we get,

$$3^3 \cdot 33^{19} \pmod{100}$$
$$\equiv 3^3 \cdot (30+3)^{19} \pmod{100}$$
$$\equiv 3^3 \cdot (19 \cdot 30 \cdot 3^{18} + 3^{19}) \pmod{100}$$
$$\equiv 3^{22} \cdot 191 \pmod{100}$$
$$\equiv 9^{11} \cdot 91 \pmod{100}$$
$$\equiv (10-1)^{11} \cdot 91 \pmod{100}$$
$$\equiv (11 \cdot 10 - 1) \cdot 91 \pmod{100}$$
$$\equiv 9 \cdot 91 \pmod{100}$$
$$\equiv \boxed{19} \pmod{100}.$$

Solutions for Chapter 13

Solution to 13.1 Letting x be the least number, we have $x \equiv 2$ (mod 3), $x \equiv 3$ (mod 5), and $x \equiv 2$ (mod 7). Let $M = 3 \cdot 5 \cdot 7 = 105$, $a_1 = 5 \cdot 7 = 35$, $a_2 = 3 \cdot 7 = 21$, and $a_3 = 3 \cdot 5 = 15$. To find a multiplicative inverse b_1 of 35 modulo 3, we have

$$35 = 11 \cdot 3 + 2, \quad 3 = 2 + 1, \quad 1 = 3 - 2 = 3 - (35 - 11 \cdot 3) = (-1) \cdot 35 + 12 \cdot 3.$$

So $b_1 = -1$. To find a multiplicative inverse b_2 of 21 modulo 5, we have

$$21 = 4 \cdot 5 + 1, \quad 1 = 1 \cdot 21 - 4 \cdot 5. \quad \text{So } b_2 = 1.$$

To find a multiplicative inverse b_3 of 15 modulo 7, we have

$$15 = 2 \cdot 7 + 1, \quad 1 = 1 \cdot 15 - 2 \cdot 7. \quad \text{So } b_3 = 1.$$

So $x \equiv 35 \cdot (-1) \cdot 2 + 21 \cdot 1 \cdot 3 + 15 \cdot 1 \cdot 2 \equiv 23$ (mod 105) and the least number is $\boxed{23}$.

Solution to 13.2 Let's look at the sequence $\lfloor \sqrt{n} \rfloor$ for non-negative integers n. It is $\{0, 1, 1, 1, 2, 2, 2, 2, 2, \ldots\}$. This is because $\lfloor \sqrt{n} \rfloor$ increases if and only if n is a square. Furthermore, there are $(n+1)^2 - n^2 = 2n+1$ numbers between any two adjacent squares. Since $\{0, 1, 1, 1, 2, 2, 2, 2, 2, \ldots\}$ is also the sequence of $\lfloor \sqrt{n-1} \rfloor$ for positive integers n, we see that $\{1, 3, 3, 3, 5, 5, 5, 5, 5, \ldots\}$ is the sequence of $2\lfloor \sqrt{n-1} \rfloor + 1$ for positive integers n. Therefore, $b = 2$, $c = -1$, $d = 1$, and $b + c + d = \boxed{2}$.

Solution to 13.3 Pick any number F. Let's consider the numbers in the sequence that starts with F modulo 12. When the first rule is applied, the remainder is doubled modulo 12. However, the remainder is the same when the second rule is applied. Since $16 \equiv 4$ (mod 12), we only need to find out which numbers are congruent to 4 (mod 12) after repeated doubling, because sooner or later, 16 will show up in the sequences that start with these numbers. We see that 1, 2, 4, 5, 7, 8, 10, and 11 all give us 4 modulo 12 after repeated doubling, but 0, 3, 6, and 9 all give us 0 eventually. So a number is "sweet" if and only it is a multiple of 3. Since there are 16 multiples of 3 among whole numbers 1 through 50, the answer is $\boxed{16}$.

Solution to 13.4 Rewriting $\dfrac{8}{15} < \dfrac{n}{n+k} < \dfrac{7}{13}$ as $\dfrac{13}{7} < \dfrac{n+k}{n} < \dfrac{15}{8}$, we get

$$\dfrac{6}{7} < \dfrac{k}{n} < \dfrac{7}{8}, \quad 48n < 56k < 49n.$$

Between $48n$ and $49n$, there are $n - 1$ integers excluding $48n$ and $49n$. If $n - 1 \geq 2 \cdot 56$, there would be at least two multiples of 56 between $48n$ and $49n$. Therefore, $n - 1 < 2 \cdot 56$. We check and see that when $n = 112$, there is a unique $k = 97$ satisfying the given condition. So the largest n is $\boxed{112}$.

Solution to 13.5 The three planets and the star are collinear now. Let l be the line passing through them. At the yth year, the angle between the period-60 star and line l is $\alpha_1 = \dfrac{y \cdot 2\pi}{60}$. Similarly, the angle α_2 between the period-84 star and line l and the angle α_3 between the period-140 star and line l are $\dfrac{y \cdot 2\pi}{84}$ and $\dfrac{y \cdot 2\pi}{140}$, respectively. For the three planets and the star to be collinear again, both $\alpha_1 - \alpha_2$ and $\alpha_1 - \alpha_3$ must be multiples of π. That is, both $\dfrac{y}{30} - \dfrac{y}{42}$ and $\dfrac{y}{30} - \dfrac{y}{70}$ must be integers. So y must be a multiple of 105. Thus, the least y is $\boxed{105 \text{ years}}$.

Solution to 13.6 Let's say that Benji bought x apples and y oranges, then

$$0.35x + 0.69y = 2.78, \qquad 35x + (70-1)y = 278, \qquad 35(x+2y) - y = 278.$$

Letting $z = x + 2y$, we get $35z - y = 278$. Taking both sides of the equation modulo 35, we get $-y \equiv 33 \pmod{35}$. Thus, $y \equiv 2 \pmod{35}$. When $y = 2$, we get $35z = 280$ and $z = 8$. So $x = z - 2y = 4$. Therefore, he bought $\boxed{4 \text{ apples}}$.

Solution to 13.7 Let's take both sides of the equation modulo 3. We get $x^2 \equiv 2 \pmod{3}$. Since perfect squares only leave a remainder of 0 or 1, (mod 3), no such integer x exists. Therefore, the answer is $\boxed{0 \text{ pairs}}$.

Solution to 13.8 Let x be the number of dollars and y the number of cents. Then

$$100y + x - 68 = 2(100x + y),$$
$$98y - 199x = 68.$$

Taking both sides of the last equation modulo 98, we get

$$-3x \equiv 68 \pmod{98}, \qquad 3x \equiv -68 \pmod{98},$$
$$3x \equiv 30 \pmod{98}, \qquad x \equiv 10 \pmod{98}.$$

Therefore, the smallest x is 10. When $x = 10$, we get $98y = 68 + 199 \cdot 10$, $y = 21$. So the smallest value is $\boxed{\$10.21}$.

Solution to 13.9 Suppose there are P pennies, N nickels, D dimes, and Q quarters. Then we have

$$155P + 195N + 135D + 175Q = 1400.$$

Let $m = P + N + D + Q$. If $m = 2n + 1$, for some n, then $155P + 195N + 135D + 175Q$ will have 5 as its ones digit. If $m = 4n + 2$, for some n, then the ones digit of $155P + 195N + 135D + 175Q$ will be zero, and the tens digit of $155P + 195N + 135D + 175Q$ will be an odd number. This is because, for any n, the tens digit of $5 \cdot (4n+2)$ is odd. Thus, m cannot be odd or of the form $4n + 2$. So it must be a multiple of 4.

Solutions for Chapter 13

Since the tallest stack made from 4 coins has length $1.95 \cdot 4 < 14$, $m > 4$. Since the shortest stack made from 12 coins has length $1.35 \cdot 12 > 14$, $m < 12$. Therefore, m has to be 8. We see that $8 \cdot 1.75 = 14$. So $\boxed{8 \text{ coins}}$ are in the stack.

Solution to 13.10 Let x be the number of coins. We have $x \equiv 3 \pmod{17}$, $x \equiv 10 \pmod{16}$, and $x \equiv 0 \pmod{15}$. Let $M = 17 \cdot 16 \cdot 15 = 4080$, $a_1 = 16 \cdot 15 = 240$, and $a_2 = 17 \cdot 15 = 255$. First we find b_1, the multiplicative inverse of a_1 modulo 17.

$$240 = 17 \cdot 14 + 2, \qquad 17 = 2 \cdot 8 + 1,$$
$$1 = 17 - 2 \cdot 8 = 17 - 8(240 - 17 \cdot 14) = 113 \cdot 17 - 8 \cdot 240.$$

So $b_1 = -8$. Next we find b_2, the multiplicative inverse of a_2 modulo 16. We have

$$255 = 16 \cdot 16 - 1, \qquad 1 = 16 \cdot 16 - 255.$$

So $b_2 = -1$. By the Chinese Remainder Theorem, one solution for x is:

$$x \equiv 240 \cdot (-8) \cdot 3 + (255) \cdot (-1) \cdot 10 \pmod{4080}$$
$$\equiv -8310 \equiv 3930 \pmod{4080}.$$

Therefore, the least number is $\boxed{3930 \text{ coins}}$.

Solution to 13.11 Since a, b, and c are positive integers, and $29a + 30b + 31c = 366$, we have $29a + 30 + 31 \le 366$. So $a \le 10$. Similarly, $29 + 30b + 31 \le 366$ gives us $b \le 10$. $29 + 30 + 31c \le 366$ gives us $c \le 9$. We rewrite $29a + 30b + 31c = 366$ as $29(a + b + c) + (b + 2c) = 366$. We observe that this equation can be satisfied with $a + b + c = 12$ and $b + 2c = 18$. We see that $a + b + c < 12$ is impossible because $b + 2c$ is at most 28. Also, $a + b + c > 12$ is impossible because $29 \cdot 13 > 366$. Thus

$$19a + 20b + 21c = 19(a + b + c) + (b + 2c) = 19 \cdot 12 + 18 = \boxed{246}.$$

Solution to 13.12 Let's calculate $\phi(49)$, which is $7^2 - 7 = 42$. Since $49 - 6 \cdot 8 = 1$, -8 is a multiplicative inverse of 6 modulo 49 and -6 is a multiplicative inverse of 8 modulo 49. By Euler's Theorem, $6^{42} \equiv 1 \pmod{49}$ and $8^{42} \equiv 1 \pmod{49}$. So

$$6^{83} + 8^{83} \equiv 6^{41} + 8^{41} \pmod{49}$$
$$\equiv 6^{41} \cdot (6 \cdot (-8)) + 8^{41} \cdot (8 \cdot (-6)) \pmod{49}$$
$$\equiv -8 - 6 \equiv -14 \equiv \boxed{35} \pmod{49}.$$

Solution to 13.13 The first four equations give us that $x \equiv -2 \pmod{3 \cdot 5 \cdot 7 \cdot 11}$. So $x = 3 \cdot 5 \cdot 7 \cdot 11 \cdot n - 2 = 1155n - 2$ for some positive integer n. Thus

$$1155n - 2 \equiv 2 \pmod{13}, \qquad 1155n \equiv 4 \pmod{13}, \qquad 11n \equiv 4 \pmod{13}.$$

Since $13 = 11+2$ and $11 = 2 \cdot 5+1$, we have $1 = 11-2 \cdot 5 = 11-(13-11) \cdot 5 = 6 \cdot 11-13 \cdot 5$. So, 6 is a multiplicative inverse of 11 modulo 13. Therefore, $n \equiv 6 \cdot 11 n \equiv 6 \cdot 4 \equiv 11$ (mod 13). So the smallest n is 11 and the smallest x is $1155 \cdot 11 - 2 = \boxed{12,703}$.

Solution to 13.14 By the Euclidean Algorithm, we have

$$43 = 2 \cdot 17 + 9, \qquad 17 = 2 \cdot 9 - 1, \qquad 1 = 2 \cdot 9 - 17 = 2(43 - 2 \cdot 17) - 17 = 2 \cdot 43 + (-5) \cdot 17.$$

Therefore for any integer k, the integer pair $(2 \cdot 1500 + 17k, -5 \cdot 1500 - 43k)$ is a solution to $43x + 17y = 1500$. To make the solution positive, we must have:

$$2 \cdot 1500 + 17k > 0, \qquad \text{and} \qquad -5 \cdot 1500 - 43k > 0.$$

Thus,
$$\frac{-3000}{17} < k < \frac{-7500}{43}.$$

The only integers k that meet those requirements are -176 and -175. Therefore, there are $\boxed{2}$ positive solutions.

Solution to 13.15 Since for any real number x, $x = \lfloor x \rfloor + \{x\}$, we can add the three equations and get:

$$2x + 2y + 2z = 568.9, \qquad x + y + z = 284.45.$$

Therefore,

$$x + y + z - (\{x\} + y + \lfloor z \rfloor) = \lfloor x \rfloor + \{z\} = 284.45 - 190.1 = 94.35.$$

So $\lfloor x \rfloor = 94$. Similarly,

$$x + y + z - (\lfloor x \rfloor + \{y\} + z) = \{x\} + \lfloor y \rfloor = 284.45 - 178.8 = 105.65.$$

So $\{x\} = 0.65$. Therefore, $x = \lfloor x \rfloor + \{x\} = \boxed{94.65}$.

Solution to 13.16 We see that $10^{290} = 2^{290} \cdot 5^{290}$. There are clearly more powers of two than powers of five in any number, so we only need to find the smallest n such that
$$290 = \lfloor \frac{n}{5} \rfloor + \lfloor \frac{n}{5^2} \rfloor + \cdots.$$

The right hand side of the equation is roughly a geometric series, so we have

$$290 \approx \frac{\frac{n}{5}}{1-\frac{1}{5}}.$$

Thus, $n \approx 1160$. Since
$$\lfloor \frac{1160}{5} \rfloor + \lfloor \frac{1160}{5^2} \rfloor + \cdots = 288,$$

Solutions for Chapter 13

we need to add two more factors of 5, which will be from 1165 and 1170. So the smallest n is $\boxed{1170}$.

Solution to 13.17 The sum has $91 - 19 + 1 = 73$ terms and each term can be either $\lfloor r \rfloor$ or $\lfloor r \rfloor + 1$. Since $546 = 7 \cdot 73 + 35$, each of the first 38 terms must be 7 and each of the last 35 terms must be 8. Thus

$$\lfloor r + \frac{56}{100} \rfloor = 7, \text{ and } \lfloor r + \frac{57}{100} \rfloor = 8.$$

Therefore, $r + \frac{56}{100} < 8$ and $r + \frac{57}{100} \geq 8$. That is, $7.43 \leq r < 7.44$. So $\lfloor 100r \rfloor = \boxed{743}$.

Solution to 13.18 First we see that $4444 \equiv 16 \pmod{18}$, so

$$4444^{4444} \equiv 16^{4444} \equiv (-2)^{4444} \equiv 4^{2222} \pmod{18}.$$

Since $\gcd(4, 18) \neq 1$, we cannot use Euler's Theorem directly. So we calculate 4^{2222} modulo 2 and 4^{2222} modulo 9 instead. We see that $4^{2222} \equiv 0 \pmod{2}$. Since $\gcd(4, 9) = 1$, and $\phi(9) = 3^2 - 3 = 6$, $4^6 \equiv 1 \pmod{9}$. So, $4^{2222} \equiv 4^2 \equiv 7 \pmod{9}$. Since the only number that is 7 (mod 9), 0 (mod 2), and less than 18 is $7 + 9 = 16$, we have $4444^{4444} \equiv \boxed{16} \pmod{18}$.

Solution to 13.19 Since 2^{2004} is a 604-digit number with leading digit 1, 2^{2003} is a 603-digit number. For every positive integer k, there is a k-digit power of 2 whose first digit is 1. So there are 603 elements of S whose first digit is 1. We see that if 2^k has a first digit of 1, then 2^{k+1} has a first digit of 2 or 3, and 2^{k+2} has a first digit of 4, 5, 6, or 7. Thus there are 603 elements whose first digit is either 2 or 3, and there are 603 elements whose first digit is 4, 5, 6, or 7. Therefore, there are $2004 - 3 \cdot 603 = 195$ elements whose first digit is 8 or 9. Note that 2^k has the first digit 8 or 9 if and only if 2^{k-1} has the first digit 4. So there are $\boxed{195}$ elements of S whose first digit is 4.

Solution to 13.20 From the equation, we see that x must be an integer. Let $x = 30n + r$, where $0 \leq r < 30$ is the remainder when x is divided by 30. Then we have

$$\lfloor \frac{30n+r}{2} \rfloor + \lfloor \frac{30n+r}{3} \rfloor + \lfloor \frac{30n+r}{5} \rfloor = 30n + r,$$

$$15n + \lfloor \frac{r}{2} \rfloor + 10n + \lfloor \frac{r}{3} \rfloor + 6n + \lfloor \frac{r}{5} \rfloor = 30n + r,$$

$$n = r - \lfloor \frac{r}{2} \rfloor - \lfloor \frac{r}{3} \rfloor - \lfloor \frac{r}{5} \rfloor.$$

We see that for each possible r, there exists exactly one corresponding n. Since $x = 30n + r$, each r gives us a unique x. Since there are 30 possible remainders, the number of solutions for x is $\boxed{30}$.

Solutions for Chapter 14

Solution to 14.1 Let's call the 100 students $S_1, S_2, ..., S_{100}$. Let N_i be the number of languages Student S_i studies. We see that for each i, $1 \le N_i \le 3$. Furthermore,

$$N_1 + N_2 + \cdots + N_{100} = 90 + 75 + 42 = 207.$$

By the pigeonhole principle, among $N_1, N_2, ..., N_{100}$, at least 7 of them must be greater than 2. So at least $\boxed{7 \text{ students}}$ take all three languages.

Solution to 14.2 Let's first assume that red and blue are the same color, say black, in order to make them indistinguishable. There are $\binom{11}{5}$ ways to place 10 black balls and five green balls in a row so that no two green balls lie next to each other. Since the 10 black balls are actually 5 red and 5 blue, the number of ways to place these 15 balls is

$$\binom{10}{5} \cdot \binom{11}{5} = \boxed{116,424}.$$

Solution to 14.3 There are 5! ways for the five people to choose the five left-handed gloves. For each arrangement of the five left-handed gloves, there are $D(5)$ ways to choose the right-handed gloves so that no one gets a matching pair. So in total, there are $5! \cdot D(5) = 5! \cdot 44 = \boxed{5280}$ ways.

Solution to 14.4 After five books are removed, there are empty slots between the remaining seven books. Since no two of the chosen books stand next to each other, there is at most one empty slot between any two remaining books. In total, there are 8 potential empty slots: at the two ends and between the seven remaining books. Any five of these empty slots uniquely determine the set of five chosen books. Therefore, there are $\binom{8}{5} = \boxed{56}$ ways.

Solution to 14.5 The problem is equivalent to placing $5-1$ bars among 14 stars. For example,

$$*|****|****|*|****$$

means "beebe" since one star would correspond to "b" and four stars would correspond to "e". So there are $\binom{14+5-1}{5-1} = \binom{18}{4} = \boxed{3060 \text{ words}}$.

Solution to 14.6 For each $1 \le i \le 4$, x_i is an odd positive integer. So we can replace it with $2y_i - 1$, where y_i is a positive integer. Then $x_1 + x_2 + x_3 + x_4 = 98$ is equivalent to $2(y_1 + y_2 + y_3 + y_4) - 4 = 98$, or $y_1 + y_2 + y_3 + y_4 = 51$. We represent 51 with 51 stars. Since each y_i is a positive number, the problem is equivalent to dividing the $51-1$

Solutions for Chapter 14

spaces between the 51 stars with 3 bars. So the number of ordered quadruples is $\binom{50}{3} = \boxed{19,600}$.

Solution to 14.7 Since every set of 4 points uniquely determines a quadrilateral and thus uniquely determines one intersection point, the maximum number of intersection points is $\binom{12}{4} = \boxed{495 \text{ points}}$.

Solution to 14.8 Let's number the balls 1, 2, 3, ..., 100, from left to right. When every fourth ball is replaced with a green ball, $\frac{100}{4} = 25$ red balls are gone. So there are 75 red balls left. After the second round, every fifth ball counting from the right end is replaced with a white ball. Balls with numbers 96, 91, 86, 81, ..., 16, 11, 6, 1 are now white. Among those, the balls numbered 16, 36, 56, 76, and 96 are not red. So, after the second round, there are $75 - (20 - 5) = 60$ red balls left. The third round replaces every sixth ball. The red balls being replaced by yellow balls are numbered 18, 30, 42, 54, 78, and 90. Therefore, at the end, there are $60 - 6 = \boxed{54 \text{ red balls}}$ left.

Solution to 14.9 Let's count how many cubes there are if we have three pairs of opposite sides with the same color. In this case there is one such cube. There is no cube such that exactly two pairs of opposite sides have the same color. If we have one pair of opposite sides with the same color, then there are three ways to choose this color. After that, the cube is fixed. So for this case, there are 3 different cubes. If there are no opposites sides with the same color, then such a cube must have opposite sides pairs (red, green), and (red, yellow). Let's place the first opposite sides pair on the top and bottom with red on the top and green on the bottom. Then counting clockwise, the other four faces can be yellow, yellow, green, red, or yellow, yellow, red, green. So there are two cubes in this case. Therefore, there are $1 + 3 + 2 = \boxed{6 \text{ cubes}}$ in total.

Solution to 14.10 We line up the first twenty positive integers in a row and consider the 14 integers that are not chosen. We use 14 stars to represent these 14 integers. Between any two of these 14 stars there is at most one empty slot, because the chosen ones cannot be consecutive. There are 15 potential empty slots: those between the 14 integers and those at the two ends. Picking any 6 slots out of the 15 uniquely determines the 6 chosen integers. For example,

$$\_*\,*\_*\,*\,*\,*\,*\,*\_*\_*\_*\,*\,*\_*$$

means that the chosen integers are 1, 4, 11, 13, 15, and 19. Therefore, there are $\binom{15}{6} = \boxed{5005}$ ways.

Solution to 14.11 The digits 1, 1, 1, 1, 3, 3, 3 can be arranged in $\binom{7}{3} = 35$ ways. We need to partition each arrangement into three integers for the prices. Using stars and bars, this can be done in $\binom{6}{2} = 15$ ways. But three of these partitions include five-digit integers: (5-digit, 1-digit, 1-digit), (1-digit, 5-digit, 1-digit), and (1-digit, 1-digit, 5-digit). Since the allowed integers are at most 9999, we have $15 - 3 = 12$ ways for each arrangement. Thus, the total number of guesses is $35 \cdot 12 = \boxed{420}$.

Solution to 14.12 We fix one face of the octahedron and color it black. The rest faces can be colored in 7! ways. Since there are three possible rotations about this fixed face that will produce indistinguishable octahedrons, the answer is $\dfrac{7!}{3} = \boxed{1680}$.

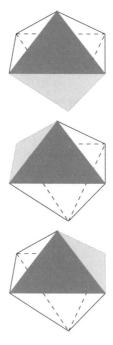

Solution to 14.13 Let's label the faces from 1 to 6. Place face 1 on the bottom and color it black. There are 5! ways to color the other faces. Since there are four possible rotations about this fixed bottom face that will produce indistinguishable cubes, the final answer is $\dfrac{5!}{4} = \boxed{30}$.

Solution to 14.14 We can arrange eight integers in 8! ways if there are no restrictions. For any one of the odd integers 1, 3, 5, and 7, there are 7! arrangements such that it is in its natural position. For any two of the odd integers, there are

Solutions for Chapter 14

6! arrangements such that these two are in their natural positions. ... For all four odd integers 1, 3, 5, 7, there are 4! arrangements such that they are in their natural positions. By the principle of inclusion-exclusion, the number of arrangements such that no odd number is in its natural position is

$$8! - \binom{4}{1}7! + \binom{4}{2}6! - \binom{4}{3}5! + \binom{4}{4}4! = \boxed{24,024}.$$

Solution to 14.15 Let $C = \{1, 2, ..., 10\} - (A \cup B)$. Since $A \cap B = \emptyset$, every number from 1 to 10 is in one and only one of the subsets A, B, and C. Thus there are three choices for each number from 1 to 10, and 3^{10} ordered triples of subsets (A, B, C). Since the elements in C are uniquely determined when the elements in A and B are determined, the number of ordered pairs of subsets (A, B) is $3^{10} = \boxed{59,049}$.

Solution to 14.16 There are $\binom{8}{5}$ ways to choose the five rings. The five rings can be arranged in 5! ways. We order the fingers from the little finger to the index finger. We order the five rings from the bottom-most ring on the first finger that has a ring to the top-most ring on the last finger that has a ring. Note that placing five rings on four fingers is equivalent to using $4-1$ bars to separate five stars. Since it is not required that each finger have a ring, there are $\binom{5+4-1}{4-1} = \binom{8}{3}$ ways to do it. Therefore,

$$n = \binom{8}{5} \cdot 5! \cdot \binom{8}{3} = 376,320.$$

The leftmost three nonzero digits of n is $\boxed{376}$.

Solution to 14.17 If 0 is one of the digits, then there are $\binom{9}{3}$ ways to choose the other three distinct digits a, b, and c. Let's assume that $0 < a < b < c$. Then there are 3 ways to arrange them in snakelike integer form:

$$ac0b, \quad bc0a, \quad \text{and} \quad ab0c.$$

If 0 is not one of the digits, then there are $\binom{9}{4}$ ways to choose the four distinct nonzero digits a, b, c, and d. Let's assume that $a < b < c < d$. Then there are 5 ways to arrange them in snakelike integer form:

$$acbd, \quad adbc, \quad bcad, \quad bdac, \quad \text{and} \quad cdab.$$

Therefore, there are

$$\binom{9}{3} \cdot 3 + \binom{9}{4} \cdot 5 = \boxed{882}$$

snakelike integers between 1000 and 9999.

Solution to 14.18 Since $360 = 2^3 \cdot 3^2 \cdot 5$, its divisors are of the form $2^a \cdot 3^b \cdot 5^c$, where a, b, and c are nonnegative integers. Let $d_1 = 2^{a_1} 3^{b_1} 5^{c_1}$, $d_2 = 2^{a_2} 3^{b_2} 5^{c_2}$, and $d_3 = 2^{a_3} 3^{b_3} 5^{c_3}$. If $d_1 \cdot d_2 \cdot d_3$ is a divisor of 360, then

$$a_1 + a_2 + a_3 \leq 3,$$
$$b_1 + b_2 + b_3 \leq 2,$$
$$c_1 + c_2 + c_3 \leq 1.$$

Since the number of ordered triples (a_1, a_2, a_3) such that $a_1 + a_2 + a_3 \leq 3$ is equivalent to the number of ordered quadruples (a_1, a_2, a_3, a_4) such that $a_1 + a_2 + a_3 + a_4 = 3$, there are $\binom{3+4-1}{4-1} = 20$ ways to choose (a_1, a_2, a_3). Similarly, there are $\binom{2+4-1}{4-1} = 10$ ways to choose (b_1, b_2, b_3), and $\binom{1+4-1}{4-1} = 4$ ways to choose (c_1, c_2, c_3). Therefore, the total number is $20 \cdot 10 \cdot 4 = \boxed{800}$.

Solution to 14.19 Let the two disjoint subsets be A and B. Let $C = S - (A \cup B)$. Since each number can be in one and only one of the subsets A, B, and C, the number of ordered pairs of subsets (A, B) is 3^{10} if we count empty sets. If A is empty and B is not empty, then the number of pairs is $2^{10} - 1$. So the number of pairs if either A or B or both are empty is $2^{10} - 1 + 2^{10} - 1 + 1 = 2^{11} - 1$. Thus the number of ordered pairs when both A and B are non-empty is $3^{10} - (2^{11} - 1)$. Since the order of A and B does not matter, the number of sets is

$$n = \frac{1}{2}(3^{10} - 2^{11} + 1) = 28,501.$$

Dividing n by 1000, we get the remainder $\boxed{501}$.

Solution to 14.20 The large triangle has one center triangle and 3 corner triangles. There are 6 ways to choose the color of the center triangle. If the corner triangles are of the same color, then there are 6 ways to choose that color. If the corner triangles are of two different colors, then there are $6 \times 5 = 30$ ways to choose the two colors. If the corner triangles are all different colors, then there are $\binom{6}{3} = 20$ ways to choose those colors. So in total, there are $6(6 + 30 + 20) = \boxed{336}$ distinguishable large triangles.

Solutions for Chapter 15

Solution to 15.1 Since it does not rain on Friday, there is only a 25% chance that it will rain on Saturday. So, the probability that there will be no rain on Saturday is $\frac{3}{4}$. Since $P(\text{no rain on Friday}) = 1$, we have

$P(\text{no rain on Saturday given no rain on Friday})$
$= \dfrac{P(\text{no rain on Friday and no rain on Saturday})}{P(\text{no rain on Friday})}$
$= P(\text{no rain on Friday and no rain on Saturday}) = P(\text{no rain on Saturday}) = \dfrac{3}{4}.$

Note that

$P(\text{no rain on Sunday given no rain on Saturday})$
$= P(\text{no rain on Saturday given no rain on Friday}) = \dfrac{3}{4}.$

Thus, the probability that there will be no rain during the weekend is

$P(\text{no rain on Saturday and no rain on Sunday}) = P(\text{no rain on Saturday})$
$\cdot P(\text{no rain on Sunday given no rain on Saturday}) = \dfrac{3}{4} \cdot \dfrac{3}{4} = \boxed{\dfrac{9}{16}}.$

Solution to 15.2 Let's place one vertex of the cube on the origin of an xyz-coordinate system. Let the three edges associated with this vertex be aligned with the x-axis, y-axis, and z-axis, respectively. We see that any continuous stripe encircling the cube has only three possible orientations: parallel to the xy-plane, parallel to the xz-plane, or parallel to the yz-plane. If a continuous stripe that is parallel to the xy-plane encircles the cube, then each of the four stripes on the faces through which this continuous stripe passes must be aligned with the xy-plane. Since there are two ways to paint the stripe on any face of the cube, the probability that all four corresponding stripes are aligned with the xy-plane is $(\frac{1}{2})^4 = \frac{1}{16}$. There are three possible orientations. So, the probability that there is a continuous stripe is

$$3 \cdot \dfrac{1}{16} = \boxed{\dfrac{3}{16}}.$$

Solution to 15.3 We use $P(B_{Da})$ to denote the probability that a child is a boy named David. Let $P(B_{Da}) = \alpha$. Similarly, we use $P(B_{De})$ to denote the probability that a child is a boy named Delta. Let $P(B_{De}) = \beta$. Since more boys are named David than are named Delta, $\alpha > \beta$. From Example 15.2, the probability for (A) is

$$P(A) = \frac{1-\alpha}{2-\alpha},$$

and the probability for (B) is

$$P(B) = \frac{1-\beta}{2-\beta}.$$

We see that $P(A) - P(B) < 0$ because

$$\frac{1-\alpha}{2-\alpha} - \left(\frac{1-\beta}{2-\beta}\right) = \frac{(1-\alpha)(2-\beta) - (1-\beta)(2-\alpha)}{(2-\alpha)(2-\beta)} = \frac{\beta - \alpha}{(2-\alpha)(2-\beta)} < 0.$$

Thus, $P(B) > P(A)$ and the probability for $\boxed{(B)}$ is higher.

Solution to 15.4 If you stick with the original door, you have a $\frac{1}{3}$ chance of winning, that is, a $\frac{2}{3}$ chance of losing. If you switch, you will lose only when the prize is behind the original door. That is, you have a $\frac{1}{3}$ chance of losing when you switch. So, the chance you will win by switching to the remaining door is $\frac{2}{3}$, doubling your original odds of winning. So the answer is $\boxed{\text{yes}}$, you should switch.

Solution to 15.5 Let's use D and ND to represent that a person has this disease, and that a person does not have this disease, respectively. Let's use T to represent the event that a person tests positive. We need to find $P(D|T)$. Since one half percent of the population has this disease, $P(D) = 0.005$. Since the test has a false negative 2% of the time, we have $P(T|D) = 0.98$. Since the test has a false positive 3% of the time, we have $P(T|ND) = 0.03$. Therefore,

$$P(T) = P(T|D) \cdot P(D) + P(T|ND) \cdot P(ND) = 0.98 \cdot 0.005 + 0.03 \cdot (1 - 0.005).$$

Thus the probability that a person who tests positive actually has the disease is

$$P(D|T) = \frac{P(D \cap T)}{P(T)} = \frac{P(T|D) \cdot P(D)}{P(T)}$$

$$= \frac{0.98 \cdot 0.005}{0.98 \cdot 0.005 + 0.03 \cdot (1 - 0.005)} \approx \boxed{0.14}.$$

Solution to 15.6 Choosing a and b uniformly at random from $(0, 1]$ is equivalent to choosing a point (a, b) from a unit square, where a is on the x-axis and b is on the y-axis. Since $\frac{1}{4} \leq c \leq \frac{3}{4}$, we have

$$\frac{1}{4} \leq \frac{a}{a+b} \leq \frac{3}{4}, \quad \frac{4}{3} \leq \frac{a+b}{a} \leq \frac{4}{1}, \quad \frac{1}{3} \leq \frac{b}{a} \leq 3.$$

So $b \leq 3a$ and $a \leq 3b$.

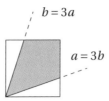

The desired probability is the area of the shaded region. It is equal to

$$1 - 2 \cdot \frac{1}{2} \cdot 1 \cdot \frac{1}{3} = \boxed{\frac{2}{3}}.$$

Solution to 15.7 Let p be the probability that you see at least one shooting star in 15 minutes. Then $(1-p)^4$ is the probability that you do not see any shooting stars in one hour. So the probability that you see at least one shooting star in one hour is $1 - (1-p)^4 = 1 - (1-0.2)^4 \approx \boxed{0.59}$.

Solution to 15.8 Let p be the probability that you see at least one shooting star in half an hour. Then the probability that you do not see any shooting stars in one hour is $(1-p)^2$. Thus

$$1 - (1-p)^2 = 0.4, \qquad (1-p)^2 = 0.6, \qquad p = 1 - \sqrt{0.6} \approx \boxed{0.225}.$$

Solution to 15.9 Since the median and unique mode are both 8, the middle two numbers of the collection are both 8 when we arrange the numbers from the smallest to the largest. So, in non-decreasing order, the numbers of the collection are:

$$a,\ b,\ c,\ 8,\ 8,\ d,\ e,\ f.$$

Since the range is 8, f is at most 16. When $f = 16$, $a = 8$. Then the numbers of the collection would be:

$$8,\ 8,\ 8,\ 8,\ 8,\ d,\ e,\ 16.$$

Since the mean is 8, this is impossible.

The next largest f is 15. When $f = 15$, $a = 7$. Then the numbers of the collection would be:

$$7,\ b,\ c,\ 8,\ 8,\ d,\ e,\ 15.$$

Since $7 + b + c + 8 + 8 + d + e + 15 = 8 \cdot 8$, we have $\dfrac{b+c+d+e}{4} = 6.5$. Since each of $b, c, d,$ and e must be at least 7, this is impossible.

The next largest f is 14. When $f = 14$, $a = 6$. Then the numbers of the collection would be:

$$6,\ b,\ c,\ 8,\ 8,\ d,\ e,\ 14.$$

Since $6+b+c+8+8+d+e+14 = 8 \cdot 8$, we have $\dfrac{b+c+d+e}{4} = 7$. So we let $b = c = 6$ and $d = e = 8$ and get

$$6, 6, 6, 8, 8, 8, 8, 14.$$

The numbers in this collection satisfy all the requirements. So the largest possible element of the collection is $\boxed{14}$.

Solution to 15.10 Let the lengths of the three parts be x, y, and z. We have $0 \le x, y, z \le 1$ and $x + y + z = 1$. Using x-axis, y-axis, and z-axis to represent x, y, and z, respectively, we see that the sample space is the equilateral triangle formed when the plane $x + y + z = 1$ cuts through the first octant. For the three parts to form a triangle, we must have $x + y > z > 0$, $x + z > y > 0$, and $y + z > x > 0$. These are equivalent to $0 < x, y, z < \frac{1}{2}$. Therefore, the feasible region is the shaded middle region of the sample space.

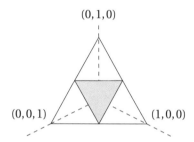

Here each vertex of the shaded triangle is the midpoint of one side of the large triangle. Therefore, the probability that the three parts form a triangle is $\boxed{\dfrac{1}{4}}$.

Solution to 15.11 Let the lengths of the four parts be w, x, y, and z. We have $0 \le w, x, y, z \le 1$ and $w + x + y + z = 1$. We use w-axis, x-axis, y-axis, and z-axis to render the sample space in four dimensions. The result is a regular tetrahedron with side length 1. The coordinates of the four vertices of the tetrahedron are $(1,0,0,0)$, $(0,1,0,0)$, $(0,0,1,0)$, and $(0,0,0,1)$. For the four parts to form a quadrilateral, we must have $w + x + y > z > 0$, $x + y + z > w > 0$, $y + z + w > x > 0$, and $z + w + x > y > 0$. These are equivalent to $0 < w, x, y, z < \frac{1}{2}$. Therefore, each of the four corners of the tetrahedron must be cut off, where each corner is a small tetrahedron with side length $\frac{1}{2}$. The resulting feasible region is a regular octahedron with side length $\frac{1}{2}$. Since each small tetrahedron has a volume of $(\frac{1}{2})^3$ of the original tetrahedron, the probability that the four parts form a quadrilateral is [3]

$$1 - 4 \cdot \left(\frac{1}{2}\right)^3 = \boxed{\dfrac{1}{2}}.$$

---

[3] With similar reasoning, it can be shown that if an interval is broken at $n-1$ points chosen uniformly at random, then the probability that the broken pieces can form an n-gon is $1 - \dfrac{n}{2^{n-1}}$.

Solutions for Chapter 15

Solution to 15.12 This is a conditional probability problem. We seek to find $P(R|B)$, where R represents that the first ball is red and B represents that the second ball is black. First let's calculate $P(R \cap B)$. If we pick Urn A in the first round, then the chance of red then black is $\frac{1}{2} \cdot \frac{2}{6} \cdot \frac{1}{2} \cdot \frac{3}{6}$. If we pick Urn B in the first round, then $\frac{1}{2} \cdot \frac{3}{6} \cdot \frac{1}{2} \cdot \frac{3}{5}$ is the chance of red then black. Thus,

$$P(R \cap B) = \frac{1}{2} \cdot \frac{2}{6} \cdot \frac{1}{2} \cdot \frac{3}{6} + \frac{1}{2} \cdot \frac{3}{6} \cdot \frac{1}{2} \cdot \frac{3}{5} = \frac{7}{60}.$$

Next let's calculate $P(B)$. If we pick Urn A in the first round, then the probability that the second ball is black is $\frac{1}{2} \cdot \frac{1}{2} \cdot \frac{3}{6} = \frac{1}{8}$. If we pick Urn B in the first round and get a black ball before getting the second black ball, then the probability is $\frac{1}{2} \cdot \frac{3}{6} \cdot \frac{1}{2} \cdot \frac{2}{5} = \frac{1}{20}$. If we pick Urn B in the first round and get a red ball before getting a black ball in the second round, then the probability is $\frac{1}{2} \cdot \frac{3}{6} \cdot \frac{1}{2} \cdot \frac{3}{5} = \frac{3}{40}$. Thus,

$$P(B) = \frac{1}{8} + \frac{1}{20} + \frac{3}{40} = \frac{1}{4}.$$

Therefore,

$$P(R|B) = \frac{P(R \cap B)}{P(B)} = \frac{\frac{7}{60}}{\frac{1}{4}} = \boxed{\frac{7}{15}}.$$

Solution to 15.13 Let's use four stars to represent the four rolled numbers. Let's use bins labeled 1, 2, ..., 6 to separate the stars. We see that there is a one-to-one correspondence between a sequence of four rolls in non-deceasing order and a way of separating the four stars with $6 - 1$ bars. Thus there are $\binom{4+6-1}{6-1}$ such sequences. So the probability is

$$\frac{\binom{4+6-1}{6-1}}{6^4} = \frac{126}{6^4} = \boxed{\frac{7}{72}}.$$

Solution to 15.14 Starting with 30 showing heads and 70 showing tails, Jenny chooses 40 pennies at random. She is expected to choose $\frac{30}{100} \cdot 40 = 12$ coins showing heads and $\frac{70}{100} \cdot 40 = 28$ coins showing tails. After turning the 40 pennies over, on average, 12 coins previously showing heads now show tails and 28 coins previously showing tails now show heads. Therefore, the expected number of pennies showing heads is $30 - 12 + 28 = \boxed{46}$.

Solution to 15.15 Let n be the number of the students in the class. Since everyone scored at least 60, we have

$$n \cdot 76 \geq 5 \cdot 100 + (n-5) \cdot 60, \qquad n \geq 12.5.$$

Next, let's see if $n = 13$ is attainable. Given 5 students scored 100 and a mean score of 76 with 13 students, the mean score of the other $13 - 5$ students would be

$$\frac{13 \cdot 76 - 5 \cdot 100}{13 - 5} = 61.$$

Therefore, when the class has 5 students who scored 100 and other 8 students who scored 61, the mean score would be 76. So $n = 13$ is attainable and the answer is $\boxed{13 \text{ students}}$.

Solution to 15.16 Let n be the number of the elements of the list. Since replacing m by $m+10$ increases the mean by 2, we have $n = 5$. So the elements of the list can be listed from the smallest to the largest as: 10, x, m, 32, 32, where $10 \leq x \leq m \leq 32$. When m is replaced by $m - 8$, the new median becomes $m - 4$. So $x = m - 4$. Now we have

$$10 + m - 4 + m + 32 + 32 = 22 \cdot 5, \qquad m = \boxed{20}.$$

Solution to 15.17 Note that the seat left for the last person is either the seat assigned to him or the seat assigned to the first person. This is because everyone besides the first person prefers his own seat and will take it when it is available. Starting from the first person, no one shows any preference to either the first person's seat or the last person's seat. So the probability is $\frac{1}{2}$ that either seat will remain. That is, the last person has a $\boxed{\dfrac{1}{2}}$ chance of getting his own seat.

Solution to 15.18 Let the probability of an even number of heads be $P(E)$ and the probability of an odd number of heads be $P(O)$. Let's consider the expansion of

$$\left(\frac{2}{3} - \frac{1}{3}\right) \cdot \left(\frac{4}{5} - \frac{1}{5}\right) \cdot \left(\frac{6}{7} - \frac{1}{7}\right) \cdots \left(\frac{2n}{2n+1} - \frac{1}{2n+1}\right).$$

For each term of the expansion, if it is positive, then it corresponds to an even number of heads. Similarly, if it is negative, then it corresponds to an odd number of heads. Therefore,

$$P(E) - P(O) = \left(\frac{2}{3} - \frac{1}{3}\right) \cdot \left(\frac{4}{5} - \frac{1}{5}\right) \cdot \left(\frac{6}{7} - \frac{1}{7}\right) \cdots \left(\frac{2n}{2n+1} - \frac{1}{2n+1}\right)$$
$$= \frac{1}{2n+1}.$$

Since $P(E) + P(O) = 1$, we have

$$P(O) = \frac{1}{2}\left(1 - \frac{1}{2n+1}\right) = \boxed{\dfrac{n}{2n+1}}.$$

Solutions for Chapter 15

Solution to 15.19 Let's represent each face of the cube with a vertex and label the vertices A, B, C, D, E, and F. We connect two vertices if and only if the two corresponding faces are adjacent. Then the cube becomes an octahedron, as shown.

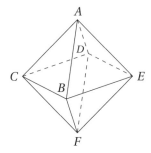

Suppose the expected number of steps from A to F is a, that from B to F is b, ..., and that from E to F is e. By symmetry, $b = c = d = e$. We need to find a, the expected number of steps for the ant to go from vertex A to vertex F. Starting from A, after one step, the ant is equally likely to be at vertex B, C, D, or E. So $a = 4 \cdot \frac{1}{4}(1+b) = 1+b$. Starting from B, the ant has a $\frac{1}{4}$ chance to go to each of A, C, E, or F. So

$$b = \frac{1}{4}\big((1+a) + (1+c) + (1+e) + 1\big) = \frac{1}{4}\big((1+1+b) + 2(1+b) + 1\big).$$

Therefore, $b = 5$ and $a = 1 + b = \boxed{6 \text{ steps}}$.

Solution to 15.20 When n soldiers are divided into groups of k, we get $\frac{n}{k}$ groups. Since we test each group at least once, there are at least $\frac{n}{k}$ group-blend tests. Since the probability that someone in a group has klep is $1 - (1-p)^k$, on average, there are $\frac{n}{k} \cdot k \cdot \big(1 - (1-p)^k\big)$ individual tests. Therefore, the expected number of tests is

$$\frac{n}{k} \cdot k \cdot \big(1 - (1-p)^k\big) + \frac{n}{k} = \boxed{n\big(1 - (1-p)^k + \frac{1}{k}\big)}.$$

Solution to 15.21 Suppose the four aces divide the cards into five piles with A, B, C, D, and F cards in them, respectively. Then we have $A + B + C + D + F = 48$ and $E(A) = E(B) = E(C) = E(D) = E(F) = \frac{48}{5}$. So the expected number of cards Richard will turn up is

$$E(A + B + C + 3) = E(A) + E(B) + E(C) + 3$$
$$= 3E(A) + 3 = 3 \cdot \frac{48}{5} + 3 = \boxed{\frac{159}{5}}.$$

Solution to 15.22 Let $E(n)$ be the expected number of steps that Sherry will take to reach 10 when she is at the number n. We have $E(1) = 1 + E(2)$ and $E(10) = 0$. For $2 \leq n \leq 9$, we have

$$E(n) = \frac{1}{2}\big((1 + E(n-1)) + (1 + E(n+1))\big), \qquad E(n+1) = 2E(n) - E(n-1) - 2.$$

Since $E(2) = E(1) - 1$, we can get $E(3)$ in terms of $E(1)$.

$$E(3) = 2E(2) - E(1) - 2 = 2\big(E(1) - 1\big) - E(1) - 2 = E(1) - 4.$$

Next we prove by induction that $E(n) = E(1) - (n-1)^2$ for all $1 \leq n \leq 9$. Clearly it is true when $n = 1$. Suppose for all $n = 1, 2, \ldots, k$, we have $E(n) = E(1) - (n-1)^2$. When $n = k+1$, we have

$$\begin{aligned} E(k+1) &= 2E(k) - E(k-1) - 2 \\ &= 2\big(E(1) - (k-1)^2\big) - \big(E(1) - (k-2)^2\big) - 2 \\ &= E(1) - \big(2(k-1)^2 - (k-2)^2 + 2\big) \\ &= E(1) - k^2. \end{aligned}$$

Therefore, by induction, for all $1 \leq n \leq 9$, we have $E(n) = E(1) - (n-1)^2$. Now we can solve for $E(1)$.

$$2(E(1) - 8^2) = 2E(9) = E(10) + E(8) + 2 = 0 + E(1) - 7^2 + 2,$$
$$E(1) = 2 \cdot 8^2 - 7^2 + 2 = \boxed{81 \text{ steps}}.$$

Solution to 15.23 Let O be the circumcircle of this regular n-gon. Let's label the n vertices clockwise from 1 to n. Note that a set of three distinct vertices forms an obtuse triangle if and only if it does not contain the center of circle O. That is, there is a diameter of the circle such that the three vertices of the obtuse triangle all lie on the same side of the diameter. Based on the parity of n, we have two cases.

Case 1: $n = 2k$. There are $\binom{2k}{3}$ possible triangles in total. Fix any vertex of the obtuse triangle, say A. We see that there are $k-1$ other vertices that lie on the same side of a diameter as A does.

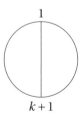

So we have $\binom{k-1}{2}$ choices for the other two vertices. Since A can be any of the $2k$ vertices, the probability that the three vertices form an obtuse triangle is

$$\frac{2k\binom{k-1}{2}}{\binom{2k}{3}} = \frac{6k(k-1)(k-2)}{2k(2k-1)(2k-2)} = \frac{3(k-2)}{2(2k-1)} = \frac{93}{125}.$$

Thus,

$$125(k-2) = 62(2k-1),$$
$$125k - 250 = 124k - 62.$$

Therefore, $k = 188$, and $n = 376$.

Case 2: $n = 2k-1$. The total number of triangles is $\binom{2k-1}{3}$. We fix a vertex A of the obtuse triangle. Again, there are $k-1$ other vertices that lie on the same side of a diameter as A does.

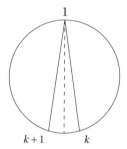

Since A can be any of the $2k-1$ vertices, the probability that the three vertices form an obtuse triangle is

$$\frac{(2k-1)\binom{k-1}{2}}{\binom{2k-1}{3}} = \frac{3(2k-1)(k-1)(k-2)}{(2k-1)(2k-2)(2k-3)} = \frac{3(k-2)}{2(2k-3)} = \frac{93}{125}.$$

Thus,

$$125(k-2) = 62(2k-3),$$
$$125k - 250 = 124k - 186.$$

So $k = 64$, and $n = 127$. Adding our two values of n, we get $376 + 127 = \boxed{503}$.

Index

n choose k, 10

acute angle, 89
acute triangle, 56, 183
AM-GM, 156
angle bisector, 62, 69, 85, 86, 101, 210, 211, 214
Angle Bisector Theorem, 51, 86, 215, 219
  converse, 51
angle chasing, 83, 85, 86, 211
apex, 75
arithmetic progression, 31
arithmetic sequence, 31
  common difference, 31
arithmetico-geometric sequence, 32
arithmetico-geometric series, 32

Bézout's Identity, 106, 113
base conversion, 107
bijective, 41
binary number, 172
binary representation, 172
binomial coefficients, 11
binomial expansion, 10, 11
Binomial Theorem, 10, 11, 110, 152–154, 156, 226

ceiling, xiv, 118, 155
center of mass, 93, 95, 97, 212, 213, 215, 217
centroid, 77, 104, 189, 213, 220
Ceva's Theorem, 52
  Trig Ceva, 86, 87, 210
cevian, xiv, 87, 94, 96, 102, 219
Chicken McNugget Theorem, 106, 108, 109, 222–225
Chinese Remainder Theorem, 113, 114, 229
circumcircle, 47, 62, 70

collinear, xiv, 85
complementary counting, 121
complete the rectangle, 8
complete the square, 8
concurrent, xiv, 52, 62, 87, 103, 219
conditional probability, 131, 241
congruent, 110
convex quadrilateral, 86, 92
coplanar, 74, 75, 200
cyclic polygon, 65
cyclic quadrilateral, 62, 68, 70, 85, 86, 192, 194, 207, 211
  phantom circle, 62, 86

decreasing function, 40
derangement, 124
dihedral angle, 74, 200
Diophantine equation, 115, 116, 122
  linear, 115
disjoint sets, 130
dodecahedron, 78, 197

Egyptian fraction, 9
Egyptian representation, 9
equilateral triangle, 70, 77, 81–83, 88, 90, 104, 130, 180, 185, 189, 191, 200, 207, 209, 211, 220, 240
Euclidean algorithm, 106, 113, 116, 225, 230
Euler's Theorem, 109, 110, 224, 226, 229, 231
Euler's totient function, 110
event, 131
expected value, 135, 138, 244
experiment, 131
exterior angle, 89
extremal principle, 4

Fermat's Last Theorem, 105, 108

247

Fermat's Little Theorem, 110, 114
Fibonacci sequence, 169
floor, xiv, 118
four dimensions, 71, 240
four-dimensional, 71
fractional part, 118
front view, 71, 78, 79
function, 7
  bijection, 41
  ceiling, 118
  domain, 7
  even, 40, 176
  floor, 118
  injection, 41
  odd, 40, 176
  range, 7
  surjection, 41
functional equation, 39
Fundamental Theorem of Algebra, 24, 26
Fundamental Theorem of Arithmetic, 105

geometric probability, 133
geometric progression, 31
geometric sequence, 31
  common ratio, 31
geometric series, 230
Golden Ratio, 84
Golden Triangle, 84
greatest common divisor, 106

hemisphere, 82
Heron's Formula, 50, 52, 193, 198, 214
hexagon, 65, 82, 204
hexagonal number, 35

icosahedron, 82, 204
incenter, 194, 195
incircle, 62, 70
increasing function, 40
indirect approach, 209
induction
  base case, 1, 40
  inductive step, 1
induction hypothesis, 179
induction principle, 1
infinite product, 31, 38, 171
infinite sum, 31
injective, 41, 179
integer, xiv
  nonnegative, xiv
  positive, xiv
interior angle, 89, 205
invariance principle, 3
invariant, 3, 4, 174

inversive geometry, 59
isosceles trapezoid, 84
isosceles triangle, 55, 57, 62, 69, 81, 83, 86–88, 90, 182, 194, 206, 207, 209–211

Langley's Adventitious Angles, xiii, 88
lattice point, xiv, 51, 82, 128, 203
lattice polygon, 51, 128
Law of Cosines, 47, 183, 207
Law of Sines, 47, 49, 64, 215
least common multiple, 107

mass points, 93, 212, 213, 215, 217
  principles of, 93, 98
mean, 134, 137
median, 97, 101, 134, 137
mode, 134, 137
modular multiplicative inverse, 113
monotonic function, 40, 118
monovariant, 3
multiplicative inverse, 113, 230

negative mass points, 93, 98, 99
net, 73, 77, 204
Newton's Sums, 27, 28, 165, 166
non-decreasing function, 118
number
  complex, xiv
  rational, xiv
  real, xiv

obtuse angle, 89
obtuse triangle, 138, 244, 245
octagon, 82, 204
octahedron, 73, 79, 130, 200, 234, 240, 243
octant, 240
one-to-one, 41
one-to-one correspondence, 41, 127, 172, 179, 241
onto, 41

parallelogram, 98, 99, 102, 104, 216
parity, 3
partial fraction decomposition, 33, 173
Pascal's triangle, 10, 11
pentagon, 58, 84, 205, 209
permutation, 124
Pick's Theorem, 51, 128, 182
pigeonhole principle, 2, 150, 232
Point-Line Distance Formula, 51, 75, 191
Point-Plane Distance Formula, 75
polynomial, 23
  degree, 23
  Factor Theorem, 23

Index

leading coefficient, 165
long division, 23, 167
  Remainder Theorem, 23, 24
  root, 24
  zero, 24
Power of a Point, 63, 64, 192, 194, 195
prime number, 105
principle
  extremal, 1
  induction, 1
  invariance, 1
  pigeonhole, 1
principle of inclusion-exclusion, 123, 170, 235
probability, 131
progression, 31
proof by contradiction, 97, 179
proof by induction, 244
Ptolemy's Theorem, 62, 65, 190
pyramid, 75, 82, 99, 104, 198, 200, 204
Pythagorean Theorem, 183, 185, 190, 192, 198, 204

quadratic equation, 24
  discriminant, 24, 25
quadratic formula, 24, 25, 167
quotient, 9, 23

radix point, 223
random variable, 134
range, 134, 137
recasting, 122, 126
rectangular parallelepiped, 75, 81
rectangular prism, 199
recurrence relation, 34, 125
  characteristic equation, 34, 36, 170
  closed form, 34, 36, 172
  homogeneous, 36, 172
  non-homogeneous, 36
recursion, 34
regular triangular prism, 200
remainder, 9, 23
rhombus, 187
right side view, 71, 78, 79

sample space, 131
scalene, xiv, 56, 89, 183

semiperimeter, 49, 50, 52, 195, 214
sequence, 31
sequence of first differences, 31, 35
sequence of second differences, 31, 35, 43, 171
series, 31
set, xiv
  intersection, xiv
  union, xiv
Shoelace Theorem, 50, 183
Simon's Favorite Factoring Trick, 8, 9, 11, 151
simple induction, 1
skew lines, 75
split mass, 95, 99, 216, 220
stars and bars, 121, 122, 234
statistics, 131, 134
Stewart's Theorem, 52, 202, 219
strategic overcounting, 123
strictly decreasing function, 40
strictly increasing function, 40, 179
strictly monotonic function, 41
strong induction, 1
surjective, 41

telescoping sum, 33
ternary number, 172
ternary representation, 172
tetrahedron, 75, 77–81, 198, 200–202, 240
three views, 77
three-dimensional, 71
top view, 71, 79
transversal, 95, 96, 216
trapezoid, 55, 57, 58, 61, 128, 186
triangle inequality, 53, 240
triangular number, 10, 37, 169
triangular prism, 79
triangular pyramid, 79, 104, 198, 199
Trigonometry
  angle addition formula, 48
  double-angle formula, 48, 49
trisect, 86, 211
trisector, 89
two-dimensional, 71

unit fraction, 9

Vieta's Formulas, 26–28, 164–166

About the Author

Karen Ge is a student at Naperville North High School in Illinois at the time of this publication. She is the 2015 Illinois State MathCounts Champion and is ranked among the nation's top 35 individuals at the 2015 MathCounts National Competition. Karen is a member of the Chicago Youth Symphony Orchestras' Encore Chamber Orchestra. Prior to that position, she served as a concertmaster of CYSO's Concert Orchestra. Karen is also the author of *Dissecting the New CogAT*, published by Aquahouse Publishing.